CARPET OF
SILVER

CARPET OF
SILVER

THE WRECK OF THE *ZUYTDORP*

Phillip Playford

UNIVERSITY OF WESTERN AUSTRALIA PRESS

First published in 1996 by
University of Western Australia Press
Crawley, Western Australia 6009
www.uwapress.uwa.edu.au

Reprinted 1998, 2006

National Library of Australia
Cataloguing-in-Publication entry:

Playford, Phillip E. (Phillip Elliott).
    Carpet of silver: the wreck of the Zuytdorp.

    Includes index.
    ISBN 1 875560 73 4.
    ISBN 978 1 875560 73 8.

    1. Zuytdorp (Ship). 2. Shipwrecks—Western Australia. I. Title.

910.45099413

Consultant editor Amanda Curtin, Curtin Communications, Perth
Designed by Robyn Mundy Design, Perth
Typeset in 10½ pt Berkeley by Lasertype, Perth
Maps drawn by Arthur Hoffman
Printed by BPA Print Group

Contents

LIST OF MAPS

Acknowledgments

My research into the *Zuytdorp* wreck could never have progressed without the willing support and encouragement of many people. The first of these was Tom Pepper, who introduced me to the wreck, and participated, with his wife Lurlie, in the 1954 and 1958 expeditions. Both Tom and Lurlie provided me with a great deal of assistance, for which I am grateful.

A large number of individuals and organizations in the Netherlands, Cape Town and Jakarta have contributed to this project. Special acknowledgment is due to the late Dr M.A.P. Meilink-Roelofsz of the Algemeen Rijksarchief in The Hague, who located and translated a great deal of information during the early phase of my research. I am also grateful to Professor Jaap Bruijn, who brought several important manuscripts and publications to my attention and provided valuable advice, and to Dr B.J. Slot, who arranged for numerous documents to be microfilmed.

My studies of the Dutch archival material have depended greatly on the assistance of Dr Cornelis de Heer, who has translated many documents relating to the *Zuytdorp*, and I would like to record my special thanks to him. Dutch wreck research in Western Australia has benefited greatly from Dr de Heer's expertise in translating early Dutch script and his extensive knowledge of Dutch ships and maritime history, in relation not only to the *Zuytdorp*, but also to the *Vergulde Draeck*, *Zeewyk* and *Batavia*.

I am grateful to Mike McCarthy, as leader of the Western Australian Maritime Museum's *Zuytdorp* project, for inviting me to join his team. This book owes a lot to him and to Geoff Kimpton for their major roles in archaeological investigations of the *Zuytdorp* wreck. Both men have courageously dived at the wrecksite many times, even when conditions were far from ideal, and they are responsible for most of what we now know about the wreck itself. Other staff of the Western Australian Maritime Museum have given me generous cooperation, for which particular thanks are due to Graeme Henderson, Jeremy Green, Pat Baker, Jon Carpenter, Ian MacLeod, Ian Godfrey, Stan Wilson, Fairlie Sawday, Myra Stanbury and Marit van Huystee.

West Australian Newspapers Ltd deserves credit for its sponsorship of two early expeditions to the wrecksite, in 1954 and 1958. Among the expedition members, I am especially indebted to Hugh Edwards, who has generously provided advice and assistance in my research over many years and has drawn my attention to several important references. I am also grateful to Jim Cruthers for his role in the 1954 expedition, and for his subsequent assistance in my research. Other members of those expeditions who deserve special thanks are Todge Campbell, John Stokes, Doug Burton, Lloyd Robinson and Ted Packer.

I would like to express appreciation to Amanda Curtin for her skilled editing of the manuscript and to Robyn Mundy for her creative design work. Thanks are also due to Graeme Henderson, Andrew Reeves, Mike McCarthy, Hugh Edwards, Cornelis de Heer, Allen Mawer, and Cynthia, Geoffrey, Julia and Katherine Playford for reading drafts of the manuscript and offering valuable suggestions for its improvement.

In addition, I would like to express thanks to the following people for their invaluable assistance and support: Tom Pepper Junior, Margaret Caunt, Elsie Wilton and Arthur Pepper, who have assisted my enquiries in many ways; Tom Brady and Max Cramer, for information on their early diving expeditions at the wrecksite; J.H. Esterhuyse, G.J. Reynecke, S. Schoeman, G.C. de Wet and D.B. McLennan, for information from the archives in Cape Town; John Legge, I.S. Wirjosapoetro, Don Zimmerman, M. Ali, D. Soemartini and M. Mangkudilaga, for facilitating access to data from the national archives in Jakarta; Arthur Hoffman, for skilled computer drafting of the maps; Simon Urbini, Murray Jones, Trevor Dods and Peter Carroll, for their assistance with photographs and other illustrations; Ann Mallard, Ivy Mallard, Geoffrey Dean, Tim Welborn, Ric Rossi and Trefor Jenkins, for advice relating to the disease porphyria variegata; Jim Henderson, for introducing me to the *Vergulde Draeck* and providing advice and assistance over many years; John Cowen, for information relating to the discovery of the *Vergulde Draeck* and related issues; Dr Naoom Haimson, for advice on Alan Robinson and the 1968 *Zuytdorp* expedition; Grace Richards, for discussions regarding her former husband, Alan Robinson; Arnold Leuftink, for advice regarding illness and mortality on Dutch East India Company ships; W.F.J. Mörzer Bruyns, for information on navigation instruments and related matters; E.W. Petrejus and L.M. Akveld, for advice and data on Dutch East India Company ships and voyages; Günter Schilder, for assistance with matters relating to early Dutch maritime history; Mollie Lukis, for assistance during my early investigations; Andrew Reeves, for facilitating access to files of the Western Australian Museum and furnishing other advice; Juliette Blevins, for information on the Nanda language; Cecil Blood, for facilitating the 1954 and 1958 expeditions; Sandra Bowdler, for guiding and participating in archaeological investigations at Wale Well; G.A. Brongers, for advice on the tobacco-box lid found at Wale Well; Ennemond Faye and Bob Cook, for information on the 1941 expedition; V. Woodward, for locating and lending photographs of the 1941 expedition, left by her late father, Victor Courtney; Ian Field, for discussions on the burning of the museum caravan and related issues; John Gibson and Ken Gregson, for arranging access to Criminal Investigation Branch files; Dominic Lamera, for advice and assistance on matters relating to the wreck and its hinterland, and for providing access to coins and other relics he has collected there; John Allchin, Joe Cremers and Ray Mickelberg, for discussions on the abalone and rock-lobster fisheries and on issues relating to the *Zuytdorp* and its treasure; David Taylor, for permission to use West Australian Newspapers Ltd's photographs; Prince Mukarram Jah, for discussing his role in exploration of the *Zuytdorp* wreck and providing other information; Peter Reeves, for advice relating to the *Zuytdorp*'s

1704 visit to Surat; Pearly Whitby and Annie Oxenham for discussions on their parents' visits to the *Zuytdorp* wrecksite; Lucy Ryder, for confirming the name of Wittecarra Spring and providing information on the Nanda people; Ginger MacDonald, Ben Carlo, Janie Winder and Jack Brand, for discussions on the Malgana and Nanda people of the Tamala and Murchison House areas; Peter Bridge, for the loan of metal-detecting equipment and bringing several references to my attention; Bob Sheppard and Tony Cockbain, for assisting archaeological and metal-detecting investigations; Evert and Thea van de Graaff, for help in obtaining copies of documents from the Algemeen Rijksarchief; Maria Pulsone Woods, for advice regarding the *Valkenisse* model; Rupert Gerritsen, for assistance in identifying a reference; and the Western Australian Maritime Museum, the Geological Survey of Western Australia, the Western Australian Chemistry Centre and West Australian Petroleum Pty Ltd, for assistance in a variety of ways.

Numerous other people have given various forms of assistance and encouragement over the years, for which I am very grateful. I hope any who should have been mentioned by name will accept my apologies.

Finally, I wish to express heartfelt gratitude to my wife, Cynthia, and daughters Julia and Katherine, for their patient love and support.

Phillip Playford
March 1996

ABBREVIATIONS

ANCODS	Australia/Netherlands Committee on Old Dutch Shipwrecks
CALM	Department of Conservation and Land Management
CIB	Criminal Investigation Branch
Historical Society	Western Australian Historical Society (later Royal Western Australian Historical Society)
VOC	Vereenigde Oost-Indische Compagnie (United East India Company)
WA Maritime Museum	Western Australian Maritime Museum
WA Museum	Western Australian Museum
WAPET	West Australian Petroleum Pty Ltd
YAL	Young Australia League

MY INTRODUCTION
TO THE *ZUYTDORP*

MY interest in the *Zuytdorp* began in July 1954, when I was working around Shark Bay as a field geologist for West Australian Petroleum Pty Ltd (WAPET). I was then twenty-two years old, had recently graduated from The University of Western Australia, and was very enthusiastic about life in the bush and the geology and human history of the areas I was visiting. On Tamala Station, south of Shark Bay, I met Tom Pepper, who had worked as a stockman on Tamala and Murchison House Station (near Kalbarri) for nearly forty years. I spent many fascinating hours in the evenings, talking with him about the old days on those stations.

One evening, several days after I first spoke with him, Tom Pepper quietly produced a grubby flour bag containing silver coins, belt buckles, brass fittings from chests, and other battered bits and pieces, together with a heavy bronze breech block from a cannon. He said that they were from the wreckage of a ship he had found in April 1927 at the foot of coastal cliffs about 65 kilometres south of Tamala. Pepper vividly recounted how he had been tracking a dingo when he first saw the wreckage, later realizing that it had come from a large wooden vessel that had been wrecked there long ago. During the following few years, he and several other people from Murchison House Station had visited the site to collect relics, including scores of silver coins, some of which he showed me that evening. Many bore the name Zeeland, suggesting that this was the wreck of a Dutch ship, and the date 1711, from which it was clear that the vessel had been lost no earlier than that year.

Tom Pepper said that he had told few people about the wreck, as he believed it could hold valuable treasure that he might eventually be able to find. However, stories of the discovery soon reached Northampton, and were relayed from there to Perth. Pepper said that these reports had led to an expedition being mounted by the *Sunday Times* in 1939 (actually it was 1941), but expedition members had been able to spend only a few hours at the site and could not identify the ship. Pepper himself had last visited the wrecksite in 1939, with his wife Lurlie and two station hands, in order to retrieve a carved figure of a woman, thought to be the figurehead of the ship.

I was enthralled by Tom Pepper's story, and immediately resolved to visit the wrecksite myself. After obtaining permission from Daryl Johnstone, the WAPET party leader, I set out early in the morning of 1 August 1954. Following directions given by Pepper, I drove my Land Rover about 60 kilometres down the extremely slow-going and rough track that followed the stockroute from Tamala to Murchison House, counting three successive rain sheds—Nyindemi, Willie's and Wattie's—until I reached the fourth, Ramyard Shed. From there, I continued along the track for another 4 kilometres, to find a derelict fence crossing the track. I followed the remains of this fence for some 6 kilometres towards the coast until it turned abruptly south near a belt of dense tea-tree scrub. From there, I headed straight on into the scrub, pushing through it with the Land Rover as far as practicable before setting out on foot.

It was an unnerving experience, crashing through that high, thick scrub. At times, the vehicle was virtually suspended above the ground on the tea-trees it had pushed over. Fortunately, I had installed scrub bars on the front of the vehicle about two weeks before, to guard against damage when driving cross-country through the bush. They had been made up for me at a garage in Northampton, and were the first to be used on a WAPET Land Rover; indeed the first that I knew of on any vehicle in the State. Similar bars soon became standard on WAPET vehicles, and

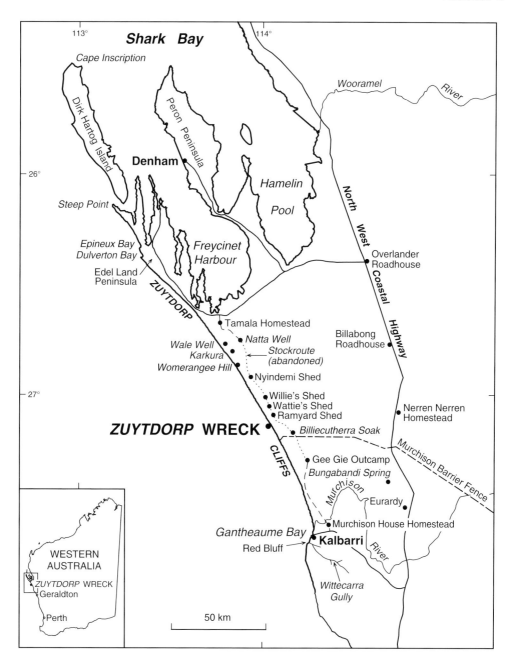

Map 1.
The area from Shark
Bay to Kalbarri

their use eventually spread to bush vehicles throughout Western Australia, becoming generally known as 'roo bars' because of the protection they afforded against damage from collisions with kangaroos crossing the road.

The place where I left the Land Rover was about a kilometre from the coast. Feeling a little concerned that I might not be able to find it again in the dense tea-tree scrub, I put up the tall telescopic aerial of my flying-doctor radio and tied a cloth sample bag to the top, so that it could be seen waving in the wind above the trees as I walked back.

After reaching the top of the spectacular sea cliffs, I walked 2 or 3 kilometres north, then south, seeking signs of the wreck, while feeling very much alone at this remote place on that cold winter's day. At last, in the mid-afternoon, almost despairing of finding the site, and facing an exhausting trip back to Tamala, I reached a place where wooden wreckage, bleached white from long exposure, could be seen at the foot of the cliffs, and fragments of green bottles lay scattered along the cliff top. Surely this was the place that I had been seeking. With mounting excitement, I scrambled down the cliff face to the wave-swept platform below, picking up a Dutch coin and a sailor's belt buckle in the thirty minutes or so that I could spend there. It was one of the most exhilarating experiences of my life.

I arrived back at Tamala at about 10 o'clock that night, tired but still elated. By then, Tom and Lurlie Pepper and some members of the WAPET party had become rather concerned, fearing that something untoward might have happened to me. Tom was being berated by Lurlie 'for letting that young fellow go to that awful place on his own'. They were relieved that I had returned safe and sound, and were soon caught up in my youthful enthusiasm about the day's events. I proudly showed them my relics—a coin, a belt buckle, and the square base of a bottle—while recounting some thoughts that I had been turning over in my mind during the slow drive back to Tamala.

The broken bottles on the cliff top seemed to be particularly significant. They suggested that some people must have survived the wreck, and had climbed the cliffs to indulge in a drinking spree while looking down on the desolate scene below. The belt buckle also seemed important, as it was lying in a position where it could not have been thrown ashore by waves. Perhaps it had come from

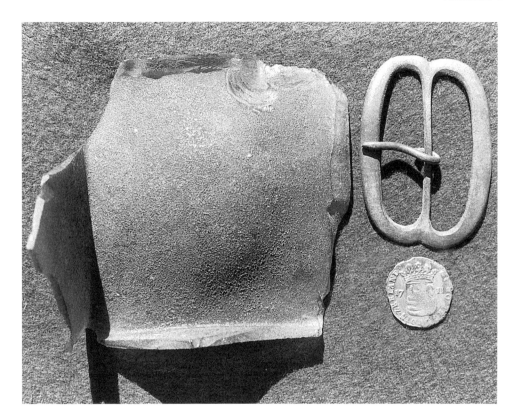

the belt of a sailor who had managed to struggle ashore. I wondered how he had died and what had become of his shipmates on the cliff top who drank to drown their despair. What was the name of this ship? Had it been carrying treasure, and why had it come to grief below these fearsome cliffs?

Little did I know then that the events of that day in 1954 would have a big impact on my life for more than forty years, marking the beginning of a saga that would involve major expeditions to the site, extensive research, identification of the wreck, treasure, arson, looting, claims and counter-claims, bureaucratic mismanagement, courageous diving feats, and indications that some of the castaways lived on to become permanent residents of this harsh land.

The object of my fascination turned out to be one of the largest ships of the Dutch East India Company, which had been lost without trace between the Cape of Good Hope and Batavia (Jakarta) during the winter of 1712. Its name was the *Zuytdorp*.

Objects found by the author during his first visit to the wrecksite, on 1 August 1954: the square base of a green glass bottle, a sailor's belt buckle, and a Zeeland schelling, dated 1711.

Photograph by the author

1. THE GOLDEN AGE

THE DUTCH EAST INDIA COMPANY

THE *Zuytdorp* was owned by the Dutch East India Company, the world's most powerful monopolistic trading concern during the seventeenth and early eighteenth centuries. The company exerted unprecedented power in the Far East, and its huge profits contributed substantially to the prosperity of the Dutch Republic during its 'Golden Age' (*de Gouden Eeuw*). As a background to the *Zuytdorp* story, it is relevant to review the history of this great company and the way in which it became involved in the history of Australia.[1]

The rise and fall of the company

The Dutch had not been the first Europeans to establish maritime links with Asia. This honour belongs to the Portuguese, whose trade with the area began in 1497–98, when Vasco da Gama succeeded in rounding the Cape of Good Hope and sailing on to India, returning with a rich cargo of spices. His successful voyage led to the development of extensive commercial ties between Portugal and Asia, and the Portuguese were able to monopolize the lucrative spice trade throughout the sixteenth century. Most of their spices were distributed through Antwerp, on the Scheldt River estuary in the southern Netherlands, which was at that time the centre of international trade in Europe.

Antwerp's dominance ended abruptly in 1585, through the brutal Spanish reconquest of that city and other areas of the southern Netherlands. Six years earlier, the seven Protestant provinces of the northern Netherlands had formed the Dutch Republic by breaking away from the ten Catholic provinces of the south. They succeeded in repelling the Spanish, at the same time mounting a successful blockade of the entrance to the Scheldt estuary. This prevented foreign shipping from reaching Antwerp, and paralysed commerce in that city. Antwerp never regained its leading status in world trade.

As a result of Spanish control of the southern Netherlands, and the associated suppression of Protestant worship, thousands of refugees streamed into the provinces of the Dutch Republic, especially Holland and Zeeland. They brought important skills and business know-how to the infant republic, which was still fighting against Spain for its very existence. However, the Spanish king, Philip II, decided in 1590 to intervene in the French civil war, a decision that proved to be a major turning point in European history. Most of the Spanish forces were withdrawn from the Netherlands, leaving only a skeleton force to face the Dutch, who immediately went on the offensive. Over the next seven years, they succeeded in doubling the area under their control, and the Dutch Republic emerged as a major military and naval power in Europe.

The demise of Antwerp in 1585 had left a vacuum in world commerce, and during the next few years it was uncertain where the new world trade centre would be established. However, by the early 1590s it had become clear that this role was steadily passing to cities of the Dutch Republic, especially Amsterdam.

The growing ascendancy of the republic in world trade owed a great deal to its maritime strength, and at the height of their power, the Dutch owned roughly half of the world's seagoing ships. As early as the fifteenth century, they had already become the leading European shippers of bulky goods, but this bulk-carrying trade, in products such as salt, did not generate great wealth. Antwerp had derived its affluence largely from the 'rich trades' in spices, sugar and textiles. When the Dutch Republic succeeded Antwerp as the centre of international commerce, it became the major marketplace for these wealth-generating commodities.

This change in the balance of world trade marked the beginning of the Golden Age of the Dutch Republic, during which this tiny nation became the wealthiest in the world, dominating international commerce for almost 150 years. This was an astounding achievement, as the Dutch Republic was the smallest of the major European nations in terms of area, population and natural resources. It ranked far behind France, Spain and England in these respects, but in commerce and wealth it soon surpassed them all. Not only did the Dutch achieve world ascendancy in commerce; they were also among the cultural leaders of Europe, being especially renowned in the field of art. The paintings of their Great Masters remain as a lasting testimony to the cultural achievements of the Dutch people during their Golden Age.

Initially, the Dutch marketed spices they had purchased in Lisbon. However, the Dutch merchants soon realized that they could capitalize on this rich trade much more by breaking the Portuguese monopoly on the direct acquisition of spices in Asia. In 1594, a consortium of nine Dutch entrepreneurs contributed the necessary funds and obtained the backing of the States General (the Dutch government) for a fleet of four ships to embark on a trading mission to the East Indies. The Compagnie van Verre (Far Lands Company) was established for this purpose.

The *Mauritius*, *Amsterdam*, *Hollandia* and *Duyfken* left Holland on 2 April 1595, under the command of Cornilis de Houtman, and returned with a cargo of pepper two years and four months later, having signed a treaty with the Sultan of Bantam in Java. This first expedition (the *Eerste Schipvaart*) was far from being a commercial success, as income from the sale of the cargo was barely sufficient to cover expenses. Moreover, only 87 out of 240 people who had left the Netherlands returned alive, and one ship (the *Amsterdam*) was abandoned in Asia.

Nevertheless, despite its disappointing financial results, the *Eerste Schipvaart* had pointed to an enormous potential for profitable commerce with Asia, and it aroused great enthusiasm in the Netherlands. Eager entrepreneurs sought to participate in the new trade, and over the next five years eight independent companies despatched sixty-five ships, in fourteen fleets, to the East Indies, India and other destinations in Asia. It was said to have been a 'goldrush for spices'.[2]

Some of the ventures were extremely successful, the vessels returning home laden with pepper, other spices, and various Eastern products such as textiles and china, all attracting high prices in Europe. The companies initially prospered in active competition with one another and with the companies of other countries, especially Spain, Portugal and England. However, this early success brought major problems. Fierce competition among Dutch merchants drove up purchase prices in Asia, while a glut of spices in the home market caused sale prices to collapse. The States General was unable to control or adequately protect the armed merchantmen of the various companies, and it quickly realized that unless a united company was formed, the trade would be ruined and (even worse) the Portuguese might regain their monopoly in Asia.

Under pressure from the States General, the various companies agreed to unite, and on 20 March 1602 they formed the Vereenigde Oost-Indische Compagnie (United East India Company, commonly known as the VOC). This was a merger of the previously existing companies of Amsterdam, Zeeland (or Middelburg), Enkhuizen, Delft, Hoorn and Rotterdam, each of which became chambers (*Kamers*) of the united company. The charter drawn up by the States General granted the VOC a monopoly over all Dutch trade east of the Cape of Good Hope. It also gave the company jurisdiction over Dutch nationals in that area, and permitted it to found colonies, prosecute the war with Spain and Portugal, raise whatever funds it needed, and regulate trade with Asia.[3]

The VOC established its Asian headquarters at a new city, Batavia, in north-western Java, on the site of an Indonesian village named Jacatra (a name that was revived as Jakarta when Indonesia gained independence after World War II). The company also set up about thirty smaller settlements in Java, Sumatra, Borneo, India, Ceylon, Arabia, Persia, Bengal, Malacca, Celebes, Timor, China and Japan, and engaged in active trade with each centre.

The VOC was administered by a board of directors, known as the *Heeren XVII* (seventeen gentlemen), who were appointed by the various chambers: eight from Amsterdam, four from Zeeland, one each from Enkhuizen, Delft, Hoorn and Rotterdam, and a seventeenth who was appointed in rotation, from Zeeland for two years and the smaller chambers for one year each. The guiding decisions of the *Heeren XVII* were implemented by the various chambers, who controlled the shipping to Asia and local operations within the republic. The duties of individual chambers entailed the building and equipping of ships, the financing of export goods and currency, and the receipt and sale of imports. Each chamber set up its own offices, warehouses and shipyards.

The most favoured months for departure from the Netherlands were December and January (the 'Christmas fleet') and April and May (the 'Easter fleet'). However, some ships departed at other times, the least favoured period being July–August, as ships leaving then were likely to experience slack wind conditions near the equator. The average voyage to Batavia lasted eight months: about four and a half months to the Cape of Good Hope, three to four weeks at the Cape, and two and a half months from there to Batavia. On the return voyage, the most frequent departure period from Batavia was October–January, with the fleet arriving home an average of seven and a half months later.

Cargoes transported to Asia by VOC ships consisted of precious metals and European merchandise for sale in Asia or use in company settlements. Precious metals were in the form of coins and ingots, commonly silver only, but sometimes including gold. They were carried in chests, packed in small bags bedded down in peat (to limit movement). The chests were bolted with two locks, nailed down with sailcloth, and sealed. They were normally secured in the captain's cabin, situated in the stern of the ship, below the poop deck.

A wide variety of silver coins were despatched, the most common being Dutch ducatons, guilders, *leeuwendaalders*, *rijksdaalders* (rix dollars), *payement* (small silver money—schellings, double stuivers and stuivers), Spanish pieces of eight (reals of eight or Spanish dollars), pieces of four and two, and Spanish-Netherlands ducatons and patagons. Among the gold coins carried, the most common were Dutch ducats.

The VOC imported into Europe many different products from Asia. Pepper was the most profitable commodity during the seventeenth century, and other spices, including nutmeg, cloves, mace and cinnamon, were also in strong demand. These were prized in Europe for flavouring the dull, bland, and often putrid food of the time, for preparing mulled wine and other beverages, and for medicinal purposes. During the eighteenth century, there was an increasing demand in Europe for Indian textiles, cotton and silk, which filled much of the cargo space in company ships. The proportion of tea and coffee imports also increased substantially, as Europeans became more fond of those beverages.

The VOC sought to monopolize the supply of spices from Asia, brutally compelling the native people to supply the company alone, at fixed prices. In this, it largely succeeded, achieving enormous profits from the spice trade. The VOC also played a major role in trade between various Asian countries, profitably buying and selling commodities such as spices, copper, tin, precious metals, opium (in which it also had a monopoly) and various dyes.

The decline of the Dutch Republic as a world power began with the Treaty of Utrecht in 1713. This ended the War of the Spanish Succession (1702–13), in which Britain, the Dutch Republic and Austria were allied against France and Spain. By 1713, the war had essentially been won by the British–Dutch–Austrian allies, but the terms of the treaty, secretly negotiated between Britain and France, constituted a political defeat for the Dutch. It heralded the decline of Dutch economic power and the concomitant rise of the British, a trend that was to continue through the rest of the eighteenth century. The demise of the Dutch nation as a major world force was sealed by its defeat in the fourth Anglo–Dutch war of 1780–83 and occupation by the French in 1795.

The effects of declining Dutch economic strength after 1713 were not immediately reflected in the performance of the VOC. However, the company had passed its peak by 1740, as witnessed by falling profits resulting from increasing British and French competition, and compounded by corruption within the company itself. The situation steadily worsened over succeeding years, and the VOC had become insolvent by the close of the eighteenth century. Its assets were taken over by the Dutch government on 31 December 1799.

The route to the Indies

VOC ships had the choice of two routes on leaving the Netherlands: either the Channel route (through the English Channel) or the so-called Back Way (around the north coast of

Scotland). Although the Channel route was shorter, the Back Way was normally preferred during times of war with England, France or Spain, or when privateers (privately owned and crewed vessels authorized to capture enemy ships) were operating out of France or the Spanish Netherlands. During such times, this route had the advantage that there was less chance of being intercepted by enemy ships. However, the weather was likely to be worse, and the voyage took an average of about one month longer.

After sailing through the Channel or rounding Scotland and Ireland, the ships headed south for the islands of Madeira or Porto Santo and from there to the Canary and Cape Verde islands, off the west African coast. South of the Cape Verde Islands, the ships entered the doldrums, where there were often sailing problems because of slack winds. If a ship was too close to the African coast, it risked being carried into the Gulf of Guinea by the Guinea Current, especially when there was little or no wind. If a ship ventured too far west, the South Equatorial Current could carry it into the Caribbean, where it might lie becalmed for long periods. In order to minimize these risks, the company navigators were directed to follow a defined seaway when sailing south from the Cape Verde Islands to the equator. Wind and current conditions were expected to be optimal within this seaway, which was known as the Wagon Way (*Wagen Weg*) or Wagon Track (*Wagenspoor*). Subdivisions of the south-western part of the Wagon Way defined variations in the route to be used at specified times of the year.

On crossing the equator, the ships continued south to south-west, taking special care to avoid the rocky Abrolhos shoals if sailing near the Brazilian coast. At latitude 36–38° south, the prevailing westerly winds were encountered, and the ships then changed course to sail eastward to the Cape of Good Hope.

From the early days of the VOC, ships used to call at Table Bay, near the Cape, to replenish water supplies and trade for fresh food with the indigenous Hottentots. It was eventually decided that a permanent settlement was warranted there, to service VOC ships, and this was founded at the Cape in 1652. A fort, several warehouses, a repair shipyard and a small hospital were constructed, along with houses, vegetable gardens, and fields for grazing animals. The Cape became a compulsory stopover point for company ships, and it was also used by foreign, especially English,

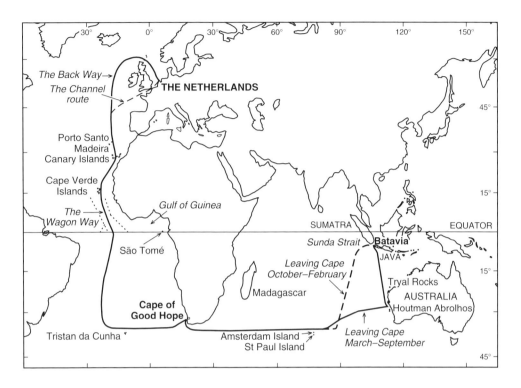

Map 2.
The Dutch East India
Company's route to
the Indies

vessels. The original hospital catered for only 30 patients, but a much larger facility, with 200 beds, was constructed towards the end of the seventeenth century. These hospitals were primitive by modern standards, but conditions for the sick were much better there than on board ship.

Most VOC ships stayed at Table Bay for three or four weeks, although this was longer than authorized by the company rules, which in 1656 specified a maximum of ten days, revised to fourteen days in 1723. The stopover at this attractive place must have been a godsend to a ship's company, escaping the dreadful conditions and poor food that had been endured on the voyage. Many crew recovered from the ravages of scurvy and other shipboard diseases during their stay at the Cape, which must have made a big difference to the survival rate on voyages to and from Asia.

During the early days of the VOC, its ships normally followed the Portuguese route after rounding the Cape of Good Hope. They would head north along the African coast, sailing on either side of Madagascar before heading north-east to the Indies, India and

Ceylon. However, this route was dangerous, as it passed many enemy Portuguese settlements. Moreover, winds were commonly adverse. In 1610–11, Commodore Hendrik Brouwer decided to experiment with another route. After leaving Table Bay, his ships headed south to below latitude 35°, where westerly winds (the 'roaring forties') prevail throughout the year. He used these winds to sail due east, as far as the estimated longitude of Sunda Strait, before turning north for the Indies. In this way, Brouwer's ships reduced the usual sailing time by several weeks, completing a very successful voyage to Bantam only two and a half months after leaving Table Bay.

Brouwer (who later became Governor General of Batavia) recommended that this new route be adopted by the company, and in 1616 the *Heeren XVII* directed that all ships sailing to the Indies were to follow Brouwer's course. The formal sailing directions (the *Seynbrief*), issued in the following year, decreed that ships should sail east between latitudes 35° and 44° south until they reached at least 1,000 Dutch miles (about 7,400 kilometres) east of the Cape, at which point they should turn north for the run to Sunda Strait.

It is clear that the expression 'east of the Cape' meant 'east of the Cape at the latitude of the Cape'—that is, at 34°24′ south, or, in round figures, between 34° and 35°. If a ship sailed east across the Indian Ocean at 35° for 1,000 Dutch miles, then headed due north, it would reach the south-west coast of Sumatra and could then sail a relatively short distance to Sunda Strait and on to Batavia. Of course, the Dutch navigators were fully aware that at higher latitudes (that is, further south), the distance to be travelled east before heading north for Sunda Strait was less than 1,000 miles, and they could readily determine the relevant distance from tables.

In practice, it was impossible for the ships to follow Brouwer's route precisely, for there was no means of reliably determining longitude at sea. The mariner had to rely on dead reckoning, which could never be accurate in a sailing ship. The distance sailed was usually measured by means of a log line, marked with regular graduations. At the end of the line was a triangular wooden float (the *schipken*) that tended to float at or near the same spot as the line was played out from a reel. Every hour (measured by means of an hourglass), the line was hauled in and the number of graduations recorded, thus measuring the approximate distance covered in that period.

It was not until the chronometer was perfected in 1759, by the Englishman John Harrison, that longitude could be measured precisely at sea. Galileo had, in 1612, devised a method of measuring longitude on land, but this depended on accurate telescopic observations of the satellites of Jupiter, and was not feasible on board ship.

On the other hand, latitude measurements at sea were reasonably reliable during the seventeenth and early eighteenth centuries, using successively the astrolabe, cross-staff, and back-staff or Davis quadrant. The VOC adopted the octant, a more accurate instrument, during the mid-eighteenth century, and the most precise instrument of all, the sextant, was introduced later in that century.

VOC navigators measured distances using 15 Dutch miles to a degree of latitude. Thus, a Dutch mile was equivalent to 4 nautical miles of modern usage, or 7.408 kilometres. Water depths were measured in fathoms, of 6 Amsterdam feet (1.698 metres), using a sounding line with a lead weight at its base.

The Land of the Eendracht

Because of the impossibility of accurately determining longitude, it was only a matter of time before one of the VOC ships travelling from the Cape to the Indies ran too far east, thereby reaching the coast of Western Australia, the Terra Australis Incognita of the earliest Dutch maps. The first ship to do so was the *Eendracht*, skippered by Dirk Hartog. On 25 October 1616, he and some of his crew landed at Cape Inscription, at the north end of what is now known as Dirk Hartog Island, leaving a pewter plate, inscribed with a record of his visit, nailed to a post. This was the first known landing of Europeans in Western Australia, although it was ten years after the first Dutchmen had set eyes on Australia. That distinction belonged to Willem Jansz and crew of the *Duyfken*, who charted the west side of Cape York Peninsula in 1606. However, at that time they believed that this land was part of New Guinea.[4]

The vast landmass discovered by Dirk Hartog became known on the Dutch charts as 't Landt van de Eendracht (the Land of the Eendracht) or Eendrachtsland, and this name persisted in company maps and documents for more than 150 years. The southern continent was also often referred to as 't Zuyd Landt (the South Land) or 't Grote Zuyd Landt (the Great South Land), and, later, as Nova Hollandia (New Holland). Many more Dutch ships sighted the coast of Western Australia during the years after Dirk Hartog's discovery, and new names appeared on the VOC maps, including Willems Rivier (1618), d'Edels Landt (1619), Frederik Houtmans Abrolhos (1619), 't Landt van de Leeuwin (1622) and Pieter Nuyts Landt (1627).

It is interesting to note that in 1623, while the ship *Leyden* was sailing alongside the coast of Western Australia, north of Shark Bay, 'Willemtgen Jansz, wedded wife of Willem Jansz, of Amsterdam, midshipman, was delivered of a son, who got the name Seebaer van Nieuwelant' (Sea-born of New Land).[5] This child can perhaps be regarded as the first white Australian. His eventual fate is unknown.

In 1627, the *Heeren XVII* issued new sailing instructions that changed the route to be followed between the Cape and Sunda Strait, and copies of these were given to each skipper and steersman on the company ships. Cornelis de Heer has translated the relevant section of these instructions as follows:

> The Cape of Good Hope having been passed it is permissible that a course be sailed eastward between 36 and 39 degrees latitude south until you have come 850 miles east of the Cape of Good Hope. Whenever after the beginning of October you find that you are about 850 miles east of the Cape of Good Hope and shall be able to make Strait Sunda with the western monsoon (which has its greatest strength in December, January, and February), shape your course thus northerly in order to be certain that you will reach west of Sunda Strait, so that when you reach 6 degrees latitude south you will be above wind of Strait Sunda and may make the same [from the west] as speedily as possible.
>
> But if sailing east from the Cape of Good Hope before the beginning of October or after the beginning of March you find yourself to be at 36 or 37 degrees latitude 800 miles east of the Cape of Good Hope and should have to make Strait Sunda with the east monsoon, then make your course as much northerly as east so that when you are at about

30 degrees latitude you estimate yourself to be 950 or 1000 miles east of the Cape of Good Hope.

These 950 or 1000 miles eastward being passed then it is permissible (if the conditions of wind and weather allow such) to run into sight of the Land of the Eendracht at 27 degrees latitude or farther north, and from there to make such a course with which you may reckon to be certain to pass by the Triall rocks, which lie at about 20 degrees latitude south, without peril, and the south coast of Java can then be made conveniently so as to reach Sunda Strait above wind and to sail [from the east] into the same Strait with speed.

Nota Bene
The way between the Cape of Good Hope and the Land of the Eendracht is in fact much shorter than shown by the plane chart and it may happen through the speed of the currents that the way is found to be even shorter than it actually is, so that the land could be sighted much earlier than could be expected; and the Land of the Eendracht has south of 27 degrees many perilous shallows and sharp grounds, therefore cautious action is needed and timely watch must be kept, and at night and in darkness it is urgent to use the lead; bottom is cast at 100, 80, and 70 fathoms for 7, 6, and 5 miles off the coast.

Thus, the instructions recognized that for ships leaving the Cape from the beginning of March to the end of September (during autumn, winter and early spring), skippers could decide to sail as far east as the Land of the Eendracht at 27° latitude or further north. In this way, they could obtain a fix on their position after the long voyage across the Indian Ocean. From the Australian coast, they should head north-north-west to meet the coast of Java, and with the south-east monsoon blowing at that time of year, the ships could readily sail west along that coast to reach Sunda Strait.

On the other hand, ships leaving the Cape of Good Hope from the beginning of October to the end of February (late spring and summer) were not allowed to sail as far east as the Australian coast. After reaching 850 Dutch miles (about 6,300 kilometres) east of the Cape, they were to sail north by east towards the coast of Sumatra. The final approach to Sunda Strait would then be from the west, driven by the north-west monsoon, which blows south of the equator during those months. If a ship tried to approach Sunda Strait from the east at that time of the year, it would be heading into these winds and would have to resort to elaborate tacking, resulting in slow progress.

The warning in the instructions to keep well clear of the 'Triall rocks' (known today as Tryal Rocks) resulted from the first known shipwreck in Western Australian waters: the *Tryall*, an English East India Company vessel that foundered in 1622, near the Montebello Islands. The skipper, John Brookes, had been seeking to follow the Dutch route to the Indies, when the ship ran, without warning, onto submerged rocks. Forty-six survivors managed to reach Batavia in two boats.[6] The ship's loss was a matter of concern to the VOC, which feared that a similar fate might befall one of its own vessels. This warning about the rocks was evidently well heeded by the Dutch skippers, as no VOC ships are known to have been lost there.

The 'many perilous shallows and sharp grounds' referred to in the instructions as occurring south of 27° are the Houtman Abrolhos Islands and their associated reefs. They had been located in 1619 by Frederik de Houtman, commander of the ships *Dordrecht* and *Amsterdam*, while following Brouwer's route to the Indies. He said that these reefs and rocks needed to be 'carefully avoided as very dangerous to ships that wish to touch at this coast'. The islands and reefs became known on VOC maps as Frederik Houtmans Abrolhos.[7]

The sailing instructions were reissued in printed form, with minor revision, in 1652,[8] and again in more detail and with further slight revision and expansion in 1748. The 1748 version directed that the Australian coast could be approached no further south than latitude 26° south (near the southern end of Dirk Hartog Island), which is 1° north of the position given in the earlier instructions. No doubt the purpose of this was to ensure that ships kept well north of the Houtman Abrolhos, which had claimed the *Batavia* in 1629 and the *Zeewyk* in 1727.

Dutch shipwrecks and explorers

It was inevitable that some VOC ships would eventually be wrecked on the little-known coast of Western Australia, given the inaccuracies of navigation methods used at that time and the lack

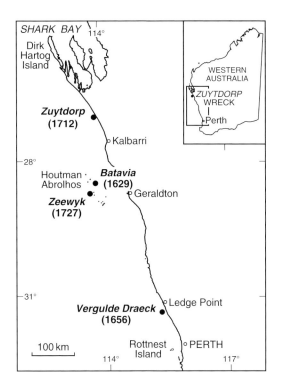

SHARK BAY
Dirk Hartog Island
Zuytdorp (1712)
Kalbarri
Houtman Abrolhos
Batavia (1629)
Geraldton
Zeewyk (1727)
Vergulde Draeck (1656)
Ledge Point
Rottnest Island
PERTH
100 km
WESTERN AUSTRALIA
ZUYTDORP WRECK
Perth

Map 3.
Ships of the Dutch
East India Company
wrecked on the coast
of Western Australia

of detailed maps and hydrographic information. Moreover, many parts of the mainland coast and adjoining islands are low-lying and fringed with reefs, and they are difficult to see from a ship, especially at night.

It is a testimony to the skills of the Dutch mariners that so few company ships were wrecked on this highly dangerous coast. Only four VOC vessels—the *Batavia* (1629), *Vergulde Draeck* (1656), *Zuytdorp* (1712) and *Zeewyk* (1727)—are definitely known to have been lost off Western Australia. However, three other ships that disappeared after leaving the Cape of Good Hope—the *Ridderschap van Holland* (1694), *Fortuyn* (1724) and *Aagtekerke* (1726)—could conceivably have foundered there.

The four known VOC shipwrecks on the Western Australian coast are included in a total of 105 company ships lost between the Netherlands and Asia over a period of some 180 years. A further 36 ships were destroyed or captured through enemy or pirate action, and about 4,700 successful voyages were completed during this period. More than half of the wrecks happened during early stages of the voyages, especially in coastal waters around Great Britain (27 wrecks), and on the Dutch coast (17 wrecks). Table Bay at the Cape of Good Hope was particularly notorious during bad weather. A violent storm there in June 1722 claimed five outward-bound ships, and another in May 1737 destroyed eight homeward-bound vessels sheltering in the bay.[9]

Put in this perspective, the hazards of the Western Australian coast were not nearly as great as those experienced elsewhere by the VOC ships. However, the wrecks that did occur on this coast, in what was then an extremely remote and virtually unknown part of the world, made a big impression on the Dutch mariners. The horrific story of the *Batavia* massacre, the mysterious disappearance of the *Vergulde Draeck* survivors, the epic journey of Abraham Leeman, and the remarkable feat of the *Zeewyk* castaways in constructing a little ship to sail to Batavia must have been legendary among successive generations of VOC sailors. At least one of these wrecks, that of the *Batavia*, was also renowned among the Dutch people through the best-selling book *Ongeluckige voyagie*, first published in 1647 and reprinted several times (most recently in 1994).[10]

The voyage from Asia to the Netherlands was more hazardous than the outward voyage. A total of 141 company ships foundered on the homeward route (over a third more than on the outward route). Half of these were lost in the Indian Ocean, but none involved the Western Australian coast, as the VOC ships did not normally pass near there on their return voyages. Many ships were wrecked as a result of cyclones around Madagascar and Mauritius. A further 28 homeward-bound vessels were lost through acts of war, mostly to the British.

Batavia

The first VOC ship to be lost on the Western Australian coast was the *Batavia*, which was wrecked on Morning Reef in the Houtman Abrolhos Islands on 4 June 1629. The story of this shipwreck and the mutiny and fearful massacre that followed is well known in both Australia and the Netherlands. Indeed, the *Batavia* saga is one of the most dramatic of the world's many stories of shipwreck, either fact or fiction, and it has been the subject of several books.[11]

About 280 people managed to escape the *Batavia* wreck to reach two small neighbouring islands. The Commodore, Francisco Pelsaert, skipper Ariaen Jacobsz, and 47 others departed soon afterwards in the longboat, intending to sail first to the mainland to seek water. They were unsuccessful in finding water, so they proceeded on to Batavia. Pelsaert returned three and a half months later in the ship *Sardam*, finding to his horror that a group of conspirators, led by the undermerchant Jeronimus Cornelisz, had massacred 125 men, women and children. Cornelisz and his group of 36 men had planned to capture the rescue ship and go pirating. They might have succeeded but for the courage and determination of 47 other men, led by Wiebbe Hayes, who held out on West Wallabi Island and managed to warn Pelsaert before the conspirators could reach his ship. Several of the murderers were executed on the Houtman Abrolhos, two were marooned on the mainland coast near the present town of Kalbarri, and others were taken to Batavia to be punished there.

After many years of speculation, the wrecksite of the *Batavia* was discovered in June 1963, on Morning Reef in the Wallabi Group. It had long been assumed that the ship had been wrecked beside Pelsaert Island, at the southernmost end of the Houtman Abrolhos, where Captain Stokes of the *Beagle* had found the wooden beams of an ancient vessel, in 1840.[12] However, a number of persons who investigated the history of the *Batavia* suggested that the wrecksite was more likely to be in the northern (Wallabi) group. The most thorough research on the matter was carried out by Henrietta Drake-Brockman, who concluded that Noon Reef was the probable site of the wreck.[13] She was nearly right; Morning Reef is only 5 kilometres east of Noon Reef.

Two select committees of the Western Australian Parliament have considered the matter of who should be recognized as the discoverers of the *Batavia* wreck. The most recent inquiry (1994) recommended that Max Cramer, David Johnson, Hugh Edwards and Henrietta Drake-Brockman be recognized as the primary discoverers, with Bruce Melrose, Graham Cramer and Greg Allen being regarded as secondary discoverers.[14]

The work of the Western Australian Museum (WA Museum) on the *Batavia* began not long after the wreck was first found, and a program of detailed marine-archaeological work got under way in 1971, when a field station was constructed on Beacon Island.

Excavation of the wrecksite began in 1973.[15] The first material to be removed consisted of 128 sandstone blocks, weighing about 27 tonnes, that had been destined for construction of a portico over an entrance to the walled grounds of the Castle of Batavia. Many other relics were recovered through careful archaeological excavation, the most spectacular (and archaeologically important) being a large section of the stern and after-side of the vessel. It now forms the principal display in the Batavia Gallery at the Western Australian Maritime Museum (WA Maritime Museum) in Fremantle, after painstaking treatment was used to preserve the wood. The portico of sandstone blocks has been erected alongside.

Vergulde Draeck

The *Vergulde Draeck*, popularly known in Australia as the 'Gilt Dragon', was the next VOC ship to be lost in Western Australian waters. It was wrecked during the night of 28 April 1656 on a reef lying 5.6 kilometres offshore, about 12 kilometres south-south-west of the present township of Ledge Point. Of 193 crew on board, 118 drowned soon after the ship foundered, and 75 landed safely on the mainland opposite the wreck. None of the cargo, which included 8 chests containing 78,600 guilders in cash, was saved. One of the ship's boats, with 7 survivors, managed to reach Batavia on 7 June. The other 68 people, including the skipper, Pieter Albertsz, were left behind on the coast opposite the wreck and were last seen trying to extricate the other ship's boat, which was largely buried in sand. Their eventual fate is unknown.[16]

Over the next few years, several VOC expeditions were sent looking for the wreck of the *Vergulde Draeck* and any remaining survivors, but without success. One of the search vessels (the *Goede Hoop*) lost eleven of its crew when they went ashore and did not return, while fourteen crew from another vessel, the *Waeckende Boey*, were abandoned on the coast in the ship's boat.[17] Led by the uppersteersman, Abraham Leeman, the abandoned men courageously set out to sail their small boat to Batavia, after raising its sides with sealskins. Several men died of thirst before they reached the south coast of Java, where the boat was destroyed after landing to obtain water. The remaining castaways were then forced to undertake a harrowing walk of hundreds of kilometres through the jungle in order to survive, and four of them, including Leeman, eventually succeeded in reaching the VOC base at Japara and were taken from there to Batavia.

The wreck of the *Vergulde Draeck* was discovered in April 1963 by Graeme, Jim and Alan Henderson, John Cowen and Alan Robinson. Graeme Henderson (now Director of the WA Maritime Museum) was the first person to recognize objects from the wreck, and he pointed them out to John Cowen, Jim Henderson and Alan Henderson, who were then in the water near him. Alan Robinson had remained in the boat, but he dived in after being shown relics brought up by the others, and assisted in confirming that they came from an ancient wreck. Robinson had been searching for the *Vergulde Draeck* in this general area for many years, and some six years earlier he had publicly claimed to have found the wreck. However, after the announcement, he had been unable to relocate the wreck, and most people were highly sceptical about his claim.

Before there was any publicity regarding the new discovery, Jim Henderson and Alan Robinson sought my opinion, bringing into my office at the Geological Survey several of the objects they had found. On the basis of this material and what they had to say about other aspects of the wreck, it seemed to me that this must be the wreck of the *Vergulde Draeck*. At Henderson's request (he was then a journalist with West Australian Newspapers Ltd), I affirmed this view to the media.[18] I accompanied the party on several diving expeditions to the wrecksite, during which material was recovered to confirm the identity of the ship.

The WA Museum began a program of marine-archaeological work on the *Vergulde Draeck* in 1966, under Dr Colin Jack-Hinton, and a significant amount had already been accomplished when Jeremy Green was recruited in 1971 to take charge of the museum's marine-archaeological program. Green's initial project was to investigate the *Tryall*, and then to continue work on the *Vergulde Draeck*, followed successively by projects on the *Batavia*, *Zeewyk* and *Zuytdorp*.

The WA Museum team recovered a large amount of important material through careful excavation of the site, operating from a museum-owned field station at Ledge Point.[19] Green introduced a high level of professionalism to the museum's wreck program, and his efforts were largely responsible for the eventual establishment of a separate maritime museum, based in Fremantle. His projects on the *Vergulde Draeck* and the *Batavia* are outstanding examples of what can be achieved in shallow-water wrecksites through properly directed marine-archaeological work.

The Select Committee on Ancient Shipwrecks recommended in 1994 that Graeme Henderson be recognized as the primary discoverer of the *Vergulde Draeck*, and that James Henderson, Alan Henderson and John Cowen be regarded as secondary discoverers.[20] The committee noted that Alan Robinson was also involved in finding the wreck, but did not formally recognize him as a discoverer because his 'conduct fell far short of the standard of public spirit and cooperation shown by other discoverers whom the Committee wishes to recognize.'[21]

Ridderschap van Holland

The *Ridderschap van Holland* (the Nobility of Holland) was the next VOC vessel to disappear on a voyage from the Cape to Batavia. This vessel belonged to the largest class of the company's ships, 160 Amsterdam feet (45.3 metres) long, with a nominal carrying capacity of 260 lasts (520 tons) and an actual capacity of 1,138 tons. Passengers on the *Ridderschap van Holland*'s fifth and final voyage to the Indies included a senior VOC official, Sir James Couper (originally from Scotland), who was scheduled to take up an appointment as a member of the Council of the Indies in Batavia. The ship disappeared after leaving the Cape of Good Hope, bound for Batavia, on 5 February 1694.

Early conjecture was that the *Ridderschap van Holland*, like the *Batavia* and the *Vergulde Draeck* before, had probably been wrecked on the coast of the South Land. In 1696, it was decided to despatch a search expedition of three vessels, under the command of Willem de Vlamingh, to seek signs of the wreck and rescue any people who might have survived.

Rumours were later received at the Cape to the effect that the *Ridderschap van Holland* had been taken by pirates based at Fort Dauphin, near the south-eastern corner of Madagascar, and in June 1698 the Cape Political Council recorded that the ship might have been lost in that way.[22] Even so, there was still hope that survivors could be found, and in 1699 two ships visiting Madagascar sought to establish the fate of the missing vessel, but without success.

Research has now shown that the fate of the *Ridderschap van Holland* was still regarded as unknown in 1713, nineteen years after its disappearance, when it was mentioned in relation to the loss of the *Zuytdorp*. The resident uppermerchant and administrator at the Cape of Good Hope, Willem Helot, wrote that 'the ship *Ridderschap van Holland*, having departed from this bay for Batavia in 1694, has never been heard of again, nor any information about the ship received.'[23] It seems that the idea that the ship had been taken by pirates at Madagascar must by then have been abandoned.

Willem de Vlamingh

The primary objective of Willem de Vlamingh's expedition in 1696–97 was to search for the wreck of the *Ridderschap van Holland* and any possible survivors, but he was also instructed to seek survivors from the *Vergulde Draeck*, even though it must have seemed unlikely that any of these people could still be alive after forty years. The three ships selected for the expedition were the frigate *Geelvinck*, the hooker *Nyptangh* and the galliot *'t Weseltje*.[24] They left the Netherlands on 3 May 1696, and reached the Cape of Good Hope on 3 September (*Nyptangh*), 7 September (*Geelvinck*) and 8 September (*'t Weseltje*). The ships stayed at the Cape for more than seven weeks, considerably longer than the time normally allowed, and Vlamingh would later be blamed for wasting time there 'feasting and merrymaking'.

The first sighting of the South Land was made in the early afternoon of 29 December, when they came upon an island off the mainland coast, which Vlamingh named Rottenest Island (now Rottnest Island) because of the many small 'bush rats' (wallabies or quokkas) that they saw there. The ships anchored off the north side of the island during the night of 29 December, and crew members from the *Geelvinck* went ashore next day, probably landing at The Basin. After exploring the island for several days, Vlamingh's ships sailed across to the mainland, and his men went ashore there between 4 and 12 January 1697. They explored the Swan River, rowing an estimated 60–70 kilometres upstream, perhaps as far as the junction with Ellen Brook. They were anxious to contact the native inhabitants, as Vlamingh had been instructed to 'catch a South Lander and bring him hither'. However, the Aborigines kept themselves well concealed, and Vlamingh's men never made contact with any, let alone capturing one. They did succeed in taking several black swans, and, because of the abundance of these birds, Vlamingh named the river the Swan.

After leaving the Swan River, the three ships sailed north along the coast, mapping it as they went and going ashore at several places, including the inlet north of Red Bluff (near Kalbarri), where Pelsaert had marooned two Dutch criminals from the *Batavia* sixty-eight years before. On 30 January, they anchored beside Dirk Hartog Island. Some of the crew climbed the cliff at what is now known as Cape Inscription, during the morning of 2 February. There they found a post standing in a fissure in the rock, and beside it lay a pewter plate, bearing an inscription recording the arrival of Dirk Hartog at this place in 1616. Vlamingh had a new pewter plate hammered flat and inscribed with the text of Dirk Hartog's original message, plus a record of his own visit. The plate was attached to a new post, probably the trunk of a Rottnest Island pine from among wood samples collected on that island, and this was set in place in the same fissure, on 11 or 12 February 1697. The plate remained there until 1818, when the Frenchman Louis de Freycinet took it to Paris for safekeeping. After World War II, the French Government presented the Vlamingh plate to the Australian people, and it is now a prize exhibit at the WA Maritime Museum.[25]

After leaving Dirk Hartog Island, Vlamingh's three ships proceeded along the coast as far as North West Cape, which they reached on 20 February. Next day, the *Geelvinck* fired five guns, and the *Nyptangh* three, 'to farewell the miserable South Land'. They arrived at Batavia, 'God be thanked for a safe voyage', on 17 March 1697.

Although Vlamingh's expedition produced little of value to the VOC, it was certainly important from the viewpoint of global exploration in the late seventeenth century. The expedition provided the first accurate map of the west coast of Australia, and resulted in the discovery and/or naming of a number of prominent geographic features, the most notable being the Swan River, Rottnest Island, Red Bluff and Dirk Hartog Island. Vlamingh's discovery of the Swan River, and the map he produced of it, became known to the British,

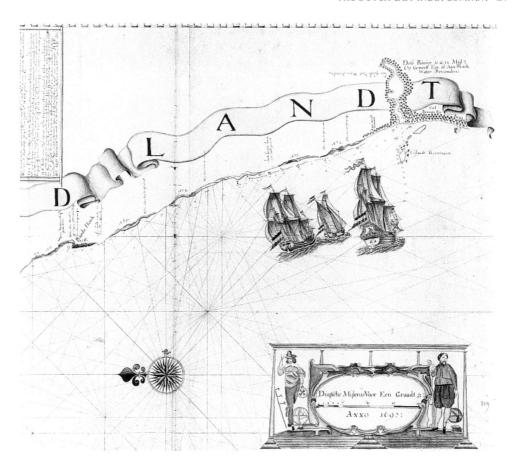

who in due course selected this place as the site for a new colony, the Swan River Colony, on the west coast of Australia.

Zuytdorp

The next VOC ship to be lost between the Cape of Good Hope and Batavia was the *Zuytdorp*, one of the great ships of the company, which left the Cape on 22 April 1712 and was never heard of again. The loss of this ship must have been a grievous blow to the company, especially as it was carrying a rich cargo, including nearly 250,000 guilders in silver coins. However, the authorities had no evidence of where the ship had been lost between the Cape and Batavia, and no vessels were ever sent to search for the wreck

Part of Vlamingh's map of the South Land ('t Zúÿd Landt), based on his exploration in 1696–97: showing his three ships (left to right), the hooker Nyptangh, *the galliot 't Weseltje, and the ship* Geelvinck, *and the coast from* Eÿlandt Rottenest *(Rottnest Island) to north of Roode Houk (Red Bluff), near the subsequent wrecksite of the* Zuytdorp.

and any possible survivors. It is now known that the *Zuytdorp* was wrecked at the foot of coastal cliffs 60 kilometres north of the present town of Kalbarri, probably during the first week of June 1712. It is the only VOC vessel known to have been wrecked on the Western Australian coast from which no survivors ever returned to tell their story.[26]

Fortuyn and *Aagtekerke*

The 1720s were disastrous years for the VOC, marked by the loss of many ships and cargoes. In 1722 alone, five ships were wrecked in a storm at the Cape, and six were destroyed during a cyclone near Mauritius. Between 1724 and 1727, three ships were lost between the Cape and Batavia: the *Fortuyn* in 1724, the *Aagtekerke* in 1726 and the *Zeewyk* in 1727. Only one of these, the *Zeewyk*, is definitely known to have been wrecked on the Western Australian coast, but the other two could have been lost there. Each was on its maiden voyage from the Netherlands to the Indies, and they all belonged to the same class of ship, 145 Amsterdam feet (41 metres) long, with a nominal carrying capacity of 140 lasts (280 tons).

The *Fortuyn*, owned by the Chamber of Amsterdam, sailed from Texel on 27 September 1723, reached the Cape of Good Hope on 2 January 1724, and sailed for Batavia on 18 January. It was never heard of again. At that time of the year, the ship was not supposed to run within sight of the South Land, but it may have inadvertently travelled too far east and been wrecked there. Alternatively, it could have been lost in some other way: perhaps being wrecked on St Paul or Amsterdam Island, or going down during a cyclone before reaching Batavia. We may never know the answer.

However, wreckage and other relics seen in the southern (Pelsaert) group of the Houtman Abrolhos by survivors of the *Zeewyk* in 1727,[27] and by Stokes of the *Beagle* in 1840,[28] could well have been derived from the *Fortuyn*, which had disappeared a little more than three years earlier. Alternatively, they could have been from the *Ridderschap van Holland*, lost in 1694. It seems less likely that the wreckage came from the *Aagtekerke*, as that ship had disappeared only a year before the *Zeewyk* was wrecked, and consequently more signs of the vessel and any survivors might have been expected.

The *Aagtekerke* was built in 1724 for the Chamber of Zeeland, receiving the same name as an earlier ship that had been lost at Plymouth in 1712. Both were named after the town of Aagtekerke in Zeeland, and each was wrecked on its maiden voyage. Following the second loss, the directors of the VOC must have decided that bad luck was associated with the name, as it was never used again for a company ship.

The second *Aagtekerke* left Rammekens on 27 May 1725, arrived at Cape Town on 3 January 1726, and left on 29 January for Batavia. Nothing was ever heard of it again, and no information has come to light to indicate its fate. The ship could have been wrecked on the coast of Western Australia, but no positive evidence of this has yet been found.

Zeewyk

The story of the wreck of the *Zeewyk* in 1727, although not as dramatic as that of the *Batavia*, is nevertheless one of the most remarkable sagas in the annals of the sea, as the survivors constructed a small ship from the wreckage and sailed it successfully to Java.[29]

The *Zeewyk* departed from Vlissingen (Flushing), on its maiden voyage, on 7 November 1726, under the command of Jan Steyns, carrying a rich cargo that included 315,836 guilders in cash, stored in ten chests. The ship arrived at the Cape of Good Hope on 26 March 1727 and departed for Batavia on 21 April. Seven weeks later, at about 7.30 in the evening of 9 June, the *Zeewyk* ran violently onto Half Moon Reef, which skirts the western side of the Pelsaert Group, the southernmost reefs and islands of the Houtman Abrolhos.

There was never any doubt that the ship had been lost. Big waves swept the deck, 2.5 metres of water soon filled the holds, and the mainmast came crashing down. With the arrival of daylight, those on board were relieved to see several islands behind the reef, but they could not leave the wreck because of the height of the surf. Six days later, they were still confined to the wreck, and by then some of the crew had broken into the liquor stores and were brought under control only under threat of death.

On the seventh day, it was decided to risk using the longboat, which was successfully launched and taken to the shallow part of the reef with twelve men. Next day, it was rowed to the nearest island (Gun Island), returning with the good news that water had been found there. The weather was fine for the following two days, and many people successfully made the trip from the wreck to the reef crest, and from there to the island. However, some refused to leave the wreck, remaining on board under precarious conditions for several months.

On 10 July, the longboat set sail for Batavia under the command of the uppersteersman, with eleven others who were generally regarded as the most capable of the seamen. They were never heard of again. The ship's officers remaining on Gun Island found it impossible to maintain shipboard standards of discipline, and there was an ever-present threat of mutiny among the crew. Fortunately, they had sufficient food from the ship's cargo and from the surrounding sea and islands, in the form of seals, fish and birds. Kegs of food were periodically obtained from the wreck, some of them floating to the reef crest. But water was soon a problem. Although it had been found on the island when they arrived there in June, the well had become salty by August, and drinking supplies were then dependent on periodic rainfall. Fortunately, this shortage was alleviated at the end of September when a good supply was found in a shallow well on a nearby island.

The survivors managed to salvage all ten money chests from the wreck, taking them to Gun Island. This was a remarkable feat, given the disintegrating state of the wreck and the fact that the total weight of the chests was more than 3 tonnes.

By the end of October, the *Zeewyk* castaways concluded that the longboat could not have reached Batavia, as otherwise a relief ship would have appeared before then. They made the courageous decision to construct a small ship from the wreckage of the *Zeewyk*, with the objective of sailing it to Batavia. The keel of this new vessel, which they named the *Sloepie* (Little Sloop), was laid on 7 November. It had to be large enough to carry eighty-eight men, over 3 tonnes of coinage, and several tonnes of water and provisions, as well as being sufficiently seaworthy to make the voyage from the Houtman Abrolhos to Batavia.

The carpenter and his mates worked hard in their little shipyard on Gun Island, using materials recovered from the wreck of the

Zeewyk plus timber from mangroves on one of the larger islands. Skipper Steyns's drawing of the vessel, on his map of the area, shows that it had a single mast, with two square sails and a jib, and flags flying bravely from the mast, bow and stern. The *Sloepie* was completed in a little over four months—an amazing achievement, considering the extraordinarily difficult circumstances. This little vessel deserves fame as the first ocean-going ship to be built in Australia, and it testifies to the remarkable courage, perseverance and resourcefulness of the VOC seamen of that time.

Of the 208 men who had departed from the Netherlands on the *Zeewyk*, and the 158 who had left the Cape, 88 remained alive to sail from the Houtman Abrolhos on the *Sloepie*. Stores and money chests were loaded, and the little sloop set sail on 26 March 1728, some 10 months after the *Zeewyk* had been wrecked. It completed a speedy voyage to Sunda Strait, arriving there on 21 April, and reaching Batavia on 30 April with 82 survivors.

In 1952, Lieutenant Commander M.R. Bromell of the Royal Australian Navy learned, during a visit to the Houtman Abrolhos, that a crayfisherman had discovered a number of cannon on Half Moon Reef. During a subsequent visit, as commander of HMAS *Mildura*, he reported finding six guns, three cylindrical pieces of iron, and two bundles of iron bars at this location. There are also some masses of nails, now welded together by rust in the shape of the barrels that originally contained them, at the site. Three of the cannon, one 12-pounder and two 8-pounders, were later raised by crews of the *Mildura* and the *Fremantle* and transported to Perth.[30]

It is clear that these relics found on top of the reef were derived from the wreck of the *Zeewyk*, as the remains of the ship were subsequently located nearby. The position of the cannon, as quoted by Bromell, is 28°52.6′ south, 113°49.7′ east. The uppersteersman's position of the *Zeewyk* wreck quoted in the ship's journal is 28°50′ south, 128°19′ east, which gives a measure of the accuracy of navigation at that time.[31] The longitude measurement given in the journal needs to be adjusted to take account of the fact that the prime meridian (0°) used at that time is not the same as that of today. Indeed, the Dutch prime meridian in the seventeenth and eighteenth centuries varied from map to map. Most navigators used either Tenerife or Ferro (Hierro) in the Canary Islands, but others used Corvo, Flores or São Miguel in the Azores, Boa Vista in the Cape Verde Islands, Fuerteventura in the Canary Islands, or Cape Verde.[32] However, it is clear from the logs of the *Belvliet* in 1711–12 and the *Zeewyk* in 1726–27 that they had adopted the peak of Tenerife (Pico de Teide) as the prime meridian. This peak rises to an elevation of 3,718 metres, and seamen at that time commonly thought of it as the highest mountain in the world. Its longitude today, in relation to the prime meridian of Greenwich, is 16°39′ west. Thus, the longitude of the *Zeewyk* wreck given in the ship's journal should be corrected to 111°40′, for comparison with present-day coordinates. This means that the wreck's position as determined by the ship's navigators was only 2.6′ (about 5 kilometres) too far north, but a massive 2°10′ (about 208 kilometres) too far west.

The first persons to locate the main part of the *Zeewyk* wreck were Hugh Edwards, Tom Brady, Harry Bingham, Max Cramer and Neil McLaughlan, in March 1968. Edwards first recognized that he was at the wrecksite when he discerned the curved shape of an elephant tusk among coral on the sea-floor. The 1994 Select Committee on Ancient Shipwrecks recommended that Hugh Edwards, Tom Brady and Harry Bingham be recognized as primary discoverers of the *Zeewyk*, and that Max Cramer, Neil McLaughlan and Colin Jack-Hinton be regarded as secondary discoverers.

Several expeditions have investigated the archaeology of Gun Island and the *Zeewyk* wreck. Most have been sponsored by the WA Museum and the WA Maritime Museum, and have returned rich collections of artefacts.[33] Several skeletons of persons from the *Zeewyk* who perished during their sojourn on the island have also been exhumed.

The *Zeewyk* was the last VOC vessel to be wrecked on the Western Australian coast. Even though hundreds of company ships sailed past that coast during the rest of the eighteenth century, none are known to have been lost there, and no new observations or maps of the area have been reported from company records of that period. The wreck of the *Zeewyk* and the voyage of the *Sloepie* brought to an end the remarkable era of Dutch discovery and shipwreck on the Western Australian coast, which had begun more than a century before, with Dirk Hartog and the *Eendracht*.

2. A SHIP OF DEATH

THE *ZUYTDORP*

The ship

The *Zuytdorp* was one of the great ships of the VOC. Of twenty-seven company ships that left the Netherlands for the Indies in 1711, none were larger than the *Zuytdorp*, and only two others were of comparable size. The ship was owned by the Chamber of Zeeland, the second largest of the VOC chambers, and it was named after a village in southern Zeeland, still known today as Zuiddorpe (south village).

The directors of the Chamber of Zeeland gave approval for construction of the *Zuytdorp* on 2 December 1700, and it was built in the chamber's shipyard, between 23 December 1700 and 22 June 1701, by a master shipwright named Penne.[34] A construction period of only six months for a large wooden vessel of this type seems amazing, from today's perspective. However, even though this was an excellent performance at the time, it was not exceptional. The Dutch had developed mass-production techniques in shipbuilding, including the use of innovative mechanical aids such as cranes and wind-driven wood saws. Moreover, the design of ships was standardized, so that uniform parts and construction techniques could be used. The result was lower shipbuilding costs, an important factor in the pre-eminence of the Netherlands as a maritime trading nation.

In April 1697, the *Heeren XVII* ruled that only three charters (classes) of ship would be built for the company, as follows, and that inspection methods would be introduced to ensure strict adherence to the specifications:

Charter	Length	Width	Depth of hold
First	160 feet (45.28 m)	40 feet (11.32 m)	17 feet (4.81 m)
Second	145 feet (41.03 m)	36.8 feet (10.41 m)	15.7 feet (4.44 m)
Third	130 feet (36.79 m)	33.6 feet (9.51 m)	14.4 feet (4.08 m)

The dimensions were measured in Amsterdam feet of 283 millimetres, giving the modern metric equivalents shown above.

The *Zuytdorp* belonged to the first, or largest, charter. Only six ships of this size were built for the company in the ten years 1700–09, compared with sixty-two of the two smaller charters. The carrying capacity of the *Zuytdorp* was listed as 250 lasts (500 tons) in 1702 and 1706, and as 200 lasts (400 tons) in 1707 and 1711. However, these capacities were nominal figures for all ships of the first charter, used in calculating the shares of company trade allocated to the respective chambers. In practice, a ship of the first charter was capable of carrying cargoes of about 1,100 tons, and for its outward voyage in 1711 the capacity of the *Zuytdorp* was quoted as 1,152 tons, the largest of all the twenty-seven ships that sailed from the Netherlands to the Indies in that year. The two other ships of the first charter that left in 1711 (the *Berbices* and *Zandenburg*) had slightly smaller capacities: 1,136 tons each. The average capacity of the other twenty-four ships that sailed in that year was 687 tons.

The spelling of the name of the ship, as with many names at that time, was variable. The most common usages in VOC records are *Zúÿtdorp, Zúÿddorp, Zúitdorp, Zúiddorp* and *Zúÿdorp,* and an individual clerk would sometimes use more than one of these. The version *Zúÿtdorp* (*Zuytdorp* for convenience in English) has been adopted here, following the advice of Mrs Meilink-Roelofsz of the Algemeen Rijksarchief that this was the most usual spelling in the archival documents.

The *Zuytdorp* was a *spiegelschip,* as its hull at the stern ended in a flat plane, the *spiegel.* It was also known as a *retourschip,* or return ship, as it was used for the carriage of goods on round trips to and from Asia. As such, it was larger and more strongly built than the average merchant ship of the time. The wide after-end provided spacious cabins for the ship's officers and passengers, in stark contrast to the extremely cramped accommodation for the crew in the mid and forward parts of the ship.

The VOC's spiegel ships differed little in outward appearance from warships, as they had to be adequately armed for defence against ships of enemy countries. The Dutch Republic was at war with various European nations (Spain, France, England and Portugal) during much of the seventeenth and eighteenth centuries, and significant numbers of VOC ships were lost through enemy action. Others were taken by pirates and privateers. The Dunkirk privateers, which preyed on ships passing through the English Channel, were especially feared.

Ships of the first charter normally carried thirty-eight guns, distributed as follows:

Location in ship	Number and size of guns
In the gun room	Four 12-pounders
Abaft the mast	Six 12-pounders
Under the half-deck	Eight 8-pounders
In the waist	Six 8-pounders
Under the forecastle	Six 8-pounders
On the half-deck	Eight 4-pounders

The *Zuytdorp* is known to have carried forty guns, made up of ten 12-pounders, twenty-two 8-pounders, and eight 4-pounders. It is uncertain to what extent the distribution of cannon on this ship differed from the standard arrangement. The eight 4-pounders were swivel cannon, probably four muzzle loaders and four breech loaders, mounted on the poop deck. These swivel cannon, and two muzzle-loading 8-pounders near the compasses, were made of gun-metal (bronze). All the rest were iron muzzle loaders.

No plans of the *Zuytdorp* or other ships of comparable design have survived. However, there are a number of contemporary models of Dutch East Indiamen of this period, including one of the sister ships *Padmos* and *Blydorp* (built in 1722), held in the Maritiem Museum Prins Hendrik, Rotterdam, and another of the *Valkenisse* (built in 1716), in the Museum of Fine Arts, Boston, Massachusetts.

These two models show that the general characteristics of ships of this period were similar: they had essentially the same layout of the upper-deck, and remarkably similar form and detailing of the stern. There is little doubt that the *Zuytdorp* would have closely resembled these ships, especially the *Valkenisse*, which was of the same charter.

Between 1972 and 1977, Dr C. de Heer built an impressive model (scale 1:50) of the *Zuytdorp*, guided by photos of models and paintings of East Indiamen of the period. This model was partly constructed with wood collected on his behalf in 1958 from wreckage of the original *Zuytdorp*.[35] From 1978 to 1990, it was shown, on loan, as the centrepiece of the *Zuytdorp* display at the WA Maritime Museum in Fremantle, before being sold to a private collection. In 1996, it was purchased by the museum, and is now on display.

The poop deck of the Padmos *and* Blydorp *model. Note the four breech-loading swivel cannon mounted on the rail of this deck and the muzzle-loading cannon extended through the gun ports on the side of the ship.*

Photograph courtesy of the Maritiem Museum Prins Hendrik, Rotterdam

*Model of the
Zuytdorp built by Dr
Cornelis de Heer.*

Photograph by Pat Baker,
courtesy of the WA Maritime
Museum

The 1702–06 and 1707–10 voyages

On 15 January 1702, the *Zuytdorp* began its maiden voyage from
de Wielingen, the shoals at the entrance to the Wester Schelde (the
western Scheldt estuary), where ships from Zeeland often waited for
a favourable wind. There were 318 people on the ship, comprising
the skipper Cornelis Jorisz, the merchant Cornelis Jongbloet, the

minister Willem Spandaun, 221 sailors, 89 soldiers, two women and three children. The vessel encountered a heavy storm in the English Channel and was forced to run for shelter to the English port of Torbay after the mainmast and bowsprit were broken by violent winds. This was an ominous beginning for a ship on its maiden voyage, and it is scarcely surprising that seven of the crew and one soldier deserted. The ship remained at Torbay for six weeks, from 24 January to 5 March, while repairs were effected.[36]

The *Zuytdorp* arrived safely at the Cape of Good Hope on 12 June 1702, six people having died on the voyage.[37] It departed three and a half weeks later, on 7 July, leaving twenty-six of its original complement behind to recuperate or join other ships, and taking aboard twelve new crew, two soldiers and a female stowaway. The ship reached Batavia on 6 October, having lost a further eight men on the voyage. A rich cargo of total value 365,591 guilders was delivered, made up of 250,000 guilders in cash (gold ducats, silver ducatons, pieces of eight, and small silver money), various types of cloth, several tonnes of lead, linseed oil, barrels of meat, butter and bacon, various types of wine and beer, paper, needles, muskets, blunderbusses, and other sundry items.

The ship remained in Asia for the next three years, voyaging between the various company trading posts.[38] In 1704, out of fifty-nine ships of the company engaged in intra-Asian trade, only three were of the first charter. The *Zuytdorp* alone among these three was said to be capable of returning to the Netherlands, as the others were worn out. An indication of the importance of intra-Asian trade to the profits of the VOC can be gained from the fact that on a trading trip to Surat, the *Zuytdorp* and other ships in the fleet sold, for 657,633 guilders, a cargo of spices and bar copper that had cost the company 166,923 guilders.[39]

Not much is known about the *Zuytdorp*'s Asian voyages, but they included travels to Surat (in India) and Mocca (in Arabia). Surat, in Gujarat Province, was at that time the centre of Indian trade with Arabia and Persia, while Mocca was the main Arabian trading centre on the Red Sea, and the stepping-off point for Muslims from India making their *hajj* pilgrimage to Mecca. The VOC had set up a major trading post at Surat, run by a director and council who answered to the Governor General in Batavia. On one of its visits to Surat, in 1704, the *Zuytdorp* played an important role in a major dispute that had developed between the VOC and Indian authorities.[40] A few details of this dispute are worth recounting, as it illustrates the way in which the VOC had become deeply involved in the local politics of its trade centres in Asia.

By the beginning of the eighteenth century, the Dutch had been in Surat for nearly 100 years, and they had built up a symbiotic association with local merchants and the Mogul government. However, relationships with the Muslim merchants were frequently very stormy. The main disputes centred around the fact that Surat ships engaged in trade with Mocca were frequently pillaged by pirates, the most notorious being William Kidd, Henry Every and Thomas Tew. Although most pirates, like these, were English, the Indians tended to group all Europeans together, referring to them as *topiwallas* ('hat-wearing men'), and insisting that it was a joint responsibility of the Dutch, English and French trading companies to ensure that Indian shipping was not molested by *topiwalla* pirates. The Indian authorities allocated to the Dutch responsibility for preventing piracy along the Arabian coast from Muscat to Jeddah, and the director at Surat was forced to sign an agreement (*muchalka*) specifying that the VOC would compensate Indian shipowners for any losses to pirates in that area. However, the Dutch insisted that although they would provide armed ships to protect convoys of Indian ships on the voyage to Mocca, the agreement would not apply to ships sailing outside those convoys.

The issue came to a head in 1701, when three ships owned by Abdul Ghafur, the wealthiest and most influential Muslim merchant in Surat, were pillaged on their return voyage from Mocca. Ghafur immediately claimed full compensation for his losses from the Dutch, citing the *muchalka* agreement. They refused to pay, maintaining that the three ships had sailed on ahead of the convoy, and were thus unprotected when the pirates struck. Eventually, in response to imperial orders from the court of Emperor Aurangzeb, the government confiscated sufficient spices from the company's store to cover the compensation payment. This resulted in a major rift in relations between the Dutch and the Muslim merchants, which was to persist for seven years.

The situation had deteriorated badly when the *Zuytdorp* arrived at Surat on 18 September 1704, after a voyage from Mocca. The Dutch residents wished to be evacuated, but they were prevented from leaving their lodge by Indian troops. The *Zuytdorp* joined a Dutch blockade, with six other VOC ships, at the entrance to the harbour. Two Indian ships that had been escorted from Mocca were seized, and the cargo being carried on the *Zuytdorp* for Surat merchants was also impounded. In addition, forty-four Indian holy men and *hajj* pilgrims returning from Mecca were detained on the *Zuytdorp*. They included a distinguished mullah named Nour-al Hak, who was returning to Gujarat after carrying the annual Mogul donations to Mecca. He held the important post of 'censor of public morals' in Ahmedabad, and was 'a prayer leader of Aurangzeb, [and] a pious descendant of the previous chief kadi of the Grand Moguls'.[41]

The arrival of the *Zuytdorp*, the most modern and heavily armed of the VOC ships, brought consternation to the Governor, who feverishly recruited troops. The detention of Nour-al Hak was especially serious because of his standing in the imperial court, and the Muslims of Surat were furious at the detention of the *hajj* pilgrims. The Governor found himself in a difficult situation. If the Dutch people in the lodge were slaughtered, the safety of Nour-al Hak would be imperilled, and that august person had made it clear that his personal security was of overriding concern. It seemed that there was only one thing that could be done: agree to an exchange of the Dutch residents for the Indian hostages being held on the *Zuytdorp*. However, the Governor hesitated to act on this because of strong opposition from Abdul Ghafur.

The situation changed with the arrival of the Dutch vessel *Eem* from Persia, with a rich cargo destined for several merchants, including a large consignment of bullion for a leading Muslim, Mahummed Taki. When this consignment was impounded by the Dutch, Taki threw his influence behind the proposed exchange, and despite furious opposition from Abdul Ghafur, it was effected on 24 December 1704. The VOC personnel and their families were escorted to the *Zuytdorp* by more than 3,000 armed men, and Nour-al Hak and the other holy men were set free.

However, the exchange of hostages did not mean the end of the blockade. The Dutch immediately presented the Governor with extravagant demands for restitution, and they succeeded in obtaining cancellation of the *muchalka*. Negotiations on the amount of compensation to be paid by the city dragged on, without resolution, and eventually the Dutch fleet left at the end of the sailing season, with the expectation that the blockade would be resumed before the next season began. In fact, the blockade was maintained for three successive seasons, until a compromise was eventually achieved and normal trade resumed.

On 1 December 1705, the *Zuytdorp* left Batavia on the homeward voyage to the Netherlands, carrying 163 people, and skippered by Arie Tats. The ship arrived safely at Rammekens (an anchorage near Vlissingen) on 26 July 1706, delivering a cargo valued at 382,204 guilders.

On its second voyage to the Indies, the *Zuytdorp* left Vlissingen on 5 June 1707, skippered by Jan Akkerman, and with a complement of 257 men. The ship reached the Cape on 11 November, after 32 people had died on the voyage, and left a month later, on 9 December. It arrived in Batavia on 29 February 1708, losing an additional seven men on the voyage. During the next 12 months, the ship was used on trading voyages in Asia, at least one of which was to Mocca and Persia. This was despite the *Heeren XVII*'s injunction of that year that it was unwise to send ships of the first charter to these destinations, as they 'suffer too much from the heat'.

On the homeward voyage to the Netherlands, the *Zuytdorp* left Batavia on 13 November 1709, with 157 people on board, skippered again by Jan Akkerman. It reached Rammekens on 16 July 1710, delivering a cargo valued at 335,299 guilders.

The final voyage of 1711–12

Departure of the *Zuytdorp* and *Belvliet*

On its third and final voyage from the Netherlands, the *Zuytdorp* left Vlissingen on 27 July 1711 and de Wielingen on 1 August, bound for the Cape of Good Hope and Batavia. The ship was accompanied by the *Belvliet*, a flute ship owned by the Chamber of Zeeland, which was also on its third voyage to Batavia.

The *Zuytdorp*'s complement of 286 people comprised 100 soldiers, four tradesmen (a stockmaker, a bricklayer, a coppersmith and a firelock maker), and 182 others—mainly sailors, but including several cabin passengers (of whom eight were on board when the ship reached the Cape). It seems likely, although this is not recorded, that the cabin passengers included some women and children. The names of the soldiers and tradesmen are preserved in the soldiers' roll and the soldiers' request book, but the names of the seamen and the cabin passengers have been lost.[42]

The soldiers' request book records the amount of money authorized for payment to each soldier's wife or the agent (*volkhouder* or crimp) who recruited him, amounting to 150 guilders for each ordinary soldier, whose wages were 11 guilders per month, and proportionally more for corporals, higher ranks, and artisans. The job of the recruiting agents, many of them innkeepers, was to persuade unemployed people to join VOC ships on voyages to Asia. The agent would provide each recruit with room and board before the ship departed, together with a set of clothing and other gear required on the voyage. The recruit would in turn give a guarantee, signed for in the request book, that the agent would receive up to 150 guilders from his future pay. In the case of the soldiers from the *Zuytdorp*, this would have amounted to more than a year's wages. After signing his employment contract, the recruit would receive an advance of two months' wages, nearly all of which would be taken by the agent in partial settlement of the debt. The total amount of each guarantee would only be paid after it had been earned in service to the company, so if a person died before the contracted amount had been earned, a proportionally smaller sum would be paid to the nominee. Consequently, after receiving the initial advance, the agent would often sell the bond to another person for a reduced sum. Because of this practice, the agents became known as 'soul sellers'.

Dutch nationals made up less than 40 per cent of the soldiers on the *Zuytdorp*. Of the 104 soldiers and tradesmen, there were 44 Germans, 39 Dutch, 11 Belgians (Spanish Netherlanders), four Norwegians, three Swiss, two Latvians and one Austrian. Nearly half of the soldiers had some literacy skills, at least to the extent of being able to sign their names in the request book. The illiterate signed with a cross, or some other mark, beside their names. The ratio of nationalities among the seamen on the ship is not known; however, it is likely to have been similar to that on the *Belvliet*, where nearly 80 per cent were Dutch. On that ship, the crew included 82 Dutch, 10 Germans, four Swedes, two Norwegians, one Swiss and one Bengali, together with one Dutch woman—the ship's steward.[43]

The pay rates for crew members on the *Zuytdorp* were no doubt the same as those on the *Belvliet*, which are known from the ship's ledger. The highest paid person was the skipper, who received 75 guilders per month. He was followed by the upper-steersman (48 guilders), senior carpenter (37 guilders), master surgeon (36 guilders), second carpenter (32 guilders), under-steersman (32 guilders), 'comforter of the sick' (30 guilders), third carpenter (28 guilders), third steersman (26 guilders), undersurgeon (24 guilders), clerk (24 guilders), master gunner (22 guilders), bosun (22 guilders), and so on down to ordinary seamen (9–11 guilders) and ship's boys (5–7 guilders). The female steward was relatively well paid, at 20 guilders per month.

Marinus Wysvliet, the skipper of the *Zuytdorp*, had not previously commanded a VOC ship, whereas Dirck Blaauw, skipper of the *Belvliet*, was an experienced VOC officer who had commanded two vessels on voyages to Asia, in 1697 and 1700. Blaauw had also been vice-commodore of the return fleet from Batavia in 1706. It seems unusual that he was not appointed as skipper of the *Zuytdorp*, as it was much larger and more valuable than the *Belvliet*. However, because of his seniority and experience, Blaauw was designated as 'skipper in command' of the *Zuytdorp* and *Belvliet* for their voyage to the Cape. In this capacity, he was responsible for routine decisions in setting the course for the two ships, which were supposed to keep together for mutual support. Major decisions were reached through joint meetings of the Broad Council of the two ships, chaired by Blaauw.

Cargo on the *Zuytdorp*

The principal payload carried by the *Zuytdorp* on its voyage of 1711–12, as on other VOC ships voyaging to the Indies, consisted of cash for the company to use in purchasing trade goods in Asia. No documents have survived that specify the precise amount carried by the ship on this voyage, but it can be deduced, by indirect means, that the cash probably consisted of silver coins valued at 248,886 guilders.

The Chamber of Zeeland despatched 925,000 guilders in cash and bullion to the Indies in 1711, equivalent in value to 9.25 tons of gold.[44] It was sent in five ships—the *Zuytdorp*, *Belvliet*, *Unie*, *Berbices* and *Vaderland Getrouwe*—and all except the *Zuytdorp* reached Batavia safely.[45] The daily journal of events (*dagregister*) at the Castle of Batavia recorded each ship's arrival there and gave details of its cargo, showing that the total value of cash and bullion carried by the *Belvliet*, *Unie*, *Berbices* and *Vaderland Getrouwe* came to 676,114 guilders. This suggests that the *Zuytdorp* must have been carrying 248,886 guilders, to give the total sent by the Chamber of Zeeland in that year. If this deduction is correct, the value of coinage carried by the *Zuytdorp* was equivalent in value to 2.5 tons of gold, worth $41.6 million in terms of today's gold values.

However, the evidence concerning the amount carried by the *Zuytdorp* is equivocal. The minutes of the Chamber of Zeeland for 21 July 1711 suggest that the *Zuytdorp* and *Belvliet* would be taking only 200,000 guilders to Batavia.[46] If this had been so, the *Zuytdorp* would have carried only 154,466 guilders, as the value of cash and bars of silver on the *Belvliet* is known to have been 45,534 guilders. Notwithstanding this, the balance of evidence favours the higher figure of 248,886 guilders, as it is similar to the amounts carried by the *Zuytdorp* on its earlier voyages and to those carried by other major ships in 1711–12.

Of the cash carried by the *Zuytdorp* and *Belvliet*, it is known that 100,000 guilders consisted of newly minted schellings and double stuivers, but the composition of the remainder is not listed in extant VOC records.[47] However, the minutes of general meetings of the Chamber of Zeeland held on 5 March and 11 May 1711 refer to the purchase, in Amsterdam, of coinage to be sent to the Indies. Accounts of the Amsterdam Wisselbank (exchange bank), which are preserved in the town archives of Amsterdam, have the following entries for 27 March and 22 May 1711 in the name of the Chamber of Zeeland:[48]

27 March 1711

8 sacks of pilaren [pieces of eight]	
at ƒ 2200 [guilders] each, plus ¼%	ƒ 17,644
2 sacks of mexicanen [pieces of eight]	
at ƒ 2200 each, plus ¼%	ƒ 4,411
11 sacks of ducatons at ƒ 2200 each, plus ¼%	ƒ 6,600
16 ducatons	ƒ 48
22 May 1711	
56 sacks of ducatons at ƒ 600 each	ƒ 33,600
10 ducatons	ƒ 30
30 sacks of mexicanen at ƒ 2200 each, plus ¼%	ƒ 66,165
Total:	ƒ 128,498

There can be little doubt that all of this money, with the probable exception of the 26 separate ducatons (which may have been for expenses incurred by the skippers), was sent to the Indies on the *Zuytdorp* and *Belvliet*. The cost of the coinage purchased from the Amsterdam Wisselbank, plus the 100,000 guilders in newly minted schellings and double stuivers, amounts to 228,498 guilders, which is about 66,000 guilders short of the total thought to have been carried by the *Zuytdorp* and *Belvliet*. This amount must have been raised separately, probably through the Middelburg Bank, where the Chamber of Zeeland conducted much of its business. However, this transaction cannot be confirmed, as the records of the bank were destroyed, along with much of Middelburg, during a German bombing raid in May 1940.

Details of the rest of the *Zuytdorp*'s payload on the voyage of 1711–12 are conjectural, because the bill of lading has not been found. However, from what is known of the cargoes carried by other ships at that time and by the *Zuytdorp* on its earlier voyages, it is expected that the holds of the ship were filled with barrels of wine, beer, butter, meat, bacon and various oils; several tonnes of lead in ingots and rolled sheets; various types of cloth; and sundry commodities such as rope, sulphur, pitch, canvas, paper, muskets, leather, copper, salt, and iron hoops and plates.

Journal of the *Belvliet*

The journal of the *Belvliet* for the voyage from Zeeland to the Cape has been preserved in the VOC archives, but the equivalent journal for the *Zuytdorp* has not survived. The *Belvliet*'s journal gives a matter-of-fact description of what took place on the voyage from Zeeland to the Cape, accompanied for most of the way by the *Zuytdorp*. It was written by Jacob Leynsen, who began the voyage as the ship's uppersteersman and was later promoted to skipper. Preserved with the journal are transcripts of resolutions reached by the Broad Council of the two ships, wills made by persons on the *Belvliet*, and details of the proceeds of auctions of the personal effects of deceased sailors and soldiers on the ship.[49]

The *Belvliet* left Zeeland with 164 people on board, including 104 sailors, 58 soldiers, and two others, presumably passengers.

Map 4 (opposite). Route followed in 1711–12 by the Belvliet *in sailing from Zeeland to the Cape of Good Hope, accompanied for much of the way by the* Zuytdorp

The journal of the ship began on 28 July 1711, a day after the two ships were released to sail from Vlissingen. As the Netherlands was at war with France and Spain (the War of the Spanish Succession), there was a danger of the ships being attacked or captured by an enemy warship or privateer, especially in the English Channel. Consequently, the *Zuytdorp* and *Belvliet* sailed to the Atlantic by the Back Way—that is, around the north coast of Scotland—joining a convoy of ships escorted by the state ship *d'Orangie Galley* and the company cruiser *d'Uyno*.

A Dutch galliot joined the convoy in the evening of 20 August, and reported that the return fleet of sixteen ships from the Indies had sailed into the Zuiderzee twelve days earlier. The *d'Uyno* and the hooker *Zeelandia* were carrying provisions for this return fleet, in case their supplies had run low, but now that the fleet had arrived at the Netherlands those provisions were no longer required for that purpose. With this in mind, the Broad Council of the *Belvliet* and *Zuytdorp* met on 22 August to consider the possibility of securing additional food supplies. It was recorded in the resolution of the meeting that since the two ships had put to sea, 'a large part of our victuals, principally beer and water, has been consumed, and we could encounter even…worse adversity in the following part of our voyage, especially in this season of the year.' Moreover, much of the bread on the *Belvliet* was said to have been infested with mites. It was decided to request the company cruiser and hooker to provide beer, water, peas and bread to the *Belvliet* and *Zuytdorp*, to be paid for from the company account.[50] These supplies were transferred on 22 and 23 August.

There is something strange about this resolution. How could a large part of the food and drink have been consumed after little more than three weeks at sea, when the ships must have left Vlissingen with enough supplies to last for more than six months? In 1713, when questions were being asked at the Cape about reasons for the disappearance of the *Zuytdorp*, it was suggested that the skipper of the ship, Marinus Wysvliet, had denied adequate food to his crew on the voyage to the Cape. It was implied that he had hoped to profit from the illicit sale of surplus food after the ship reached Batavia. Perhaps Dirck Blaauw of the *Belvliet* was also involved in such a scheme, and a deal had been struck with the skippers of the two supply vessels in the North Sea.

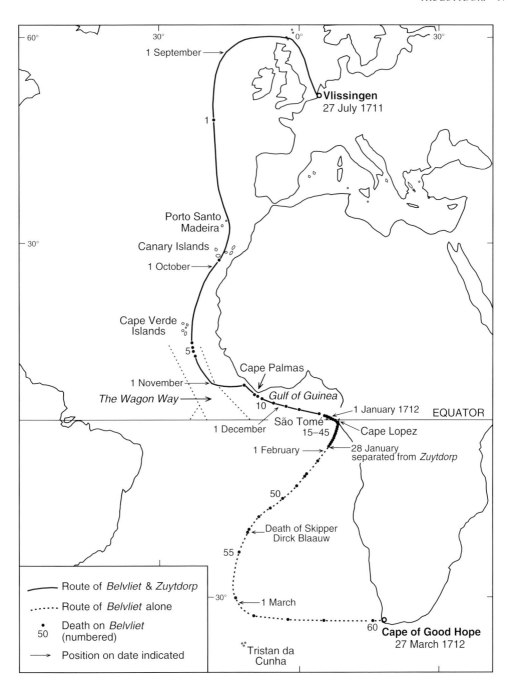

60°   30°   0°   30°

1 September ⟶

Vlissingen
27 July 1711

1

— 30°

Porto Santo
Madeira °
Canary Islands °
1 October ⟶

Cape Verde °°
Islands

5

Cape Palmas
1 November ⟶
The Wagon Way ⟶
10   *Gulf of Guinea*   1 January 1712   EQUATOR
São Tomé   Cape Lopez
1 December   15–45
1 February ⟶   28 January
separated from *Zuytdorp*

50

Death of Skipper
Dirck Blaauw
55

— 30°   ⟵ 1 March

60   **Cape of Good Hope**
27 March 1712

°° Tristan da
Cunha

Route of *Belvliet & Zuytdorp*
Route of *Belvliet* alone
Death on *Belvliet*
50 (numbered)
⟶ Position on date indicated

The ships sailed between Fair Isle and the northernmost islands of the Orkneys on 23 August, and turned south in the Atlantic on 1 September. Each day, the position of the *Belvliet* was deduced by dead reckoning in terms of both latitude and longitude, the latitude being measured more precisely whenever it was possible to sight the sun at noon.

The first death on the *Belvliet* occurred on 15 September, seven weeks after leaving the Netherlands. The island of Porto Santo was sighted on 23 September, an estimated 9–10 Dutch miles (65–75 kilometres) away, and after passing that island and others in the Madeiras, the ship sailed on through the Canary Islands, passing between Fuerteventura and Gran Canaria. The log reports that various ships of the fleet separated from the *Belvliet* and *Zuytdorp* from time to time, the last being a galliot on 30 September.

Progress for the month of September had been relatively slow, but steady, until the ships entered the doldrums after crossing the Tropic of Cancer on 29 September. On 6 October, it was estimated that they had covered only 8 Dutch miles (60 kilometres) in the previous twenty-four hours, and were drifting in a dead calm. Progress was better on 8 and 9 October (20 miles and 19 miles), but at midday on the 10th the ships were again becalmed, and had covered only 5½ miles in the previous twenty-four hours. The crew of the *Belvliet* cleaned the ship between decks and sprinkled their quarters with vinegar. No doubt the vinegar was used to alleviate the stench from the crew's quarters, which must have intensified after they entered the tropics and scurvy became more prevalent.

The ships entered the northern end of the Wagon Way, south of the Cape Verde Islands, on 8 October, and Blaauw signalled the *Zuytdorp* to sail south-south-east within this sea lane. However, the two ships progressed only very slowly, with little or no wind, and the *Belvliet's* log contains entries such as 'dead calm, drifted back and forth', 'dead calm and overcast sky and rain'. The rain did at least enable them to replenish their water casks. Once again, they cleaned and fumigated the ship between decks. In the twenty-six days up to 3 November, the two ships had progressed only 110 Dutch miles, or an average of little more than 4 Dutch miles (30 kilometres) per day, and had drifted close to the eastern boundary of the Wagon Way.

On 3 November, after a gust of wind and rain at sunrise, they were again becalmed. In the afternoon, Blaauw called a meeting of the Broad Council to decide on the best course to adopt, and for this purpose the skipper, undermerchant and uppersteersman of the *Zuytdorp* came on board the *Belvliet*. The minutes of the meeting record that scurvy had become prevalent, and there were now many sick people on both ships. On the *Belvliet*, twenty-eight people were listed as suffering from scurvy, and forty-eight on the *Zuytdorp*, most being unfit for duty. Nine of the sick people on the *Belvliet* and eight on the *Zuytdorp* had been laid up in their bunks for some time, and it was recorded that they were unlikely to recover unless fresh food and water could soon be obtained. The council concluded that 'means should be devised to find some relief for our sick, who still increase daily.' Consequently, it decided to sail east towards the African coast at Cape Palmas, in order to obtain a firm position, after which it might be desirable to continue on to the islands of Annabon or São Tomé, the latter being judged 'very suitable for comforting our sick and to provide us again with water'.[51]

The coast of Africa was sighted on 6 November, and presumably a final decision was made at about that time to proceed to the island of São Tomé. However, it took the ships nearly six weeks to reach the island, and three months to sail out of the Gulf of Guinea.

The health of the *Belvliet*'s crew continued to deteriorate, and many died, as they sailed towards São Tomé. At this stage, many of the crew must have had serious doubts about their ability to survive the voyage, as several men made their wills, which were written and certified by Frederick Lieffers, secretary of the *Belvliet*. They are still preserved among the ship's papers. An example is the will of twenty-three year old Alexander Wisse of Zierikzee, the ship's second carpenter, who

> being somewhat sickly heretofore, but being up and about, and having good control over his speech, mind and memory, and being of brave appearance…but having considered the fragility of the life of man, that nothing is more certain than death and nothing more uncertain than the hour thereof, has therefore taken counsel, before departing from this vale of tears, to make dispensation of those temporal goods granted him by Almighty God in this life…

After requesting that he be given a Christian burial, 'be it on land or at sea', Wisse bequeathed to

> Willem de Vries of Middelburgh, sailing in this ship as third mate, the sum of one hundred guilders…to the collective officers of this ship a similar sum of one hundred guilders…to his mate Jan Willemsz Koot of Moordreght, also sailing on this vessel as ship's carpenter, all his clothes, sleepware, and further [illegible] outside his chests in the forward part of the forecastle of the ship…and finally he the testator declares as his universal heir [to receive the residue of his estate]…the Reformed Poor at Zierickzee…for the benefit of the poor mentioned before, without opposition by anybody.

The will was witnessed by Cornelis Miris, boatswain, Jan Cornelisz, quartermaster, and Hendrick Helm, rigger, before Frederick Lieffers, 'in the ship *Belvliet* sailing now at the northern latitude of 3 degrees and 12 minutes'.[52] However, Alexander Wisse was to survive the voyage to the Cape of Good Hope, and on to Batavia, as did the two friends identified in his will.

The ships arrived at São Tomé (just north of the equator) on 11 December, anchoring in the roads near the Portuguese settlement on the island. By then, fourteen people had died on the *Belvliet*, and sixty were listed as sick, more than double the number of sick when the ship had left the Wagon Way. The invalids were carried ashore four days later, and the remaining crew cleaned between the decks. While at São Tomé, the ship acquired ten cows, twelve and a half boatloads of water, and two and a half boatloads of firewood. The ship was also careened on the shore of the island.

Eight men from the *Zuytdorp* and two from the *Belvliet* deserted at São Tomé. They may have hoped to join a Portuguese ship in due course, although the island was not on a busy trade route. In any case, these men probably felt that they had nothing to lose, and that the uncertainties of life on São Tomé were preferable to the prospects of death on the *Zuytdorp* and *Belvliet*.

After carrying the sick back on board, the two ships set sail from São Tomé on 3 January, and dropped anchor on 9 January beside the African (Gabon) coast at Cape Lopez, then known as

Cape de Lopez Gonsalves. The death rate rose catastrophically immediately after they left the island, nineteen dying during a period of two weeks. Many of the dead were buried on shore at Cape Lopez, including the commander of the soldiers, Anthony van Dolle of Dordrecht. Unlike others of lower rank, he was interred in a coffin.

After leaving Cape Lopez on 16 January, the two ships had little success in sailing south along the African coast, because of contrary winds and currents, and they separated inadvertently during the night of 28 January. Soon afterwards, the *Belvliet* set course away from the coast, sailing towards the central Atlantic and finally escaping from the disastrous Gulf of Guinea.

The skipper, Dirck Blaauw of Vlissingen, died on 22 February, having been ill for some time. Next day, they 'gave the dead body of the deceased skipper…a seaman's burial, fired 22 guns in all and carried him three times around the ship.' Only six days before dying, he had granted power of attorney to the uppersurgeon, Pieter Calland of Middelburg, and the understeersman, Hendrick Fret of Vlissingen, directing that 'if he should come to die of this, his present disease, or in the course of this voyage', they should take his belongings to two named merchants in Batavia for sale there on behalf of his wife in Middelburg.[53] Blaauw must have decided that more would be realized if his goods were sold in Batavia than if they were auctioned on the ship, like those of other people who had died on the voyage. Moreover, he may not have wished his personal belongings to be subject to the scrutiny of all on board at a public auction.

The records of such auctions list the possessions of the sailors and soldiers who died, and the value of such items when purchased by their shipmates. Perhaps the most pathetic of these were the personal effects of Matthys Roeloffsz of Suydeham, seaman, who left 'solely a little tobacco, a few short pipes, and some old odds and ends, which altogether was sold by public auction to Jan Swart of Stockholm, seaman-gunner, for 2 guilders and 10 stuivers.'[54]

More typical was Steven Dircksz of Amsterdam, gunner-seaman, who left a linen undershirt and underpants, a blue-striped undershirt and pants, a watchcoat, an old mattress, an old woollen shirt, an old linen shirt, two white shirts, a blue shirt, a pair of new shoes, a pair of old shoes, an old English bonnet, a handkerchief, a pair of scissors, and a knife. These items sold in five lots at auction for 16 guilders and 18 stuivers.[55]

A midshipman, Johannes Vermeer of Rotterdam, left some of the most valuable personal effects, which were auctioned, in forty-one lots, for 344 guilders and 12 stuivers. They included two gold rings, a signet ring, a silver toothpick, a pair of silver buckles, a cane with a silver knob and tassels, a silver snuffbox, a prayerbook with a silver mounting (purchased by the skipper, Dirck Blaauw, for 7 guilders), a jacket with golden buttons, a damask waistcoat, steersman's instruments, and a parcel of books including *The life of Cromwell*, *The Amsterdam secretary*, *The complete secretary* and *The condition of Germany*. The jacket and waistcoat were sold for 55 guilders, whereas the parcel of books realized only 2 guilders. This young man, who must have been well educated and from a wealthy family, was probably expected to follow an illustrious career with the VOC, only to lose his life on what may have been his first voyage.[56]

Opposite: Page of the journal of the Belvliet on its voyage of 1711–12 from the Netherlands to the Cape of Good Hope, covering the period 29 February to 3 March 1712. Death no. 56, that of the quartermaster Jan van Dalen of Middelburg, occurred on 29 February.

After the death of Dirck Blaauw, it was necessary to appoint a replacement skipper, and consequently a meeting of the ship's council was called on 25 February. This meeting resolved to appoint as skipper the uppersteersman, Jacob Leynsen, at a monthly stipend of 60 guilders. At the same time, the understeersman, Hendrick Fret, was promoted to uppersteersman at 40 guilders per month, and the third steersman, Willem de Vries, to understeersman at 29 guilders per month. It was acknowledged that these promotions would be subject to the approval of the High Noble Governor General and Councillors of India at Batavia, or of the Noble Lord Governor and Council at the Cape of Good Hope.[57]

Leynsen's appointment was evidently confirmed, for he continued as skipper of the *Belvliet* on the voyage from the Cape to Batavia, and on its homeward voyage from Ceylon in 1715–16. He was skipper of the *Steenhoven* when it sailed to Batavia in 1721–22, but was not listed as such on its homeward voyage or on that of any other VOC ship. Probably Leynsen's fate, like that of so many company personnel, was death from disease in Asia. Throughout the history of the VOC, only one in three company personnel returned to the Netherlands after departing for Asian destinations.[58]

By the last day of February 1712, the death toll on the *Belvliet* had reached fifty-six. It seems remarkable that there were still

A° 1712 Int' Schip Belvliet Zeylende van Patria

29 m: Z ter af de
gissing bevonden 29 m: Z ⅔ ... fyn als de gissing, naar midd: d'wint ...
A 4 gr: 5 m Nording
door twee peylings als vooren voorts snaggts d'wint want 'O tot Z O ...
4 gr: 00 m Nording bramz en lab: hoelt, moij weer, inde naggt maanschijn

Maandagh ultimo feb smorgens en in d'voormidd: d'wint O en ON.
teerden d'masten lab bramz hoelt reelijk klaar weer; teerden d'mast
met d'boot
haaldend'z op en d'boot gaalden de z koij uijt, visiterende d'seijlen,
op d midd: gissen d'hoelb en vergeijd to: 't etmaal op ...
Bevonden Z 8 ... 30
gr: 13 m Z 16 mijl, hout op d gegiste Z 8 van 30 gr: 15 m en lengt
coers verandert als vooren naar midd: wint N O hoelt als vooren ...
N° 56 ... Jan van den Z O aan, met d 2 gl in dito naggt is overleden Jan
Dalen quartm van Dalen ... middels quartiermeester, voorts snaggts d
wint N O en N N O bramz en frisse hoelt, reelijk
klaar weer

Dinsdagh Prijmo maart smorgens en in de voormidd: d'wint N N O
braaude de schuijt bramz en dito frisse hoelt braanden d ... uijt op d midd
gissen d'hoelb en vergeijd vant etmaal op Z O ½ Z 23 m
Bevonden Z 8 ... hout volgens dien d gegiste Z 8 ... 31 gr: 23 m: lengt
31 gr: 20 m
coers verandert ... 3 gr: 21 m: naar midd: d wint en weer als vooren
frinden O Z O aan voorts snaggts d wint vant N N O tot
N O t O bramz hoelt

Woonsdagh den 2 ... smorgens, en inde voormidd: d wint vant N O
tot O N O bramz hoelt op d midd: gissen hoelb en ...
Bevonden Z 8 ... to: 't etmaal op Z O t O 19 mijl: hout den volgens op d gegist
... 32 gr: 0 m Z 8 ... 32 gr: 2 m lengt ... 4 gr: 36 m, naar midd: d wint
vant O N O tot N N O hoelt als vooren, voorts snaggts
d wint N O en N O t O aan O bramz en lab: hoelt klaar ...

Donderdagh den 3 ... smorgens en in de voormidd: de wint N O en ON.
lab bramz hoelt moij weer, op de midd: gissen d'hoel
en vergeijd to: 't etmaal op Z O t O 47 mijl; hout den
Bevonden Z 8 ... volgens op d gegiste Z 8 ... 32 gr: 47 m lengt ... 5 gr 43
32 gr: 47 m
naar midd: de wint als vooren lab hoelt en still klaar
weer, voorts snaggts de wint vant N t O tot N O t N lab
hoelt betrokke luggt

enough able-bodied people left on board to keep the ship sailing and otherwise well constituted, after nearly eight months of this tragic voyage. However, Leynsen, as the newly appointed skipper, must have been determined to ensure that the *Belvliet* would be in good shape on arrival in Cape Town, despite the appalling death toll. Over three days of the final run towards the Cape, the living quarters between the decks were cleaned, the ship was tarred, and the barge and longboat were scraped and painted. On 18 March, the bower and stream anchors were put in place, ready for the ship's arrival at the Cape.

On 26 March, the ship's position by dead reckoning was latitude 33°37′ south, longitude 39°24′ east, according to which they should already have reached land. However, a great deal of seaweed was seen floating in the sea, indicating that land was not far away, and indeed it came into sight next day. The ship entered Table Bay on 27 March, the yards were lowered and the topmasts struck in the afternoon, and two anchors were dropped during the evening. The *Zuytdorp* had arrived there four days earlier and was lying at anchor in the bay. Two months had passed since the two vessels were last in contact near the coast of Africa.

In his journal, Leynsen hailed their arrival by writing 'God be praised and who else accompanied us.' No doubt he and many of the ship's complement had wondered whether someone other than God had been on board during much of that hellish eight-month voyage. Certainly, fate was against them when the ill-considered decision was made to leave the Wagon Way and sail into the Gulf of Guinea. This prolonged the voyage by at least two months, resulting in scores of deaths that would not otherwise have occurred (about two-thirds of all fatalities during the voyage to the Cape of Good Hope happened in the three months spent in the Gulf of Guinea). If Dirck Blaauw and Marinus Wysvliet had survived to reach Batavia, both may have been held to account for this decision, as it had contravened VOC sailing instructions, with disastrous consequences.

The daily journal of events at the Cape recorded the arrival of the *Zuytdorp* on 23 March, stating that it had 'out of 286 crew lost 112 men, and brings in 22 sick'. This information was repeated in a letter from the Cape authorities to the *Heeren XVII*, dated 27 March 1712, which added that a further eight men had deserted the ship at São Tomé, and the *Zuytdorp* was 'well constituted in other respects'.[59] A postscript to the letter advised that the *Belvliet* had arrived on 27 March, also 'well constituted', with 60 dead and 18 sick (out of 164 crew), after losing two by desertion at São Tomé. No doubt the most important thing in the eyes of the *Heeren XVII* was that each vessel was still 'well constituted'.

The voyage to the Cape by the *Zuytdorp* and *Belvliet* had taken eight months, or nearly double the usual time. Of the other twenty-five ships that left the Netherlands for the Indies in 1711, most took about four months to reach the Cape. Some completed the voyage in less than this time, and none took longer than five months, apart from one ship that lost its masts in a storm and had to put in to Lisbon for repairs. The reasons for the very slow voyages of the *Zuytdorp* and *Belvliet* were: first, the departure from the Netherlands at an inappropriate time of the year, resulting in the ships experiencing very calm weather in the equatorial area; and second, the imprudent decision to follow a course into the Gulf of Guinea, thereby prolonging the voyage by at least two months.

After returning to the Netherlands in 1716, the *Belvliet* sailed on its fourth voyage to the Indies, on 28 January 1717, arriving at Batavia on 24 September that year. It was then used for trading voyages within Asia over the next twelve years, before being laid up in Batavia in 1729. By that time, the *Belvliet* had given twenty-five years of faithful service to the company.

Deaths on the *Zuytdorp* and *Belvliet*

Of the people who left the Netherlands on these two ships, nearly half had died, deserted or become seriously incapacitated through illness before reaching the Cape of Good Hope. The death rate amounted to 39.2 per cent on the *Zuytdorp* and 36.6 per cent on the *Belvliet*. These levels of death and sickness were extremely high, even for those times. In the period 1700–10, the average death rate on all voyages from the Netherlands to the Cape was only 4.6 per cent.[60]

Scurvy was the main killer during most of the history of the company, until it was found, in the second half of the eighteenth century, that sauerkraut (pickled cabbage) in the shipboard diet could alleviate the disease. It had long been known that fruit and vegetables would prevent and cure scurvy, but they could not be kept fresh for very long, whereas sauerkraut could last and retain its effectiveness for many months.

In some cases, a ship's company would suffer an epidemic of an infectious disease such as typhoid or typhus, resulting in many deaths, but there is no evidence that this was the case for the *Zuytdorp* and *Belvliet*. It is clear that scurvy was the primary illness on board these two vessels. However, Dr Arnold Leuftink, who made a special study of health care on VOC ships, suggested that tropical malaria, contracted when the ships visited São Tomé, was almost certainly responsible for the steep increase in deaths during the period immediately after the visit to that island. This type of malaria can take a violent course, resulting in death within a few days or even hours. Enteric diseases, like typhoid and dysentery, contracted on the island, might also have induced deaths among people who were already weakened by scurvy.[61]

It would be difficult to imagine a more harrowing occupation than that of master surgeon or undersurgeon on one of these ships of death, trying to cope with the ravages of disease among large numbers of incapacitated people, under dreadful conditions in the cramped quarters between the decks. Knowledge of disease and its treatment was at best rudimentary, and the conditions of hygiene on board were appalling.

The Dutch East Indiamen were certainly magnificent vessels to behold on the outside, with their attractive lines, spectacular decorations, colourful paintwork, and many flags and streamers. However, it was another thing inside the ships. Living conditions for the sailors and soldiers were squalid and unhygienic. The men had to swing their hammocks, store their belongings and eat their meals in the extremely confined spaces between the decks. In ships of the largest charter, like the *Zuytdorp*, it was common for 300 or more men to be crammed between the decks in this manner. Limited amounts of light and ventilation came through the gun ports and a few hatches, which had to be closed during adverse weather, making conditions dreadfully hot and humid in the tropics. On the other hand, there was no heating when the ships were in cold latitudes, so many on board suffered greatly from colds and influenza. Severe pulmonary diseases such as pleurisy and pneumonia often claimed many lives, especially in the North Sea during winter.[62]

Although there was a strict requirement for people to relieve themselves over the sea, using the heads (gratings) at the bow-end of the ship, this was impossible to enforce during bad weather or when people were incapacitated through sickness. Consequently, there was an ever-present problem of human excrement and vomit between the decks. The stench that emanated from the quarters occupied by the sailors and soldiers, especially when there were large numbers of seriously ill and dying people, or when many were seasick, must have been overpowering.

Weather and sea conditions permitting, walking invalids were treated by the master surgeon in the open air beside the mainmast, twice a day.[63] Sick parades were held immediately after or before morning prayers, when the provost would strike his baton against the mainmast, chanting:

> *Kreupelen en blinden* [Cripples and blind]
> *Komt laat U verbinden* [Come to be bandaged]
> *Boven bij den grooten mast* [Up by the mainmast]
> *Zult gij den Meester vinden* [Shall ye the master find]

On VOC ships, the master surgeons were required to have relevant health care training and experience, but their assistants commonly had little or no prior training. If the master surgeon died, one of his assistants was liable to be thrust into the senior position, even if he lacked the necessary qualifications. Similarly, unqualified persons among the crew could be made undersurgeons if the need arose.

From 1695 onwards, master surgeons were required to maintain a journal in which the symptoms, diagnosis, treatment and progress of individual patients were detailed. Those journals that have survived show that many surgeons were conscientious in looking after their patients, despite the trying work conditions. Two excellent examples of such journals are those for the *Geelvinck* and *Nyptangh*, on their voyages to the Cape in 1696, which have been translated by Cornelis de Heer in Günter Schilder's book on Vlamingh's expedition.[64] The surgeons on these two ships were clearly dedicated people who really cared about their sick patients, and their treatments for some maladies seem to have been quite successful. However, there was little that could be done about scurvy, because of the deficiency of vitamin C in the shipboard diet. Three months after leaving the Netherlands, during August, the master surgeon of the *Geelvinck* reported that about twenty people were incapacitated with scurvy. He noted the following symptoms:

> Rigid limbs, in particular in the juncture of the chin, and with purple spots and a bluish rash, a constriction above the heart, and short of breath, pale complexion, fatigue of the body, all this together with a sound heart, but had difficulty in biting, the mouth being in a poor condition through spongy and rotten gums and loose teeth. I had their legs bathed every morning with the following liniment and their mouths washed with the following wash, and internally administered twice a day these spirits, to be taken in brandy fortified with horseradish. Their nourishment was beer and bread or a rusk with butter or cheese for those who could bite it and a glass of sack and for the rest whatever they liked and could be supplied on board. With this I sustained them until they arrived at the Cape of Good Hope.

At the Cape, these sick people would have entered the company hospital, hopefully to be cured of scurvy through a diet of fresh fruit and vegetables, although some must have succumbed to other maladies.

The surgeons on both ships showed a caring and sympathetic attitude towards their patients, but there were signs of mild reproach for those who had alcohol-induced or venereal illnesses. The master surgeon of the *Geelvinck* commented on his treatment of one patient as follows:

> I was called to Jan Dirx, of Workum, who complained to me of a great pain in his chest with throwing up of bloody phlegm, and some fever, which did not strike me as strange since his was a much debauched body, particularly with alcohol. I prepared for him a mild laxans of folia sennae, since he had no motion for 2 to 3 days. I made him take every day balsamum sulfuris therebintinati and a decoctum of the radix China and sarsaparilla. Occasionally he improved, but he could not get up. For nourishment he took mostly an egg soft boiled and sometimes a caudle of wine with sugar and

herbs and further whatever he liked and could be given. The 20th ditto he became very weak and very feverish, against which I administered elixir cum spiritu salis armoniaci. The next day he was a little better, when the fever had left him. To sustain his strength, which gradually waned, I administered a nourishing chicken soup, and further he lay abed. A little fever took him on 28th August, with which he entered his eternal rest.

The master surgeon of the *Nyptangh* commented thus on health problems experienced during August in the vicinity of Tristan da Cunha:

The people began to complain of fatigue and stiffness all over their bodies; it being the beginning of scurvy…further since most ailments occurring in the Hon. Company's ships are severe colds, both north and south of the equinoctial line, mostly caused by a lack of clothing, particularly those who are fitted out by the so-called crimps, making them believe that they will soon come to warm regions and providing linen clothes instead of woollen ones, and consequently they fall into burning fevers, a pale and leaden colour, short and stinking breath, a constriction over the heart, little appetite, blue swollen rotten gums, blue and green spots over the whole body, and others like fleabites on the shins, rigidity through all the limbs, headaches, etc. The main cure for this consists of a good fortifying diet and more clothing.

The health problems on the *Geelvinck* and *Nyptangh*, bad as they seem today, were not unusual for the time. When Vlamingh's ships arrived at the Cape, the Governor and Council reported that they had arrived 'without dead or sick people worth mentioning', even though on the *Geelvinck* alone seven had died, seventeen were hospitalized, and most of the others were ill with scurvy. However, Vlamingh's voyage from the Netherlands to the Cape had taken only four months, compared with eight months for the *Zuytdorp* and *Belvliet*. On those two ships, where many more died or were seriously ill, it must have been impossible for the surgeons to provide appropriate care for the sick, or to maintain an adequate journal. One master surgeon, Jan Loxe, in his journal of

1699, explained why he had problems in finding time to write up individual case histories:[65]

> The first thing in the morning, we must prepare the medicines that have to be taken internally, and give each patient his dose. Next, we must scarify, clean, and dress the filthy stinking wounds, and bandage them and the ulcerations. Then we must bandage the stiff and benumbed limbs of the scurvy patients. At noon we must fetch and dish out food for sometimes forty, fifty, or even sixty people, and the same again in the evening; and what is more, we are kept up half the night as well in attending to patients who suffer a relapse, and so forth.

The master surgeons and their assistants on the *Zuytdorp* and *Belvliet* must have experienced overwhelming problems from the time that the ships entered the tropics, in trying to look after large numbers of sick and dying patients. Arent Blankert, the master surgeon of *d'Unie*, which was lying at anchor with the return fleet from Batavia when the *Zuytdorp* arrived in Table Bay, recorded that

> the *Zuyddorp* called, about 8 months from Zeeland, having had 114 dead by scurvy, hot diseases, and raging fevers. The chief-surgeon and both his mates had jumped overboard in their delirium and ragings, notwithstanding all conceivable precautions.[66]

Given the appalling sickness and loss of life that occurred on the *Zuytdorp*, these suicides are not surprising. The three surgeons must have found it impossible to cope with the conditions on board, with death their only release.

The 166 people who were still alive when the *Zuytdorp* reached the Cape were said to consist of '8 cabin guests and 158 crew'. Of these, 22 were listed as 'sick', and must have been hospitalized, although most of the rest were also 'extremely ill', according to the resident uppermerchant at the Cape, Willem Helot. The ship remained at Table Bay for a month, during which time the overall health of many of these people would have improved greatly, with the provision of vegetables, fruit and other fresh foods. Most of those who had been moderately ill with scurvy, but were still fit enough to look after themselves, would probably have recovered reasonably well within two or three weeks. However, some would still not have recuperated sufficiently to join the ship when it departed on 22 April, and it seems unlikely that any of those who were hospitalized on arrival would have been fit enough to resume the voyage.

A letter from the Governor and Council at the Cape to the Governor General and Council in Batavia, dated 2 April 1712, advised that the '*Zuytdorp* and *Belvliet* will be replenished and the dead crew members will be replaced as far as possible.'[67]

Disappearance of the *Zuytdorp*

On 21 April, it was reported that the *Zuytdorp* and *Belvliet* had been ready to sail for Batavia for seven to eight days, but had been delayed by contrary winds. The *Zuytdorp* left, in company with the *Kockenge*, on 22 April,[68] but the *Belvliet* remained at the Cape until 9 May. The *Zuytdorp* and *Kockenge* were supposed to keep together, if possible, on the voyage to Batavia. However, the *Zuytdorp*, which was the faster of the two vessels, pulled ahead of the *Kockenge* a day after leaving the Cape. It disappeared from sight, never to be seen or heard from again.[69]

The *Zuytdorp* left the Cape with 200 people (referred to as 'eaters') on board. It is not known how many of these were recruited at the Cape, but, using figures for the *Belvliet* as a guide, it is likely that eighty to ninety were new to the ship. Most would have been people transferred from other vessels that had arrived at the Cape without significant crew losses, but a few may have been recruited from among the resident population at the Cape.

The *Belvliet*, which had arrived at the Cape with 18 sick, left 29 people behind and took on board 62 newcomers (37 sailors and 25 soldiers) when it departed for Batavia on 9 May 1712.[70] In other words, nearly 46 per cent of the crew were newcomers. Of those people, 42 are known to have been recruited from the *Oostersteyn*, the *Zuyderbeeck* and the *Popkensburg*, which had recently arrived at the Cape from the fatherland.[71] The *Belvliet* arrived safely at Batavia on 18 July with 134 on board, having lost only one person (a sailor) on the voyage.[72] It is notable that of the 58 soldiers who left the Netherlands on the *Belvliet*, only 14 completed the voyage to Batavia on that ship.

On 28 April, six days after the *Zuytdorp* departed from the Cape, two cases of interest to the present story were heard before the Council of Justice.[73] In the first, seaman-gunner Harmen Hendrix was charged with absenting himself from the ship *Zuytdorp*, to which he had been transferred from the *Kykuyt* (a recent arrival from the Netherlands). Hendrix was said to be 'still vagabonding free', although it was presumed that he had 'absconded aboard one of the recently departed English ships'. If so, he was extremely lucky: had he continued on the *Zuytdorp*, he would have disappeared with that ship, never to return to his homeland. If he failed to escape on an English ship, he would eventually have been caught by the Cape authorities, in which case he was to be 'bound in chains, in which to labour for a period of twelve months on Robben Island'. Hendrix was also to forfeit three months' wages and his sea-chest, which he had left behind, but which contained 'nothing worth mentioning'.

The second case concerned a seaman, Jacobus Phillipse, who failed to join his appointed ship, the *Zuytdorp*, and instead had 'vagabonded ashore'. However, he gave himself up to the prosecutor, and was thereupon condemned to work for six months at the company's fortification work on Robben Island, bound in chains, without wages, and forfeiting three months' prior wages. Despite this harsh sentence, Phillipse may have considered himself lucky. The *Zuytdorp* no doubt already had a reputation as a ship of death, and he would have felt even better after learning of its disappearance on the voyage to Batavia.

As the *Zuytdorp* had left the Cape later than the beginning of March, the sailing instructions gave the skipper the option of running to within sight of the Land of the Eendracht at latitude 27° south (or further north) before setting course towards Sunda Strait. Unfortunately for those on board the ship, this option was apparently accepted, as the ship was wrecked on the Western Australian coast at latitude 27°11′13″ south, close to the specified latitude for ships to sight that coast. The wreck probably happened in about the first week of June, some six or seven weeks after the ship left the Cape, as the voyage from the coast of Western Australia to Batavia normally took three to four weeks, and the *Kockenge*, which left the Cape with the *Zuytdorp*, arrived in Batavia on 4 July.

It is worth noting that the wreck would never have occurred if the *Zuytdorp* had followed normal instructions on its voyage to the Cape of Good Hope. By visiting São Tomé in the Gulf of Guinea, contrary to the sailing directions, the voyage was delayed by about two months. Without this delay, the ship would have left the Cape in February, when vessels were directed to sail to the Indies without approaching the Western Australian coast.

The non-arrival of the *Zuytdorp* in Batavia was referred to in various letters from the Governor General and Council there. In one dated 25 November 1712 to the *Heeren XVII* in Amsterdam, it was stated: 'to our regret the fine ship *Zuytdorp* has not arrived yet, in spite of the fact that it set sail from the Cape to here on 22 April'.[74] In another letter of the same date to the directors of the Zeeland Chamber, it was said that 'the ship *Zuytdorp*, which departed from the Cape of Good Hope as early as 22 April has not arrived so far, which causes us no small concern for this ship.' On 30 January 1713, the directors in Middelburg were again advised of the non-arrival of the ship in Batavia.[75] However, no mention is made of the ship's loss in minutes of meetings of the *Heeren XVII* and the directors of the Chamber of Zeeland. This seems surprising, as the *Zuytdorp* was carrying a rich cargo, and its loss must have been a serious blow to the company.

No attempt was ever made to trace the *Zuytdorp* after it failed to arrive in Batavia, and indeed such would have seemed a hopeless task, as there was no indication of where the ship had been lost. Memories must have remained of Vlamingh's fruitless, and costly, voyage of fifteen years earlier, seeking traces of the *Ridderschap van Holland*, a ship that had similarly disappeared after leaving the Cape.

A year after the *Zuytdorp* had disappeared, a rumour reached the Cape from Batavia that the ship had been inadequately provisioned by the authorities at the Cape, and that this was the reason for its loss. The rumour was strenuously denied by the uppermerchant and administrator at the Cape, Willem Helot. He wrote a letter on the matter to 'The Most Noble Hon. Lord Joannes van Steelant, Councillor Extraordinary of India and Commissioner of the Cape Government etc. etc.' and arranged for a number of relevant affidavits to be presented by persons before the Court of Justice. In his letter, dated 30 March 1713, Helot stated:[76]

It has come to the ears of the undersigned, Uppermerchant Willem Helot, with the utmost astonishment and no less distress of the mind, that in Batavia a rumour has been spread with regard to the delayed arrival of the ship *Zuiddorp*, departed on 22 April 1712 from here for the capital, as if the undersigned had come to such a degree of negligence as to have permitted that vessel to depart without a store of victuals sufficient for a three-monthly voyage; that a plausible rumour has been spread by hostile persons...who cannot have knowledge of the kind and nature of the matter concerned...wherefore the undersigned is at peace in his mind that regarding this matter he has done nothing nor acted in any way contrary to the service of the Hon. Company; much less that he could have exposed such a costly vessel to any immediate peril or calamities.

Thus the undersigned states that with regard to the provisions and further necessities supplied to the said vessel, he refers to the charge account of same, enclosed herewith in authenticated copy, which, signed by the skipper [Marinus Wysvliet], is plain evidence that he was content and fully satisfied with the supply, also has raised no objection against confidently continuing the voyage from here therewith...The more so as no members of this Council are aware that this skipper has ever lodged any complaints that he had not sufficient victuals on board for the remainder of the voyage. Furthermore, the undersigned could have demonstrated plainly and clearly, in order to remove any remaining hesitation that might linger in this respect, what quantity and what nature of provisions that ship was still carrying upon her departure from here if...the log kept by the skipper during the voyage from the fatherland were to be found here; which the secretary Pieter de Meyer upon whom it is incumbent to claim the ships' logs from all skippers coming out...upon express enquiry by the undersigned, advised not to be at the secretariat. Then in order to cast more light on the matter as much as feasible, the undersigned most humbly submits for Your Honour's reflection and consideration: that the ship in question, *Zuiddorp*, put to sea on 27 July 1711 with 286 crew and put in here on 23 March 1712; having meanwhile, on account of an excessive number of sick people, after already having a large party of dead men, stopped at Sao Thomé from December 13 until January 4 for refreshment; and landed here with 22 sick and a loss of 112 men in addition to 10 runaways in the aforesaid place, being more than two fifth parts of the whole; moreover the ship departed from here…with 200 crew and thus with 86 eaters fewer than the number with which they put to sea; and was well known previously to have been provisioned so well that the vessel must have had on board such a copious supply of victuals that she was able to undertake the voyage from here with perfect confidence…It further appears from the enclosed extract from the log kept by skipper Hayman de Laver who departed in *Kokkenge* in the company of *Zuiddorp* on the day mentioned earlier: that *Zuiddorp* on the day after putting to sea sailed on ahead without waiting for *Kokkenge*, etc.; from which it can be inferred and concluded that if the officers of *Zuiddorp* had raised objections regarding any foreseeable shortage of provisions, they, as being the faster vessel, would not have left *Kokkenge* behind, since in case of sudden need or difficulty could have been assisted by them.

Now it is almost certain that the aforesaid ship *Zuiddorp* has been lost at sea either through heavy weather or through negligence or ill management, or has foundered elsewhere, seized by mutineers, or through a relapse of the crew's health, who upon their arrival here were mostly extremely ill, could have fallen into such a weakened and impotent state that the ship could no longer be properly directed and thus had to be surrendered to the mercy of sea and winds, of which vicissitudes there are numerous examples, in particular of the ship *Ridderschap van Holland*, which having departed from this bay for Batavia in 1694 has never been heard of again, nor any information about the ship received.

The copy of the charge account that accompanied this letter showed that the store at the Cape had provided the *Zuytdorp* with 1,813 pounds of fresh meat and ten live sheep, an unspecified amount of vegetables and potherbs (at no charge), 2 hundred-weight of beans, 2 hundredweight of peas, 300 pounds of rice, and numerous other items, ranging from sail yarn to window panes and medical stores.[77]

The affidavits presented to the Court of Justice on this matter are revealing.[78] One, by conveyance clerk Jeronimo Snitquer, stated that when the *Zuytdorp* was in port the year before, he heard that its skipper, Marinus Wysvliet, had vaunted that he still had sufficient provisions for the voyage to Batavia and needed little or nothing else. On hearing this claim, another person, believed to be a steersman, responded: 'that is no wonder, for on the voyage he has ill treated his people and has given them all but nothing to eat.'

Another affidavit, by uppersteersman Jan de Heere, stated that in the previous year (1712) he had been aboard the ship *Oostersteyn*, lying in Table Bay, when the *Zuytdorp* arrived. The *Zuytdorp*'s skipper, Marinus Wysvliet, had come on board and spoke there to the skipper of the *Oostersteyn* and de Heere, together with several of their shipmates. One of the matters discussed was the protracted voyage of the *Zuytdorp*, and when Wysvliet was asked about the sufficiency of the provisions on this voyage, he replied, 'I have stores enough to continue my voyage to Batavia.' To this, de Heere responded, 'then you have denied or stolen their meat from your people', drawing the further reply from Wysvliet: 'I was sparing with the provisions at the beginning of the voyage and I have had many deaths, but henceforth on the voyage between this place and Batavia I shall prove that I am an honest man and issue plentiful rations to the people.'

This evidence suggests the possibility, referred to earlier, that Wysvliet had been 'sparing with the provisions' because he was hoping to profit from the sale of excess stores in Batavia, a practice that was not unknown among VOC skippers at the time.

It seems that the *Zuytdorp* was soon virtually forgotten, although its disappearance was briefly mentioned in a few publications, with speculation as to whether the ship had been wrecked on the Houtman Abrolhos or elsewhere on the Australian coast.[79] It was not until 1958, 246 years after its disappearance, that the fate of this long-lost ship was conclusively established: the *Zuytdorp* was wrecked on the coast of Western Australia, approximately midway between the mouth of the Murchison River and Shark Bay, at the foot of the coastal cliffs that now bear its name.

3. COINS, CANNON AND A GHOSTLY WOMAN

THE WRECK

Identification of the wreck

When I returned to Perth after that first exhilarating visit to the wrecksite, in August 1954, I sought advice from Malcolm Uren, a senior executive of West Australian Newspapers Ltd and well known for his book *Sailormen's ghosts*, on Dutch shipwrecks on the Houtman Abrolhos. Uren expressed his intention to research the wreck, with the objective of publishing a historical account, but his initial enquiry with the Netherlands produced nothing and he did not persist.[80] So in 1957, I decided to take up the research myself, and began a prolonged correspondence with various archives and museums in the Netherlands, Cape Town and Jakarta, with a view to discovering the identity of the ship and learning all that I could about it. I established a key contact in the Netherlands, Mrs (later Dr) M.A.P. Meilink-Roelofsz, Keeper of the First Section in the Algemeen Rijksarchief (National Archives) in The Hague, who gave me a great deal of assistance and showed remarkable patience and interest in promptly answering my correspondence.

The identity of the wreck was not proved conclusively until 1958. However, in 1954 I had already deduced that this was very likely the wreck of the *Zuytdorp*. Using the details I already knew—

that the ship was clearly Dutch, as many coins bore the name Zeeland, and it could not have been lost earlier than 1711, the date shown on the coins found at the site—I had consulted records held by the State Library and the Western Australian Historical Society (Historical Society). These suggested that the wreck could be one of three Dutch ships that had disappeared after leaving the Cape of Good Hope for Batavia: the *Zuytdorp*, in 1712, the *Fortuyn*, in 1724, and the *Aagtekerke*, in 1726. It seemed to me that the *Zuytdorp* was the most likely of these, as it was owned by the Chamber of Zeeland, had left the Netherlands in 1711, and could easily have been carrying a consignment of newly minted coins.

My correspondence in 1957–58 with the Algemeen Rijksarchief and the provincial archives in Zeeland showed that this deduction was correct: the wreck was certainly that of the *Zuytdorp*. The coins were the key to its identity.[81]

The directors' minutes of the Chamber of Zeeland showed that on 16 February 1711, the Middelburg Mint was authorized to coin 100,000 guilders in schellings and double stuivers. The Mint-Master, Adolf de Groene, fulfilled the order, and the coins were produced before 20 May 1711. The consignment of newly minted coins, valued at 100,000 guilders, was originally supposed to be sent to Ceylon (via Batavia) on the *Belvliet*. However, most, if not all, of the consignment must have been taken on the *Zuytdorp*, as the *Belvliet* carried only 45,534 guilders in cash and bars of silver to Batavia. Thus, the discovery at the wrecksite of large numbers of schellings and double stuivers bearing the date 1711, the name Zeeland, and the mint-mark of the Middelburg Mint proved that the wreck was that of the *Zuytdorp*.

In this way, the mystery of the loss of this great ship was solved, nearly 250 years after it disappeared en route from the Cape to Batavia. However, the human mystery of what happened to its survivors still remains (see Chapter 6).

The wrecksite

The *Zuytdorp* was wrecked on the Western Australian coast when it crashed into coastal cliffs at latitude 27°11′13″ south, longitude 113°56′09″ east, almost midway between the present town of Kalbarri and the southern shores of Shark Bay. The wrecksite is

Schellings and double stuivers minted in 1711 by the Middelburg Mint in the province of Zeeland. The mint-mark of that mint (a small castle) can be seen at the top of each coin in the right-hand view.

Photograph by the author

located at one of the most spectacular stretches of the Australian coast, at the foot of a line of precipitous cliffs, up to 250 metres high, that extend almost unbroken for 250 kilometres, from near the mouth of the Murchison River to the northern end of Dirk Hartog Island. The cliffs are only interrupted at two small inlets, Dulverton Bay (False Entrance) and Epineux Bay (Crayfish Bay), and at the narrow passage between Dirk Hartog Island and the mainland (see Map 1). In 1958, the Geographic Nomenclature Committee accepted my proposal that this stretch of coast be given the name Zuytdorp Cliffs.[82]

The Zuytdorp Cliffs must have been observed from hundreds of Dutch ships on voyages to the Indies, as the VOC ships were authorized to sail within sight of the coast at latitude 27° south (near where the *Zuytdorp* was wrecked), or further north, during autumn, winter and early spring. The cliffs could be seen from far out to sea, presenting a forbidding sight, and it is unlikely that a ship would run into them without warning. However, the square-rigged ships of that time could do little but run before gale-force

winds, and the *Zuytdorp* was probably the hapless victim of an early
winter storm, which drove the ship unerringly into the cliffs.

Pelsaert, in 1629, recorded that this stretch of coast was
'very steeply hewn, without any foreshore or inlets as have other
countries, but it seemed to be a dry cursed earth without foliage
or grass,'[83] and Vlamingh, in 1697, described it as 'high steep
land and very precipitous, so that it is impossible to land', and
'altogether high and bare, without any green thing on it and very
steep up to the top as if it had been chopped off by an axe, without
any beach at its foot, with heavy surf that is a wonder to see; kept
away from shore as far as we could.'[84]

Vlamingh's reaction of seeking to keep well away from the
cliffs was no doubt that of all Dutch skippers, and indeed of the
French and British navigators who came later. This stretch of
coast continued to be shunned after British settlement in Western
Australia, and reliable maps of the area were not produced until
the mid-1950s, following the advent of aerial photography. When
I first went there in 1954, the coastline between the mouth of the
Murchison River and the south end of Dirk Hartog Island was one

of the least known parts of Australia. It had never been surveyed from the sea or on land, and was consequently marked on most maps of Australia as a dashed line—the only part of the continent to be shown in that way. Tom Pepper, in 1927, may have been the first European to visit this stretch of coast after the *Zuytdorp* survivors, and Daryl Johnstone and I, in 1954, were the first geologists to go there.

The Zuytdorp *wrecksite, looking north-west.*

Photograph by the author

The Zuytdorp Cliffs between Tamala and Murchison House are still among the least accessible parts of the Western Australian coast, visited by few people each year. The coastal area in the vicinity of the wrecksite is included in a nature reserve, administered by the State Department of Conservation and Land Management (CALM). Until recently, it had the status of a national park, but this was changed to nature reserve status because there is no provision for public access to the site. The reserve is bounded on one side by the Indian Ocean, and is surrounded on land by the Tamala Station pastoral lease. Most of this part of the lease has never been used to pasture sheep or cattle, but it now supports a large population of feral goats. These animals have already caused a lot of environmental degradation along parts of the Zuytdorp Cliffs.

There is no easy way to drive to the wrecksite, and people can easily become lost if they are not familiar with the many sandy tracks that crisscross this remote and desolate area. The most direct route from the North West Coastal Highway is 75 kilometres long, passing along the Murchison Barrier Fence, a series of oil-exploration tracks, the old stockroute, and my 1954 track (see Maps 5 and 6). Four-wheel drive and high clearance are essential, and the sections of the tracks that cross limestone are extremely rough. However, it is illegal to travel along the barrier fence without the written permission of Agriculture Western Australia. The main purpose of this barrier is to prevent emus from migrating into agricultural land to the south.

Map 5.
The area around the
Zuytdorp *wrecksite*

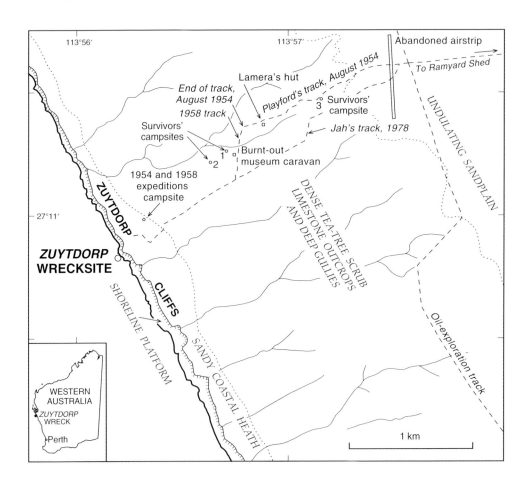

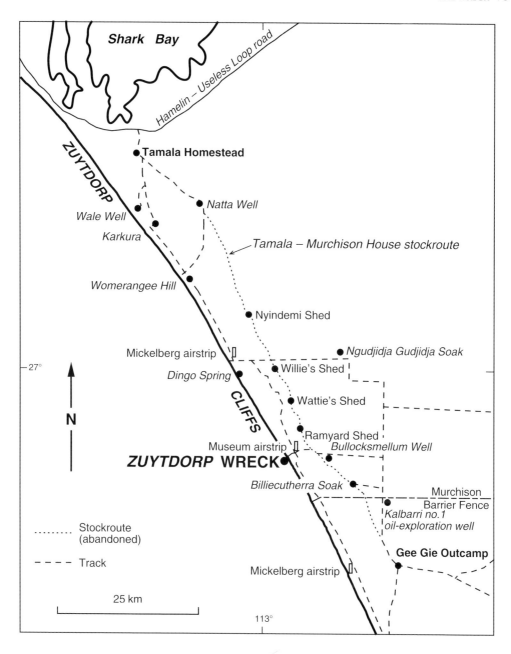

Map 6.
Principal tracks in
the area and the
abandoned stockroute
from Tamala to
Murchison House

The oil-exploration tracks are part of a rectangular grid of lines bulldozed by Oceania Petroleum in 1971–72 for a geophysical (gravity) survey. The company also drilled one oil-exploration well, Kalbarri no. 1, just south of the barrier fence. Most of the company tracks have now virtually disappeared, but some are kept open for coastal access by abalone divers, who have also made many tracks of their own.

The wrecksite itself is protected, under the *State Museum Act*, by the Zuytdorp Cliffs Reserve, covering an area of 7.3 hectares around the site. Entry to this reserve is prohibited without formal approval from the WA Museum. It is also illegal, under provisions of the *Commonwealth Historic Shipwrecks Act*, to dive or disturb the sea-floor within a radius of 500 metres around the wreck. The *Zuytdorp* is the only historic wreck in the State to be protected by such an exclusion zone, although it has never been adequately policed. Many people are known to have dived at the site without authority, but none have been charged for doing so, and only one person has been prosecuted for the removal of relics, despite the massive looting that has occurred (see Chapter 5).

The Zuytdorp Cliffs are formed of limestone, which originally accumulated as enormous sand dunes during the Pleistocene glacial epochs, more than 10,000 years ago, when sea-level was as much as 150 metres lower than today and the prevailing winds were much stronger.[85] The cliffs probably mark a fault in the earth's crust that last moved several thousands of years ago, after the Pleistocene dunes had accumulated. Movement along this fault is thought to have been responsible for the steep, straight scarp that forms the line of cliffs and deeply incised gullies. The cliffs in the southern part, for some 25 kilometres north of Kalbarri, are lower and less distinct than those in the north. Discontinuous beaches have developed along the shoreline in that area, with some bright-pink beach sands containing high concentrations of the mineral garnet. Such sands, which are mined commercially in the Hutt Lagoon area, have been derived by erosion of the garnet-rich metamorphic rocks around Northampton. The garnet sand along the Zuytdorp Cliffs has been carried to the sea by the Murchison River and then swept north by the prevailing longshore current.

The Zuytdorp Cliffs reach their highest point at Womerangee Hill,[86] 35 kilometres north-north-west of the wrecksite, where they are 250 metres high and drop precipitously into deep water.

If the *Zuytdorp* had been wrecked anywhere along this section of the cliffs, no one could have survived and no trace of the wreck may have been found. Other missing VOC ships could easily have been wrecked in this area without leaving any visible signs at the surface. Airborne magnetic methods, able to detect the presence of iron cannon and anchors, may be the only practicable means of finding any such wrecks.

At Womerangee Hill, the Zuytdorp Cliffs form one of the most awe-inspiring sights on the Australian coast. About eighty years ago, a rabbit-proof fence was constructed to meet the cliffs at Womerangee, and it was taken right down the 250-metre cliff face—an amazing feat. Only a few remnants of this fence remain on the cliff face today, but it was still reasonably intact when I first visited there in 1954, as the fence was being maintained as the southern boundary of Tamala Station. I have climbed the cliff twice at this locality, but never again!

At the *Zuytdorp* wrecksite, the cliffs are relatively low, extending only 30–35 metres above sea-level. The scree slope fronting the cliff scarp consists of a jumbled mass of limestone boulders and sand eroded from the scarp. Most of the largest boulders have reached the base of the slope, and some have rolled onto the adjoining shoreline platform. This platform, averaging about 20 metres in width, and standing some 2 metres above sea-level, has been cut almost horizontally into the limestone cliff by marine erosion during the past few thousand years. The platform surface is encrusted with oysters and other shellfish, which would have provided a ready source of food for the wreck survivors. When I first went there during the 1950s, the shellfish on the platform included abundant abalone, but these are now rare in the more readily accessible areas because of exploitation by commercial abalone fishermen.

A striking feature of the Zuytdorp Cliffs area is the presence of remarkable rimmed terraces, termed 'paddy-field terraces', which form the tops of some shoreline platforms. Water from the swash of breaking waves cascades from one terrace to the next, in spectacular fashion. Individual sets of terraces can attain a vertical relief of as much as several metres. Similar paddy-field terraces occur elsewhere along the limestone coast of south-western Western Australia,[87] but they are best developed along the Zuytdorp Cliffs. Their origin has yet to be adequately explained.

An extensive system of caverns extends from the sea beneath the shoreline platform at the wrecksite, and coins and other relics were collected from some of the smaller dry caverns near the rubble at the base of the cliff during the 1954 and 1958 expeditions (see Chapter 4). In some areas, the seaward part of the platform has collapsed into the cave system, forming a jumbled mass of large blocks. At one place, the platform has collapsed 5–12 metres from the seaward margin, resulting in a large hole (the 'bathtub pool') where the water rushes in with each wave (see Map 7).

Water also surges in and out of the caves in response to wave action, and some of the caverns reach the surface as blowholes, ejecting water or spray and blasts of air with successive waves. One 'dry' blowhole, close to the limestone rubble at the base of the cliff, and 30 metres from the edge of the platform, normally ejects only air, although during storms it can also blow water and sand (see Map 7). The vertical hole can often be descended by rope into the dark cave below, where the water rises and falls, successively blowing and sucking air through the pipe. The cave is usually open from autumn to early summer, but it can become completely blocked with sand during mid-summer.

A windswept belt of limestone and sand, 200–400 metres wide, extends behind the cliffs. It supports low heath vegetation that is salt and wind tolerant. Further inland, this bare strip passes into a belt of dense scrub, about 2 kilometres wide, consisting mainly of tea-tree (*Melaleuca cardiophylla*), with patches of mallee (*Eucalyptus* sp.) growing on limestone with little soil cover. This belt is deeply incised by a regular system of gullies, about 300 metres to 1 kilometre apart, and up to 15 metres deep and 2 kilometres long, that are cut into the limestone at right angles to the cliff face. The gullies flow for short periods after heavy downpours of rain, especially those associated with periodic summer cyclones. There are no permanent water sources in the area, but rainwater collects in a few places in the gullies and in gnamma holes (small natural rockholes) below the limestone surface between the gullies. Aborigines scooped soil out of these holes, to maximize the amount of water they could hold, and they commonly placed slabs of stone over them to limit evaporation and prevent intrusion by animals. Some of the larger gnamma holes could probably hold as much as 50 litres of water. Most have filled with soil since Aborigines left the area, and they now hold little water.

East of the tea-tree belt, the country consists of undulating sandplain, covered with low stunted scrub that includes stands of banksias, eucalypts and acacias. This scrub presents a drab spectacle for most of the year, but many plants flower brilliantly in spring, and others in autumn. The closest permanent fresh water to the wrecksite used to be at a soak known as Billiecutherra, 13 kilometres to the south-east. The soak would certainly have existed as an Aboriginal waterhole when the *Zuytdorp* was wrecked. It still contained permanent water as recently as 1958, but is now dry, after being filled with drifting sand. However, digging in the sand would still yield water there.

Scores of similar shallow soaks occur in the sandplain east of the wrecksite. They were excavated by Aborigines over thousands of years, forming bare circular depressions up to 10 metres deep and 50 metres across. Most now dry out completely in spring or summer, although a few may retain water throughout the year, because feral camels still roam in the area and they need access to permanent water in order to survive.

The Zuytdorp *wrecksite from the air, in 1995. The vehicle track shown top centre has since been closed and rehabilitated.*

Photograph by the author

Aboriginal knowledge of the wreck

The wrecksite of the *Zuytdorp* and the story of the shipwreck must have been well known to the Aboriginal inhabitants of the area between Shark Bay and the Murchison River prior to British colonization in the nineteenth century. In 1834, just five years after the founding of the Swan River Colony, a story was received in Perth, through local Aborigines, of a shipwreck said to be situated about thirty days' walk north of Perth. It is probable that this story referred to the wreck of the *Zuytdorp*, 122 years before.

The story first appeared in the *Perth Gazette* on 5 July 1834, and the Colonial Secretary was officially advised about it in a letter from a farmer named Stephen Parker, dated 6 July. Further information was provided in subsequent issues of the *Perth Gazette*, and the report was also discussed in the diary of George Fletcher Moore.[88] Each of these accounts differs in some details.

It appears that two Aborigines, Tonguin and Weenat, were the first to report the wreck, speaking to Stephen Parker and his sons on 2 July 1834, at the Parkers' farm near Guildford (10 kilometres north-east of Perth). The story had been 'handed down from tribe to tribe' until it eventually reached blacks in the Perth area, no doubt becoming garbled to some extent during the process. The wreck was said to be situated about thirty days' walk (presumably a walk of 'one moon'), or about 650 kilometres, north of Perth, and the report was attributed to blacks known as Wayl (alternatively Waylo or Weel) men. The most distinctive feature of the wrecksite, repeated many times by the informants, was the presence of a great deal of 'white money' (silver coins), scattered for about 30 yards (27 metres) along the shore in front of the wreck. One graphic account recorded that the coins were stacked one on top of another, 'as thick as seed vessels under a red gum tree'. The 'gabby' (surf) was said to break with a very great noise where the money was lying, and as it ran back the Wayl men would run forward and pick up coins. The ship was apparently torn apart ('broke'), and surf surged between the ruptured sections. It had three masts, with 'blankets' (sails) flapping around, and one of the later informants indicated (by repeatedly tilting his woomera) that the ship had been lying on its side when it was driven ashore.

Most colonists assumed that the report referred to a recent wreck, possibly with survivors waiting to be saved. Advice from the Aborigines was uncertain on this point. Parker was told that the ship had broken up, with water rushing through the wreckage, and that all the people who had been on board were now dead. However, later advice suggested that some might still be alive, and that they included tall white men, with women and children. Relations between these people and the Aborigines were said to have been good. The men had given the Aborigines food ('biscuit'), and received spears and shields in return. The survivors had been living in five 'houses'—two large and three small—constructed of wood and canvas, situated on the open coast. One account referred to a river in the vicinity (probably the Murchison). It was believed from the initial report that the ship might have been wrecked only six months before, but a later account suggested that this was either the time that it had taken for the report to filter through to Perth, or the last time an informant had been at the site.

This story and the resulting conjecture caused quite a stir in Perth. The conclusion reached by the authorities was that the wreck must be located somewhere between Gantheaume Bay and Shark Bay (that is, along the Zuytdorp Cliffs), and that some survivors could be awaiting rescue. They decided to send a party, commanded by Assistant Surveyor H.M. Ommanney, to search the coast in that area.[89] The party departed from Fremantle on 18 July aboard the *Monkey*, a small schooner skippered by Captain Walter Pace.

A few days before, George Fletcher Moore had independently taken steps to send a message to the possible survivors, via a Perth Aborigine named Weeip, who was at that time subject to arrest because of his alleged role in the murder of a colonist. Weeip set out on about 12 July, and returned after twenty-two days, without getting as far as the territory of the Wayl men. He reported that 'he made enquiry, everywhere, of all the black men, if they know of any white men on the coast, or any ship, [but] they all said that they did not.' However, Weeip insisted that 'they all tell him there is "money plenty" on the shore…that the pieces of money lie on the top of one another…and…cover a good space of ground.'

This information, which seemed fairly reliable, arrived after the *Monkey* had already departed. The schooner returned on 2 October, without having found the supposed wreck, although expedition members had seen a lot of driftwood at the south end of Dirk Hartog Island—'great quantities of broken timber that had been washed up from some wreck, but many years since: some was washed up very high and some still washing among the reef.'[90]

Ommanney reported that he and his party had landed on the south side of Freycinet Harbour, in the Tamala–Carrarang area, intending to walk, with a single pony, to Gantheaume Bay. However, this plan soon had to be abandoned because they were unable to find water in the area, even though it was winter. Eventually, they obtained water by digging between sandhills on Peron Peninsula, on the other side of Freycinet Harbour. There they encountered about thirty Aborigines, all of them very tall men. Ommanney then decided to proceed south in the *Monkey*, to Gantheaume Bay, recognizing that it was a likely place to obtain advice on the supposed wreck from Aborigines. However, a north-westerly gale blew up and it proved impossible to land, much to Ommanney's regret. They were compelled to sail back to Fremantle, arriving there on 2 October 1834.

Later that year, there was speculation that the wreck reported by the Aborigines could have been that of the *Mercury*, a small barque that had disappeared after leaving Calcutta for King George Sound on 3 October 1833.[91] However, this seems unlikely. The most distinctive feature of the wrecksite described by the Aborigines was the presence of masses of silver coins lying on the shore. There is no evidence to suggest that the cargo of the *Mercury* included silver coinage, whereas the *Zuytdorp* was carrying a consignment of some 250,000 guilders in silver coins.

In fact, a later account suggested that the *Mercury* was probably wrecked near the mouth of the Greenough River. Aborigines from that area reported in 1851 that a ship had been wrecked there about sixteen years before, and there was speculation in Perth that this could have been the *Mercury*.

The results of the *Monkey* expedition, plus the information obtained from Weeip, suggested that there was little or no chance of finding any survivors, whether or not the wreck was that of the *Mercury*. Nevertheless, the authorities decided to send another search expedition to Gantheaume Bay, in the colonial schooner *Ellen*, which departed on 14 November and returned three weeks later.[92] Again, no sign was found of any wreck, and some colonists concluded that the original story must have been concocted by the Aborigines. A few people might have guessed that the wreck was of an old, unknown ship, but it is unlikely that any would have thought of a Dutch ship that had foundered more than 120 years before.

However, in the light of what we know now about the *Zuytdorp* wrecksite, this seems to be the most probable explanation of the story. The largest and most important Aboriginal encampment and waterhole near the *Zuytdorp* wrecksite was at a well known as Wale, 50 kilometres to the north, where at least one relic derived from the *Zuytdorp* has recently been found. It seems highly likely that the 'Wayl men' of the 1834 report were Aborigines from Wale Well (see Map 6) or its vicinity.

Other features of the 1834 report correspond well with the *Zuytdorp* wrecksite. First, the position of the reported wreck, as deduced by the colonists, was between Gantheaume Bay and Shark Bay, and this agrees with the site of the *Zuytdorp* wreck. Second, the description of abundant silver coins, strewn one on top of another 'as thick as seed vessels under a red gum tree' for about 30 yards along a surf-swept shoreline, closely matches the situation at the *Zuytdorp* wrecksite in 1927, when the surface of the shoreline platform was studded with silver coins. Third, evidence at the site shows that the survivors camped near the wreck, probably in shelters made from the ship's timbers and sails, which would be in accord with the Aborigines' description of 'houses'.

The sudden appearance of this shipwreck on the coast, and of the white people who scrambled ashore, must have had a big impact on the Aboriginal people of the area. There can be no doubt that the story of this major event would have been handed on during the 122 years from 1712 to 1834. Indeed, grandchildren of Aborigines who had seen the wreck and its survivors in 1712 could still have been living in 1834, with clear memories of what their grandparents had had to say about that dramatic event. The impact would have been even greater, and the stories even more detailed, if some of the castaways had joined and interbred with local Aborigines.

Early settlers in the Murchison House and Shark Bay areas may well have heard about the wreck and its survivors from the local Aborigines. However, there is no known documentary evidence of this. Indeed, almost nothing is known about interaction between the European settlers and the indigenous people when pastoral leases were first taken up in this area during the 1860s. However, it seems clear that the Aboriginal population declined rapidly. Some Aborigines must have been killed as a result of clashes with the settlers, but the biggest toll would probably have been from infectious diseases introduced by Europeans. According to Tom Pepper, the last tribal Aborigines in the Murchison House area died out during the early 1920s, having essentially starved to death because their traditional food-gathering grounds had been taken over by the station. The remaining people were forced to forage for sparse food in the sandplain country outside the boundaries of the sheep stations, especially along the gorge of the Murchison River, where they eventually died.

Modern discovery of the wreck

In recent times, there have been conflicting claims that the wreck of the *Zuytdorp* was first found by Tom Pepper, or Ada and Ernest Drage, or Charlie Mallard. There is no doubt that each of these people visited the wrecksite and collected relics there in about 1927, but now they are all deceased and it is impossible to prove who among them was the first to see the wreckage.

Both Ernest Drage and Charlie Mallard had died before I visited the area. I never had any discussions with Ada Drage and was unaware of any controversy about the discovery until long after her death in 1960. However, I did on many occasions discuss the discovery with Tom Pepper, and had no reason to doubt his version: that the wreckage was first discovered by him in April 1927 when he had been dingo trapping in the area.

Pepper told me that at that time he had been asked by the manager of Murchison House Station to go from Gee Gie Outcamp to Bullocksmellum Paddock, where several dingoes had moved in from the open country between Murchison House and Tamala and were killing and maiming sheep. Pepper believed that there were eight or nine dingoes involved, and he set about trying to catch them. After attacking the sheep at night, the dogs would move into dense tea-tree scrub (described by Pepper as 'jungle') that formed a belt about 2 kilometres wide between the sandplain and the coastal cliffs. This rough and impenetrable belt of scrub was of no use for pasturing sheep, and station people had previously had no reason to go there.[93]

Pepper took three days to find a suitable route and cut a horse pad through the 'jungle' in order to get through to the coast with the dingo traps. At the top of the cliffs, he found a well-marked dog pad, leading north to a little spring (which I have named Dingo Spring; see Map 6) about 15 kilometres north of the wrecksite, where the dogs were obtaining water. He eventually succeeded in trapping and shooting them all.

On the day that Pepper found the dog pad, the sea was quite calm, and he thought he might try to catch a fish or two for his evening meal. He usually carried a fishing line in his horse pack, with a piece of kangaroo meat for bait, in case such an opportunity arose. He found a suitable place to climb down the cliffs, noting in passing that there were some broken bottles scattered along the cliff top. At the foot of the cliffs, he saw wooden wreckage scattered around, including what he thought was a piece of a mast (actually it was part of a yardarm) about 7 metres long. He took little notice of this, thinking vaguely that it was debris from a wrecked fishing boat.

He soon caught a snapper and a tailor, more than enough for his meal. On the way back to the cliff top, he observed about eight green cylindrical objects with handles (now known to be bronze breech blocks of cannon) lying together at the foot of a large rock in the rubble below the cliff. He picked up a couple of them, not knowing what they were, but noting that they were heavy. He scratched one with a knife, penetrating through the green oxide coating into the metal below. He also picked up about eight small green metal discs, without realizing that they were coins. According to one account, Tom Pepper claimed that the coins were lying on the ground near the breech blocks, but in a recorded interview with me he said that they were in shallow water on the platform, which seems more likely. He snapped several of the discs between his fingers and put the rest in his pocket. At this stage, Pepper was unaware that he had found the wreckage of a very old ship.

In an interview with Jim Cruthers in 1954, Pepper said that on the way back to Gee Gie Outcamp he called at Bullocksmellum Well,[94] where Ernest Drage, a station contractor, was camped, and he showed Drage the metal discs, saying where he had found them.[95] Later, at Gee Gie, Pepper showed the discs to another station employee, Fred Dickerson, who guessed that they were coins, and tried cleaning them in acid. This dissolved away the thin green film of copper carbonate coating the coins (schellings and double stuivers, which were made from an alloy of 41.7 per cent copper and 58.3 per cent silver), allowing the inscription Zeeland and the date 1711 to be seen. Tom Pepper then realized that he had found the site of an ancient wreck, and guessed that it was probably Dutch.

Pepper said that a few days later he set out for the site again, in order to collect more coins, and on the way there he called at Bullocksmellum. He learned that Ernest Drage had followed his directions to the wrecksite, and had picked up about thirty coins from the shoreline platform. Drage was said to have been 'elated' about his find and promised that after he had cleaned the coins he would give Pepper half, but he never did so. Pepper went back to the site and found about thirty more coins, now known to have been schellings, double stuivers, ducatons, and pieces of eight, but described originally by Pepper as 'sixpences, threepences, five-shillings, and silver ingots'. He also picked up a ducaton dated 1670, and part of a metal instrument (cannonball callipers) near the breech blocks. He later gave this ducaton, which was particularly well preserved, to David Hunter, the Commissioner of Police. Close to the breech-blocks locality, he also noted a large piece of wood, carved as the figure of a woman, wedged in the rocks. He believed that this was the ship's figurehead, but it was actually a carved console from the stern of the ship.

Pepper returned to the wrecksite with his wife, Lurlie, on several occasions, mainly to collect pieces of sheet lead to use in making bullets for a .44 carbine rifle. The lead that he picked up was scattered in front of the rubble at the foot of the cliffs, except for one large rolled sheet, weighing about 9 kilograms, which he found in a small cave at the cliff top. Altogether, Pepper estimated that he obtained some 25 kilograms of lead from the wrecksite, all of which was melted down and made into bullets.

Ernest Drage and his wife, Ada, also visited the wrecksite several times, to collect coins and other material (including breech blocks), and a number of other station employees went there with the Peppers or the Drages, to collect relics. I was told by Tom Pepper that Charlie Mallard was first taken there by his daughter, Lurlie Pepper.

In 1939, Tom Pepper heard rumours that an expedition intended visiting the wrecksite, and that Ernest Drage was planning to recover the 'figurehead', which was still at the site.

Carved figure from the stern of the Zuytdorp, found by Tom Pepper in 1927 and recovered from the wrecksite in 1939. The figure is that of a pregnant woman, her head wreathed and her bust in the form of a stylized lion's head.

Photograph by the author

Pepper resolved to get there first, in order to remove the figure and any other objects that might be of value. He set off on horseback with Lurlie and two station hands, Jack Ryan and Tommy Bonner. Ryan told me, during an interview in 1994, that they carried the 'figurehead' to the cliff top, leaving it there for a day or so while they went back to Gee Gie for a packhorse to carry it away. Pepper

The stern of the Padmos and Blydorp model. Note the eight carved figures (consoles) below the windows of the great cabin; each is in the form of a pregnant woman, closely resembling the figure found at the Zuytdorp wrecksite.

Photograph courtesy of the Maritiem Museum Prins Hendrik, Rotterdam

wrapped the figure in a sheet and put it under a bed at Gee Gie Outcamp, where it remained for the next nine years. Lurlie was not particularly happy with this, as she regarded the carved woman's figure as a rather frightening ghostly object.

When the Peppers moved to Tamala in 1950, Jack Ryan took the figure to Murchison House in a spring cart, and from there it was transferred to the home of Tom Pepper's sister at Moonyoonooka, near Geraldton, where I first saw it. I later brought it to Perth temporarily, so that a replica could be made for the WA Museum. Some twenty years later, the original was placed in the Geraldton Museum, on loan from the Pepper family, where it now forms the centrepiece of the *Zuytdorp* display. The replica can be seen at the WA Maritime Museum in Fremantle.

This carved figure, known as a console, from the stern of the ship is the most impressive relic from the *Zuytdorp*.[96] It is in the form of a pregnant woman's figure, the symbolic significance of which is lost today. The small plump face has a placid expression, and is turned upwards. A wreath surrounds the head, and the bust is in the stylized form of a lion's head. The back of the carving is moulded to fit against the curved counter of the ship, below the square stern section on its starboard side. Contemporary models of VOC ships of that period (the *Padmos/Blydorp* and the *Valkenisse*) show eight similar figures mounted below the windows of the great cabin of each ship, where the skipper had his quarters.

The earliest published reference to the discovery of the wreck appeared in the *West Australian* of 5 February 1931, under the heading 'Moore River relics'. The main part of the report dealt with the discovery of coins and an old skeleton near the mouth of the Moore River, but the following statement, attributed to Dr J.S. Battye, was also included:

> The probability that the *Vergulde Draeck* was not the only vessel wrecked on that coastline is strengthened by the fact that about two years ago a collection of Spanish and Dutch coins was gathered on the shore slightly north of the mouth of the Murchison River, and about 30 miles from Murchison House. Those who found the coins said that some remains existed, particularly a large block of wood which seemed to have formed part of the figure-head of a ship, that the overhanging cliff had fallen over the spot, and that if anything did happen to be there it would probably be buried under many tons of rock and sand. The spot where these last-mentioned coins were found is practically unapproachable by sea, and is so forbidding that any vessel driven on the rocks would not have the slightest chance of being saved. In this case again, however, there is not sufficient information to enable any authoritative statement to be made, and without some further discoveries it would be quite useless to ask the Dutch authorities at either Batavia or Amsterdam to search [their] records for possible missing ships.

Eight years later, another account of the wreck appeared in the *West Australian* of 12 May 1939, headlined 'Treasure trove, coins and ingots found'. The first part of the article, under the subheading 'Relics in North-West', read as follows:

Coins, small ingots of silver, parts of a lock, breeches from cannon, and other objects, evidently belonging to a ship wrecked on the coast many years ago, were found recently by a native about 40 miles north of the Murchison River. This information was given yesterday by Mr E Drage of Northampton, before he returned to Geraldton by the afternoon train. One of the coins, he said, clearly showed the date 1711, the word 'Zeeland', and a crest. A particularly interesting relic was a heart-shaped brass plate with a keyhole in it, which at one time apparently formed part of a chest of some description.

The native who made the discovery was fishing on a reef in shallow water when he noticed a coin at his feet. He made a closer examination and found that the reef was studded with coins, pieces of brass, and other relics, most of them firmly adhering to the rock. In some places the relics almost covered the reef, and the coins, etc., had to be chiselled off with an iron bar. The silver ingots were mostly a couple of inches long and of various shapes, some of them looking like a wedge. At the blunt ends was the impress of a small cross. A brass tray with a spout or lip at one corner and the breeches of two cannon were among the finds. Several of the silver coins brought to Perth by Mr Drage were as large as present day five-shilling pieces.

No mention was made in this article of the 1931 report on the discovery of the wreck. The latest report was attributed to Mr Eusebius Drage, usually known as Hughie ('Euie'), a prominent pastoralist at Northampton and former owner of Murchison House Station, who was later to join an expedition, sponsored by the *Sunday Times*, to the wrecksite (see Chapter 4). According to his son Keith, the 'native' referred to was Ernest Drage, Hughie's half-Aboriginal half-brother. Hughie Drage's parents were both European, but his father, Tom Drage, fathered Ernest by an Aboriginal woman, Polly Glass of Coolcalalaya, before he married.

The second part of the article, with the subheadings 'A theory that fits' and 'Possible link with the Zeewyck [sic]', was attributed to Malcolm Uren, and the text was as follows:

The discovery of Dutch coins and pieces of plate of ancient shape near the mouth of the Murchison River conjures up a number of fascinating theories concerning possible links between the relics and reported and unknown Dutch casualties on the coast of Western Australia over 200 years ago. The first thought is that they are part of the wreckage of a Dutch ship, which, bound from the Cape of Good Hope to the Dutch East Indies, carried on too far westward [sic] and came to grief on the scantily known coast of the great South Land.

If the relics mark the graveyard of a Dutch ship, they might be from the wreck of any of four Dutch vessels reported missing around 1700 on a voyage to the Dutch East Indies. These ships were the Ridderschap van Holland, the Fortyn [sic], the Aagtekerke, and the Zutydorp [sic]. All belonged to the Dutch East India Company, whose officers, because they were meticulously careful about such things, recorded the non-arrival of these ships at Batavia.

There are rather unsatisfactory references to the wreck of the Zutydorp on the Abrolhos in 1711, and if that date is right the coins now found must have been newly minted, which is unlikely. There are even less convincing theories that wreckage seen by castaways from the Dutch ship Zeewyck near Pelsart Island in 1729 [sic] were part of the missing Fortyn or Aagtekerke. One date given for the disappearance of the Ridderschap van Holland is 1694, which would rule out that ship as a possibility because of the finding of the coin dated 1711.

There is, however, a much more likely theory that fits the facts much closer than the previous necessarily wild guesses. That theory would link the relics found on the reef near the Murchison River with the wreck of the Zeewyck. This wreck occurred in 1729, and 11 of the 93 who escaped from the wreck and landed on a small island, now called Gun Island, were dispatched in a ship's boat to Batavia to bring succour. They were never heard of again. This little boat would have headed north, and, under the influence of the strong south-westerlies that are the prevailing winds along that part of the coast, particularly in June, the month of the wreck, could easily have been blown towards the mainland and been dashed to pieces on the reef north of the Murchison River.

A chest would almost certainly be carried on such a boat for the purpose of storing the crude navigation instruments and any money made available to the man in charge for the purpose of purchasing stores from any friendly ship or peoples. What more likely that a boat in 1729 would be carrying coins minted in 1711?

The finding of the breeches of two cannon weakens this theory to some extent and lends colour to a belief that the wreck was larger than the ship's boat and probably large enough to carry cannon. But the finding of breeches without any sign of the rest of the cannon suggests that the breeches were being carried separately and, if that were so, they might have been used as ballast for a ship's boat. A brass tray with a spout at one corner, which was included in the discoveries, could be a utensil used for filling wine flagons, and might well have formed part of the equipment of a boat setting out for Batavia.

As another link with the early Dutch voyagers off our coast, the discovery is interesting, but as an historical fact it is too isolated to permit more than a theory as to possible origin. Unless additional evidence is forthcoming, the origin of the relics found north of the Murchison River will remain enveloped in mystery, and join, in uncertain but romantic interest, such other relics eloquent of centuries-old stories of the sea, as the Portuguese carronade found on Carronade Island in Napier Broome Bay, and the old flintlock pistol found several years ago on Lovers' Island, Port Hedland.

This remarkable interpretation, linking the wreck with the ship's boat of the *Zeewyk*, was hardly 'a theory that fits'. Uren dismissed the possibility of the wreck being that of the *Zuytdorp* by stating that it was unlikely that a ship would be carrying newly minted coins. He thus disregarded the key piece of information that led in due course to identification of the wreck. The *Zuytdorp* was indeed carrying several hundred thousand newly minted coins, 1711 being both the year of minting and the year that the ship left the Netherlands.

A further report appeared in the *West Australian* on 9 September 1939, under the headings 'Treasure trove' and 'More finds near Murchison River'. The text repeated much of the information given in earlier accounts of the discovery and of relics that had been found, then went on to say:

The party, Mr Drage wrote, 'reported that it had secured a piece of timber which seemed to have a woman's face and a lion's head on it. In addition, a fastener of a trunk or chest and several pieces of iron, and about 20 feet of a ship's mast, were recovered. The members of the party stated that there seemed to be other remains of the wreck under the reef but these would need blasting out. About 70 or 80 coins and pieces of silver were found on this occasion'.

Essentially the same story also appeared in the *Geraldton Guardian* of 12 September 1939 and in Malcolm Uren's book *Sailormen's ghosts* (1940).

The next published reference to the wreck was by Victor Courtney, printed in two issues of the *Sunday Times Magazine* in June 1941, following an expedition to the site (see Chapter 4) sponsored by that newspaper and guided by Charlie Mallard (the father of Lurlie Pepper and Ada Drage). In his articles, Courtney refers to both Tom Pepper and Charlie Mallard, but he does not mention Ernest or Ada Drage. This omission would seem surprising if Hughie Drage, who was an expedition member, believed that Ernest or Ada Drage had made the original discovery.

There is also no suggestion in Courtney's articles that Charlie Mallard was the finder. On the other hand, although Tom Pepper is not specifically identified as the person who discovered the wreck, that is implied in the text. Courtney states that Tom Pepper was 'the finder of the original figurehead on this spot', inferring that he was also the first to visit the site, and that the wreck had been found by 'a man hunting a dingo, [who] went back and collected a few coins and told a few people'. This is consistent with Tom Pepper's account of how he found the wreck.

A specific account of the discovery appeared in parts of seven articles by Jim Cruthers, published during December 1954 in the *Daily News*, under the pen-name 'Jay Winter'.[97] These articles describe an expedition to the site that I organized (see Chapter 4), accompanied by Tom and Lurlie Pepper, John Stokes, Jim Cruthers and Todge Campbell. Cruthers discusses early visits to the wrecksite by Tom Pepper and Ernest Drage, and unequivocally identifies Pepper as the person who first found the wreck. These articles attracted a lot of public attention at the time, and no one came forward to dispute the conclusion that Tom Pepper had made the first discovery.

However, members of the Drage family with whom I have discussed the matter sincerely believe that Ada Drage (née Mallard), alone or with her husband Ernest, was the first to make the discovery. Pearly Whitby (née Drage) told me that her mother, Ada Drage, found the wreck while 'poking around' for oysters and other shellfish at the foot of the cliffs, at a time when Ernest was repairing the fence that ran towards the wreck from near Ramyard Shed. She said that Ada was accompanied on this visit by her small son Bertie, and that she afterwards told her brother-in-law Tom Pepper about her find, causing him to visit the site.

A submission made by Pearly Whitby to the Select Committee on Ancient Shipwrecks, dated February 1994, reads as follows:

> My mother and father were both of Aboriginal descent and could not read and write. They had 16 children. I was the third eldest, and was born on 1st September 1919. My older brothers and sisters and I never learnt to read and write.
>
> Because in the early days nobody took much notice of what Aboriginals said, they were used to staying in the background, and because none of us could read or write, no full record of our story was recorded. Now, because the Government has asked for submissions, I have asked my friends and relatives to help me do just that. I do not pretend that these exact words are my own, but I swear that the story is true in every detail. I am one of only three people alive today who saw the first Zuytdorp relics when they were found by my mother.
>
> For many years I have listened to stories of Tom Pepper Senior making the first discovery, and it has caused me great pain. My only reason for making a claim on my mother's behalf is our wish to be able to afford headstones for our parents' graves and to have a monument erected at the wreck site to commemorate our mother's find.
>
> It is necessary to understand the circumstances near the wreck site around 1926–27. My father was working on Murchison House Station erecting fences, windmills, tankstands, and sheds, as well as trapping dingoes, cutting fence posts, and similar jobs. By then my mother had I think

eight children under the age of about eleven, so we all had
to bog in and help. At the time of the find I was about seven
years old. We lived in a camp at Bullocksmellum Well, about
six miles south east of the wreck site. At the time, Tom
Pepper Senior, who was a white man, was in charge of about
five Aboriginal stockmen. Some of the men who worked there
about that time were Tommy Bonner, who was a full blood,
George Mallard, Jack Ryan, Ben Kelly, and Jack Mallard. They
were camped at Gee Gie Outcamp, 18–20 miles south east of
the wreck.

My mother kept a hammer and chisel in her saddle
bag, and used these tools to gather oysters, periwinkles, and
other shellfish when she was able to get down to the sea. My
father did not like her going down because the sea was often
dangerous. Also the scrub was so thick towards the coast he
thought she might injure herself.

One day my mum and dad arrived back at our home
with three jugs [now known to be breech blocks]. Two were
about 18 inches high and one was 12 inches high. They also
had three small plates and a handful of coins. Over the years
my parents always told the same story, and this is how it
happened:

Dad was going to check dingo traps on horseback,
and Mum and Bertie, my brother, went with him on their
own horses. One dingo had been caught in a trap and had
chewed his own foot off. This is not uncommon, as most
bushmen know. Dad decided to track the dingo and try to
shoot him. As they were quite close to the ocean, Mum
said she would go down and gather shellfish. Depending on
the weather, it was sometimes possible to catch crayfish by
hand or spear. People today do not realise how boring our
diet was then, as we only went shopping in Northampton
about every six months. Mum used to add to our diet
with seafood.

Mum was quite surprised to find the relics, and she and
Bertie spent some time collecting what they could find. They
met Dad later and they all went back to our camp. All of the
horses were fitted with saddle bags and wagga bags those
days. Wagga bags are large bags which fit over the horse's
rump, and large objects can be carried in them.

People today ask me how can a mother with so many children have time to go fishing? They do not realise that we had to help with all the work from a very young age. Also, at that time we had Bronco Brand and his wife staying with us, as well as two full bloods. They all used to help my parents. Because of this, Mum was sometimes able to get away from the hard work at our home and go with Dad or go fishing.

People today just do not know what hard work is. When I was less than ten years old I gathered firewood, milked the cow, helped make butter, bread, and salted meat, mind my brothers and sisters, and a thousand other jobs. As I got older I had to do all the men's jobs, including: cut fence posts, dig the holes for them, bore the posts and run the wire, harness the camel team to the four-wheel wagon and drive it, harness the horse to the spring cart and drive it, and shoot and skin kangaroos. My favorite rifle those days was an old forty-four. I used to make my own bullets. I even did the mail run from Murchison House to Ajana on a horse…

I think it was some weeks after finding the relics, Mum went with my brother Bertie and Bronco and his wife to the wreck site. Bertie was one year younger than me and had a little pony called 'Billy-goat' because he was so small. They went to the wreck site and the main thing they found was what appeared to be a wood carving of a woman. It was wedged in some rocks and I do not remember if any other relics were found on that trip.

Because of the type of work that Dad did, we used to shift camp from time to time, and I think it was about a year later that Mum and Dad, Tom and his Aboriginal wife Lurley, and young Bertie went to the wreck site. The carving was still there and they carried it well up the cliff. I am quite sure that was the first time that Tom Pepper saw any of the Zuytdorp relics. I am well aware that he did find and remove various relics over the years. I am also aware that various land and sea parties have removed relics, but my mother was the first person with white blood to find the site…

One cannot fail to be moved by the sincerity of Pearly Whitby's telling of this story. She similarly impressed me with her candour when I interviewed her on the subject in 1993. However, it must be remembered that her account is based on childhood memories of more than sixty-five years ago, and such memories may or may not have changed with time.

Pearly Whitby's sister, Annie Oxenham (recently deceased), also maintained that Ada was the discoverer. She said that her mother was looking for shellfish when she visited the site and noted masses of green coins on the reef top, which she collected and took back to their camp, at Bullocksmellum, in a golden syrup tin. She also picked up a number of plates and 'jugs' (breech blocks). Annie Oxenham said that her mother later showed the coins to Lurlie and Tom Pepper and told them how to find the wrecksite.

The account given by Annie Oxenham's daughter Ann, as reported in the *Geraldton Guardian* on 30 May 1968, is slightly different. She credited the discovery jointly to Ernest and Ada Drage, and stated that they were accompanied on the initial visit by an Aboriginal man named Nyarda (others have told me that his name was actually Nyardu).

Ernest and Ada Drage had seventeen children, sixteen of whom survived and were brought up in bush camps on Murchison House and Tamala, never living in a normal house, although Ernest constructed large bough-sheds with brush roofs that were remarkably watertight. He was a skilled and resourceful bushman and station worker, and the memorials to his skills include a number of impressive stone tanks on Tamala and Murchison House, including those at Yalthoo (near Murchison House Homestead), and Wale Well. He also constructed Ramyard Shed, 7 kilometres north-east of the *Zuytdorp* wrecksite, on the stockroute from Tamala to Murchison House. Much of Ernest and Ada Drage's income was derived from hunting dingoes, kangaroos, emus, foxes and goats. Ernest died of a brain tumour in 1943, soon after he and Ada had retired to Ajana, for the first settled existence of their married lives. Ada died in 1960, leaving sixty-four grand-children and five great-grandchildren.

It may be significant that, as far as can be determined, none of the Mallard siblings ever backed the claim that their sister Ada or brother-in-law Ernest Drage had discovered the wreck. Some maintained that it was found by Tom Pepper,[98] while others claimed that their father, Charlie Mallard, was the real finder. Charlie Mallard's claim was strongly advocated by his daughter Louise Dickerson (recently deceased) and his daughter-in-law

Ivy Mallard (widow of Joe Mallard). Both were adamant that Tom Pepper, Ernest Drage and Ada Drage had nothing to do with the find and that Charlie Mallard was solely responsible.

Charlie Mallard was born at Lynton as the son of a part-Aboriginal teenage girl. He knew nothing of his father, but was brought up as the foster child of a Mr and Mrs Mallard. Mallard Senior had come to Western Australia as a convict from England, where he had been a baker, and after obtaining his ticket-of-leave he worked in the Northampton area. His young foster son grew up with the name 'Charlie Doughey', apparently because he had been brought up by a baker, but he later adopted the name Mallard.

Charlie Mallard lived and worked in the Lynton–Northampton–Murchison House–Tamala area throughout his life. He married Alice McMurray, a part-Aborigine. She had previously been married to a Scot named McMurray, by whom she had borne two children. Charlie and Alice Mallard had thirteen children, four of whom—Ada (married Ernest Drage), Joe (married Ivy Poland), Lurlie (married Tom Pepper) and Louise (married Fred Dickerson)—are involved in the *Zuytdorp* story.

Members of the Pepper family are totally convinced of the validity of Tom Pepper's claim to have been the discoverer. Although there are some differences in detail between the various accounts, all maintain that the find was made when Pepper was tracking dingoes along the cliff top, and that visits to the site by Ada Drage, Ernest Drage and Charlie Mallard took place after Pepper's initial discovery.

It seems clear that the conflicting claims made by or on behalf of Tom Pepper, Ada and Ernest Drage, and Charlie Mallard cannot be reconciled, and it is unlikely that incontrovertible proof, one way or another, will ever be established. However, I believe that the available evidence is consistent with the view that Tom Pepper was the original discoverer. Counter-claims made by the Drage and Mallard descendants are based solely on hearsay of more than sixty years ago. There are no contemporary records of what Ada Drage, Ernest Drage and Charlie Mallard themselves had to say regarding their supposed roles in the discovery. On the other hand, Tom Pepper's claim is backed by tape recordings of his own words on the matter, plus the detailed transcript of an interview with Jim Cruthers in 1954.[99] Moreover, Pepper was renowned for his honesty and fundamental sense of decency, and his version of the discovery has been accepted without question in almost all published accounts over the past forty years.

Members of the Select Committee on Ancient Shipwrecks also decided that the evidence pointed to Tom Pepper as having been the first person to find the *Zuytdorp* wreck in modern times, and he was recognized as a primary discoverer. I was designated as the second primary discoverer, as my research had been responsible for identifying the ship. Ada Drage, Max Cramer, Graham Cramer and Tom Brady were each named as secondary discoverers. Awards were made to each of the discoverers by the Minister for the Arts, at a special ceremony held in Geraldton on 22 February 1996.

Tom Pepper

Tom Pepper was born on 7 February 1900 at Shelford in the County of Cambridge, England. He was the eldest of five children born to Richard and Mary Pepper. The Peppers came originally from the Cotswold Hills, moving to a farm at Little Abbington, near Cambridge, in about 1909. Richard Pepper found that gravel and sand on his property was suitable for construction purposes, so he proceeded to develop the deposit, using steam-driven trucks for haulage. Unfortunately, these trucks cut up the roads and he was successfully sued for repairs by the Cambridge Council, driving him into bankruptcy. As a result, the Peppers decided to start a new life in Australia, migrating to Western Australia in 1911, when Tom was eleven. He received no further schooling after this move.

On arriving in Western Australia, the Peppers travelled by ship to Port Gregory, in order to take up a block of 1,000 acres (405 hectares) nearby at Balline. However, Richard Pepper had no understanding of Australian farming conditions, and he and the two elder boys had cleared 300 acres (122 hectares) before realizing that the block was far too small to be viable. They abandoned this property in about 1914, to take up a pastoral lease of 30,000 acres (12,150 hectares) at Bungabandi Spring, between Eurardy and Murchison House stations. They built a small house there, still marked today by its paving stones, and Tom Pepper and his brother Jack put up fence posts around much of the property. However, there was no money for wire to complete the fence. The station was never stocked, and they had to abandon it after two years.

After leaving Bungabandi, Tom and Jack stayed on to work in the area around Shark Bay, Northampton and Murchison House, while their parents and the other children moved to the south-west of the state. On 6 March 1926, Tom married Lurlie Mallard (aged eighteen), the part-Aboriginal daughter of Charlie and Alice Mallard, in Carnarvon. At that time, it was most unusual for a European man to marry an Aboriginal woman, although many lived together in de facto relationships on the stations. Tom's parents were opposed to the marriage—indeed, they never became fully reconciled to it. However, Tom was a highly moral person, without the racist outlook that was common at that time. Lurlie was an attractive and spirited young woman, and theirs was to be a loving and stable marriage that lasted for forty-one years.

In 1926, the newlyweds set up home at Gee Gie Outcamp on Murchison House Station, remaining there continuously until 1950 (Lurlie used to say that they 'spent twenty-three Christmases at Gee Gie'). Their little galvanized-iron home had three rooms—a kitchen/living-room and two bedrooms—with a verandah on one side. The house had been built during the early years of the twentieth century, and it was still standing in 1995, although urgently in need of repairs, having been unoccupied for about thirty years.

Tom and Lurlie had five children while they were at Gee Gie: Elsie, Tom, Margaret, Laura (died 1977) and Arthur. They were a well-matched couple, who were content with life in the bush, hunting, trapping, and working with sheep, horses and camels. Lurlie was an excellent bush cook, specializing in camp-oven cooking. Although she never learned to read or write, she had an excellent memory and could recount stories of long ago, many of them highly amusing, in extraordinary detail. She and Tom were determined that their children would be suitably educated, sending them to schools in Ajana, Northampton and Geraldton. Providing for the children's board, clothes and books was a major expense for the Peppers, when Tom's wages on the station were only £2 ($4) a week. However, they managed to earn a lot of additional income by hunting dingoes, emus, kangaroos, foxes and eagles.

When Tom Pepper began working on Murchison House Station in the early 1920s, dingoes were a serious problem, killing hundreds of sheep every year, and consequently a lot of effort was put into eliminating them. Pepper became a skilled dogger (dingo hunter), trapping and shooting as many as sixty or seventy a year.

The standard bounty paid was £2 ($4) for each dingo scalp and tail, although a station would pay more for a particular dingo that was causing a lot of damage and proving difficult to catch. Pepper finally hunted down and killed the last dingo in the area, at the remote Ngudjidja Gudjidja Soak, in about 1950.

It was through his dingo-hunting activities that Tom Pepper first found the *Zuytdorp* wreck, in 1927. When I first met him, he had not been back to the wrecksite since 1939, when he went there to collect the carved figure. However, every year he would pass within 5.5 kilometres of the site while droving sheep from Tamala to Murchison House. The stockroute between the two stations had long been established—it was probably first used during the 1860s. There had originally been a serious obstacle to droving sheep along this route: the lack of reliable water on the

Tom Pepper (1958).

Photograph by Maurie Hammond, courtesy of West Australian Newspapers

60-kilometre stretch between Natta Well on Tamala and Gee Gie on Murchison House. This problem was overcome, some time before the end of the nineteenth century, when the Shark Bay Road Board built a large rain-catchment shed, Willie's Shed, approximately midway between the two places. The original shed was pulled down and replaced, in 1929, by a new one covering an area of 150 square metres, with six tanks, to store 41,500 litres of water.[100] A 5,000-gallon (18,927-litre) tank was later added, and the shed was last renovated, by Tom and Arthur Pepper, in 1957. As far as I know, Willie's is the largest rainshed in Western Australia, and was still standing, in restorable condition, when I last visited it in 1993.[101]

Prior to moving to Tamala in 1950, Tom Pepper periodically had assisted in droving sheep from Tamala to Murchison House, and sometimes from there into Northampton. However, after moving to Tamala, it became an annual event for him to take between 4,000 and 5,000 wethers down the stockroute to Murchison House after shearing had been completed in November. Cecil Blood, who was then manager of Tamala, told me that between 1951 and 1963 Pepper took 49,000 sheep to Murchison House, losing almost none on each trip—a remarkable droving achievement.[102] The stockroute has not been used since 1963.

The Peppers remained at Tamala until 1964, when Tom was appointed as manager of Peron Peninsula Station, Shark Bay. He set about revitalizing the station, which had become badly run down. He and Lurlie enjoyed working and living there, even though it was outside their normal 'home range' of Murchison House and Tamala. Three years later, in 1967, tragedy struck the family when Lurlie died suddenly of a heart attack, at the age of fifty-nine. After her death, Tom continued working on Peron Peninsula until, at the age of seventy-six, he accepted the old-age pension for the first time. Two years later, his health failed and he was moved to Carnarvon, and from there to a nursing home in Geraldton, where he died on 23 September 1985, at the age of eighty-five.[103]

Tom Pepper will be long remembered, not only for his role in discovering the *Zuytdorp* wreck, but also for his skills as one of the most outstanding stockmen and bushmen in the history of the lower Murchison and Shark Bay areas.

4. The Glint of Silver

Early Expeditions

The *Sunday Times* expedition, 1941

I first heard of the *Sunday Times* expedition during my earliest discussions with Tom Pepper. He said then that the visit had taken place 'just before the war', in 1939, and that participants had included Victor Courtney of that newspaper and David Hunter, the Commissioner of Police. This '1939' expedition was later mentioned by Jim Cruthers in his *Daily News* articles of 1954, although at that time we had almost no information about it or the participants. In 1958, I telephoned Victor Courtney to enquire about the expedition and the relics he was said to have brought back to Perth, but, inexplicably, he denied having any knowledge of either. So we remained very much in the dark about the expedition.

When the WA Museum's Mike McCarthy invited me, in 1987, to recommence my research into historical aspects of the *Zuytdorp*, I realized that one of the matters that needed to be followed up was the *Sunday Times* expedition. The way in which my enquiries into this matter were conducted illustrates how historical research and detective work are closely related. Similarly, there are parallels between the approaches adopted in historical and geological research, both of which involve piecing together disparate items of information to produce an integrated picture of the past.

There was no mention of the expedition in 1939 issues of the *Sunday Times*, so this was no help. However, I remembered that, as a result of his 1954 story in the *Daily News*, Jim Cruthers had been telephoned by a Robert Cook of Cottesloe, who said that he and E. Faye had participated in the *Sunday Times* expedition. On consulting the 1954 telephone directory, I found that although there was no R. Cook of Cottesloe listed, there was an R.H. Cook in Mosman Park. That entry continued until 1981, and its deletion was not followed by a new listing in the Karrakatta Cemetery register of deceased persons. However, a few years before, I had learned that a man then living in Geraldton was reported to have taken part in the *Sunday Times* expedition. Could he have been R.H. Cook? Sure enough, the country telephone directory for 1982 showed this name, with a Geraldton address, and it was still listed there in 1987. On telephoning the number, I was told that Bob Cook had left there two or three years earlier and that the present occupant of the house had no idea where he had gone. So it looked as though this line of enquiry had come to a dead end.[104]

My remaining lead was E. Faye, who was known to have been on the expedition with Robert Cook. Could he have been the father of Claude Faye, whom I knew as a member of the Perth Rotary Club? On telephoning Claude, he confirmed that his father, Ennemond Faye, had indeed been on the trip, and that he was still alive and resident in England, estranged from his Perth family. Moreover, Claude said that he might be able to find a film of the expedition, which his father had left behind in Perth about forty years before. Several weeks later, after some prompting, Claude found the film and loaned it to me for copying on to videotape, copies of which I donated to the State Archives and the WA Maritime Museum. The film is a fascinating record of the expedition, the people who took part, and the vehicles that they used. It includes scenes taken at Gee Gie, featuring Lurlie Pepper, the carved stern figure from the wreck, and a camel team.

Claude Faye told me that he remembered Bob Cook, but had no idea of his present whereabouts. However, he suggested that I contact Cook's sharebroker, who might be able to help. When I did so, the person concerned advised that he had not heard of Bob Cook for some years, although he understood that his son was a real estate agent in Mosman Park.

A Mosman Park agent listed in the telephone directory gave me Bruce Cook's telephone number, and, on speaking to him, I learned that his parents were then living with him. In this circuitous way, I was able to meet Bob Cook and speak to him about the *Sunday Times* expedition, showing him the video of Faye's film to refresh memories of forty-six years before. He had kept in touch with Ennemond Faye, and gave me his address in Bristol, so I was able to write to him there, sending a video copy of his film of the expedition. Faye had been divorced from his Australian family for forty years, and he was delighted to have the video copy so that he could show his later English family 'that he had been young once'.

Cook and Faye both reiterated that the expedition had been in 1939, 'just before the war', but they could not explain why there was no account of it in the *Sunday Times* of that year. It then occurred to me that the Commissioner of Police, David Hunter, must have taken leave in order to go on the expedition. Enquiries with the Police Department showed that he took leave from 11 to 24 July 1939 and 1 May to 3 August 1941.

Shortly afterwards, Bob Cook's wife remembered she had made her debut, at Government House ballroom, at the time of the expedition, and consequently Bob had been unable to partner her at the ball. This prompted her to look through some old scrapbooks, and in due course she telephoned to say that the debutante ball was held on 14 May 1941. Thus, I learned that the *Sunday Times* expedition had taken place in 1941, not 1939 as everyone had claimed, and I was then able to locate Victor Courtney's articles on the expedition, published in the *Sunday Times Magazine* of 8 and 15 June 1941.[105]

This confusion of 1941 and 1939 was no doubt due to the fact that World War II became a stark reality for most Australians in December 1941, after the attack on Pearl Harbor and the subsequent threat to Australia of Japanese invasion. Before that time, the distant war in Europe and North Africa had made relatively little impact on the Australian people, and so an expedition that took place in May 1941 would be remembered long afterwards as having been 'just before the war'.

The origin of the *Sunday Times* expedition can be traced to the articles published in the *West Australian* in May and September 1939, describing relics found at the wrecksite, which were also discussed in Malcolm Uren's book *Sailormen's ghosts*, published in 1940.[106] These accounts aroused considerable interest, and in 1941 a number of prominent Perth people decided to mount an expedition to visit the site, believing that the wreck might be that of the fabled *Gilt Dragon* (*Vergulde Draeck*). The expedition was sponsored by the *Sunday Times*, and the two major shareholders in that paper, J.J. Simons and Victor Courtney, were expedition members. Also participating were Ennemond ('Pacha') Faye (a director of the *Sunday Times* and son-in-law of Claude de Bernales, the well-known mining entrepreneur), David Hunter (Commissioner of Police), Hughie Drage (pastoralist of Northampton), Claude McKinlay (photographer and racing-car driver), Bob Cook (cadet journalist, who had been a ward of Simons as a child), Charlie Mallard (guide to the expedition and father of Lurlie Pepper), and a miner named Geoff (surname unknown).

J.J. Simons, usually referred to as 'Boss' Simons, was a prominent citizen of Perth at that time, known principally for his leadership of the Young Australia League (YAL), which he had founded in 1905.[107] That organization is little known today, but during the 1930s and 1940s everyone knew about the YAL, and it had a membership of more than 100,000 young people throughout Australia. A principal objective of the organization was 'Education by Travel', accomplished through overseas and interstate tours by young men and women. Simons made friends in many countries through his leadership of these tours, and the YAL was acclaimed by several world leaders, including King George V and President Hoover.

Simons had, as a young man, been an outspoken political activist and advocate of Australia and Australian values, and some of his nationalistic views would still receive wide support today. However, the motto that he espoused in 1907—'A White, Self-Contained, Self-Reliant Nation'—would hardly be acceptable in today's multicultural Australia. In 1904, when Simons was only twenty-two, he created a sensation by organizing a pageant in Perth to commemorate the fiftieth anniversary of the Eureka Stockade. Several survivors of that rebellion took part in the parade. Simons felt that Eureka should be celebrated as a symbol of the struggle of democracy against colonial tyranny, whereas many in the Perth establishment saw it solely in terms of radical rebellion by a poorly organized rabble.

Simons and Victor Courtney, who had got to know one another through the YAL, became the joint owners of a small newspaper, the *Call*, in 1917, and in 1935 they purchased the *Sunday Times*, running it as a very successful partnership. By the time that Simons died in 1948, at the age of sixty-six, he had become a wealthy man. He never married, and on his death a significant part of his estate was left to the YAL.

Simons and Courtney enlisted their fellow *Sunday Times* director, Ennemond Faye, to join the expedition. Faye was a French citizen who had, at the age of twenty-two, married Daphne de Bernales, daughter of Claude de Bernales, the charming, elegant and wealthy entrepreneur who played a major role in Western Australia's gold boom of the 1930s. At the time of the expedition, Faye was responsible for administering the de Bernales mining interests in Western Australia while de Bernales himself was resident in England.

I visited Faye in Bristol during October 1989, in order to discuss the 1941 *Sunday Times* expedition, having corresponded with him for some time before then. Faye is a great raconteur, and he entertained me at lunch with amusing descriptions of his role in the expedition, Western Australia during the 1930s and 1940s, and his subsequent life in England.[108]

David Hunter, the Commissioner of Police and a friend of Faye's, was also a member of the expedition. Faye told me that the rationale behind this was that with Hunter's presence the police force would help if the expedition got into trouble. Hunter had once been a constable in Northampton, where he became acquainted with Hughie Drage, another member of the party. Hunter had no doubt seen relics from the wreck that Drage had acquired from his part-Aboriginal half-brother, Ernest. Keith Drage, Hughie's son, remembers the expedition well, because as they were passing through Northampton, Hunter arranged for him to be issued with a driving licence, while he was still only sixteen, a year below the minimum age.

Claude McKinlay was another useful member of the expedition, in two ways: first, he was responsible for the photographs and movie film taken of the trip; and second, as a racing-car enthusiast, he was a skilled driver. The miner, Geoff, was brought along as a truck driver and also because of his skills with explosives, as the group intended doing some blasting at the wrecksite. The only problem with this plan was that they forgot to take the detonators—a fortunate omission in view of the damage that might otherwise have been done to the site.

The party of seven men left Perth on about 3 May 1941, and drove to Northampton, where they were met by Hughie Drage and Charlie Mallard. At the Drage home, they were shown a number of relics from the wreck, including coins, several with the date 1711, and a copper (or brass) tray, all of which whetted their appetites for the adventure ahead.

Charlie Mallard with the carved figure from the stern of the Zuytdorp, *at Gee Gie Outcamp (May 1941).*

Photograph by Claude McKinlay, courtesy of the *Sunday Times*

The party left Northampton on 5 May, travelling along the North West Coastal Highway to near Eurardy Homestead, and from there along a bush track past Bungabandi Spring to Gee Gie Outcamp (see Map 1). They were equipped with three vehicles: a small truck (provided by Ennemond Faye), a new Plymouth sedan car (provided by Boss Simons, and driven by McKinlay), and a Chevrolet utility (provided by Hughie Drage). The party reached Gee Gie in the early evening, camping there overnight. Tom Pepper had left for sheep-crutching at Tamala, but Lurlie Pepper, the children and several station hands were there to meet the party. Margaret Caunt, then Margaret Pepper, aged ten, vividly remembers seeing the lights of the three vehicles coming along the track into the outcamp. It was a big event in their lives, as Gee Gie was a remote place that was rarely visited by anyone other than occasional station personnel.

The Murchison House camel team was being used at the outcamp at the time, and the film taken by McKinlay has several hilarious scenes of members of the party attempting to ride camels. On seeing the video of this film, Margaret Caunt was able to identify several of the camels by name—King, Maud, Nugget and Sally.

Members and vehicles of the 1941 Sunday Times *expedition, at Gee Gie Outcamp.*

Photograph by Claude McKinlay, courtesy of the *Sunday Times*

Four or five years later, these camels were released to fend for themselves, and a number of their descendants still live in the country east of the wrecksite, outside the limits of pastoral stations. Unfortunately, some of them have been shot from time to time by station personnel and staff of Agriculture Western Australia (because they are feral animals), which seems a pity as they are causing little or no harm. Certainly, any damage resulting from camels is minuscule compared to the devastation caused by feral goats.

The utility used by the *Sunday Times* party was left behind at Gee Gie, while the truck and sedan car were driven to within a few kilometres of the wrecksite. Both were only two-wheel-drive vehicles (four-wheel drive was unknown in Western Australia at that time), and it was a remarkable achievement to have taken them so far. Simons was upset that his new car suffered damage to its bodywork, but it is amazing that such a vehicle, designed for city use, ever succeeded in traversing the sand tracks on Murchison House Station. The car was frequently bogged, but it nevertheless got through. Fortunately, rain had fallen not long before—Tom Pepper's records at Gee Gie show that 85 points (22 millimetres) fell there from 27 April to 2 May—making the sand tracks much firmer than they would otherwise have been.

The party apparently camped about 4 kilometres south of Ramyard Shed, and 5.5 kilometres from the wrecksite, near the spot where the stockroute track passed through an old fence (the same one that I would follow thirteen years later, on my first visit to the wrecksite). Next morning, members of the party walked from their camp to the wrecksite, guided by Charlie Mallard. It was a long and exhausting hike for them all, and they were tormented by myriads of flies; however, photographs show that the dapper Frenchman Ennemond Faye wore a tie throughout the walk.

The group made a general reconnaissance of the site over a few hours, and collected several coins (including pieces of eight) and other artefacts. They also dug in low caves behind the top of the cliff, finding a coin and pieces of rusty metal, which suggested to them that some survivors had probably sheltered there. They deduced, incorrectly, that the remains of the ship were buried under tons of rubble derived from the collapse of part of the cliff face.

The party left in the afternoon for the long walk back to their camp, a little disappointed at having not found more after so much

effort. Next day, they drove back to Gee Gie, where Lurlie Pepper, in Tom's absence, agreed to show them the 'figurehead'. This relic impressed them greatly, to the extent that about two years later the Commissioner of Police threatened Tom Pepper with legal action if he did not relinquish it to the state. Pepper's retort was that if action were taken against him, he would take the object back to the wrecksite and throw it into the sea. Nothing further was done by the police, and in any case it seems unlikely that they had any legal powers to act.

Keith Drage told me that his father gave all the relics in his possession to Police Commissioner Hunter, to pass on to the WA Museum. Ennemond Faye and Bob Cook said that the relics collected on the expedition were supposedly passed to the museum, via Simons and Courtney. However, I am advised by the museum authorities that none of this material was ever lodged at the museum, and its eventual fate is unknown.

Members of the expedition had originally set out with the belief that this wreck could be that of the *Vergulde Draeck*.

Members of the 1941 Sunday Times expedition en route to the wrecksite, with Charlie Mallard pointing the way. The other expedition members (left to right) are Victor Courtney, Hughie Drage, 'Boss' Simons, David Hunter, Bob Cook and Ennemond Faye.

Photograph by Claude McKinlay, courtesy of the *Sunday Times*

However, the coins from the site, with dates as recent as 1711, proved that this could not be so, as the *Vergulde Draeck* was wrecked in 1656. In his articles on the expedition, Courtney concluded that it could conceivably be the wreck of the *Zeewyk*, although he should have been aware that that ship was already known to have been lost on the Houtman Abrolhos, even though the wreck itself had not been located at that time. He may have been confused by Malcolm Uren's earlier theory that the wreck was that of the *Zeewyk*'s longboat. Courtney summed up by saying that 'the identity of the ill-fated ship can't be traced from anything that was found'.

The *Daily News* expedition, 1954

During my first visit to the wrecksite, on 1 August 1954, I resolved to organize a properly equipped expedition to investigate the wreck. Returning to Perth in late August, I approached Malcolm Uren, seeking the support of West Australian Newspapers Ltd in financing such an expedition. I showed him the coin and other relics that I had found during my visit there. Uren was enthusiastic about the proposal, expressing confidence that he could arrange sponsorship by the newspaper. He also said that he would like to participate himself, and agreed that we should invite John Stokes, who had been recommended by my father as a skilled diver, to join the team. Uren suggested that we form a legal syndicate, so that all members of the group would know where they stood if any treasure were to be found. I agreed to this proposal, and arranged for a family friend and prominent Perth lawyer, Frank Downing, to draw up an appropriate document.

The New Holland Syndicate was consequently constituted, 'for the purpose of exploring and recovering treasure from the wreck now lying on the North-West Coast of Western Australia, approximately 40 miles north-north-west from the mouth of the Murchison River'. Members of the syndicate were listed as Phillip Elliott Playford (geologist), Malcolm John Leggoe Uren (editorial executive), John Gerrard Stokes (assistant mill superintendent), and Thomas Pepper (station overseer). West Australian Newspapers agreed to provide two vehicles, food, and camping equipment for a three-week visit to the site, beginning in the first week of November 1954. A photographer would accompany the party, and Malcolm Uren would be responsible for writing a series of articles for publication in the *Daily News*, Perth's popular evening newspaper.

Tom Pepper had told me that the calmest periods of the year for diving at the site were in spring and autumn. He said that for a few days at those times of the year, the sea could be quite smooth, with little or no swell. Clearly, our expedition should be timed to coincide with one of those periods. We considered it unwise to wait for autumn 1955, because of the possibility of word leaking out and someone else getting there first. The earliest practicable time seemed to be early November, which could be a little late for the calm periods that were expected in spring. However, taking everything into consideration, we finally settled on that month for the trip.

I then had to obtain permission from my employer, WAPET, to take leave at that time. Having been with the company for only seven months, I was not yet eligible for annual leave, and therefore special permission had to be obtained from the Managing Director, Jim Kirby. I was unable to tell him why I wished to take leave, as members of the syndicate were bound by legal agreement to maintain secrecy. However, he did find out somehow that I was going back to the same area where I had recently been working in the field, and he enquired of my immediate supervisor, Ross McWhae, whether I might have 'got a girl into trouble up there'. In the straitlaced world of 1954, this would indeed have been an interesting piece of scandal, and Jim Kirby was probably a little disappointed when he eventually learned of the true reason.

When the time came for the party to leave, Malcolm Uren was delayed because of a pressing business issue, so John Stokes and I set off alone on 5 November, in a short-wheel-base Land Rover provided by West Australian Newspapers. The amount of gear that we could carry was very limited because of this vehicle's small size. We drove to Gee Gie and the wrecksite via the Eurardy route (the same way that the *Sunday Times* party had gone, thirteen years before), without meeting anyone after leaving the North West Coastal Highway.

From a study of aerial photographs of the area, I had decided that the most practicable way through the belt of dense tea-tree scrub would be about 2 kilometres north of the route I had followed three months earlier. This plan worked out reasonably well, and I was able to drive safely to the wrecksite, although some steep, sandy slopes and deep creeks had to be negotiated. John Stokes (who had not experienced such cross-country driving before) was rather concerned when I headed nonchalantly into steep-sided creek beds, commenting that I drove the vehicle 'like a tank'. On reaching the wrecksite in the late afternoon, we set up camp about 300 metres from the site, in a slight hollow that gave a little protection from the strong south-westerly winds (see Map 5). The same campsite was also to be used four years later, for the 1958 expedition.

Next day, we were joined by Tom and Lurlie Pepper, who had ridden down from Tamala with two riding horses and a packhorse. They camped at Ramyard Shed and brought water to our camp each day.

It had been arranged that I would go back into Northampton a few days later, to meet Malcolm Uren and the photographer, who would be driving from Perth in another Land Rover. John Stokes remained at our camp near the wrecksite, while I drove back to Northampton, needing a full day to get there. On telephoning Perth, I was told that Uren could not come because of industrial trouble at the newspaper, but that Jim Cruthers would take his place, and he would arrive in Northampton later that evening with a photographer, John ('Todge') Campbell.

So the eventual make-up of our party was Tom and Lurlie Pepper, John Stokes, Jim Cruthers, Todge Campbell and me. The Peppers, John Stokes and I spent three weeks on the expedition, while the others were with us for a little more than two weeks.

In an album of photographs presented to each expedition member after we returned to Perth, Jim Cruthers described our group as follows:

Tom Pepper [54]: Overseer of Tamala Station and well-known Murchison identity. Tom first discovered the wreck, and refused to lose interest in it. A good hand at making improvised cray drop-nets—and catching crays. The only man in the camp who shaved *every* day.

Mrs (Lurlie) Pepper [46]: The firm friend of the 'city slickers' among the party, who enjoyed her kangaroo stew and marvelled at her bread. Mrs Pepper was by far the most diligent and successful searcher, and her finds on the cliff-top made a valuable contribution to the party's discoveries.

Phillip Playford [22]: When Phillip Playford—a geologist with WAPET—was working in the Murchison area, Tom Pepper told him about the wreck and Phil made moves to form the expedition. He enjoyed the search more than anyone else, worked out more theories than anyone else, attracted more bull-ants and ticks than anyone else, and showed greater concern than anyone else when John Stokes used wood from the wreck for a camp table.

John Stokes [31]: Engineer Stokes, of Cottesloe, was the handyman of the expedition. He made a camp table and seats (what did it matter if they were collectors' pieces—wreckage more than 240 years old!), a splendid fireplace, did a bit of skindiving (playing up to the cameraman of course), caught an occasional fish, blasted away boulders so that we could find more coins, made a kangaroo-tail stew that survived a week, and a damper—and what a damper!

John ('Todge') Campbell [28]: A well-built newspaper photographer, who, in the interests of the job, was prepared to undergo—with admirable philosophy—the rigours of outdoor life. Nevertheless, he will probably talk about this 'tough' assignment for some time. Todge claimed he was the only 'Injun' in the camp. Frequently heard to make mention of a person named Humble—obviously a city acquaintance [he was the West Australian Newspapers stores officer, who was light-heartedly blamed for any deficiencies in the stores and equipment].

Jim Cruthers [29]: A somewhat odd fellow who seemed to spend most of his time writing in a little book. A very average and quite unsuccessful searcher who finally had to borrow a couple of coins from Todge so that his friends in Perth would not disbelieve his story about treasure hunting. A very sound driver, particularly when overtaking on the North-West Highway. [Jim had been a pilot during the war, but he had only recently learned how to drive a car, not particularly well.]

To my surprise, Jim Cruthers and Todge Campbell arrived at Northampton in a two-wheel-drive Ford utility—I had expected a

Map 7 (opposite). Zuytdorp wrecksite, showing locations of onshore relics, and guns, anchors and other relics on the sea-floor. Also showing successive positions of the ship: A—when it first struck the sea-floor; B—when it swivelled around parallel to the coast and its bottom was torn out; and C—when it broke into three segments, which were driven close to the edge of the shoreline platform

'Bathtub pool' in use by members of the 1954 expedition.

Photograph by John Campbell, courtesy of West Australian Newspapers

second Land Rover. Clearly, this would be a problem, because the sand tracks were very soft, and long stretches would be impassable for a two-wheel-drive vehicle. It was unlikely that the utility could reach Gee Gie, let alone the wrecksite. We decided that we would go as far as we could in the utility, then leave it beside the track after loading essential gear into the Land Rover, and proceed in that vehicle for the rest of the way.

We stayed overnight in Northampton. Jim Cruthers had a spot of bother in the bar of the Railway Hotel, as Todge introduced him to some young Aborigines as 'Jimmy Carruthers', who was then very well known in Australia as our first world boxing champion. One of the Aborigines suggested that Jim accompany him outside to see who really was the best fighter. Jim did not accept the challenge.

Next day, we set out for the wreck. The utility was eventually left behind when it became badly bogged some 10 kilometres east of Gee Gie. A lot of gear had to remain in the utility (including Malcolm Uren's 'thunder box' portable toilet—a source of some amusement), so our camp at the wrecksite had only the bare minimum requirements for two weeks of living in the bush.

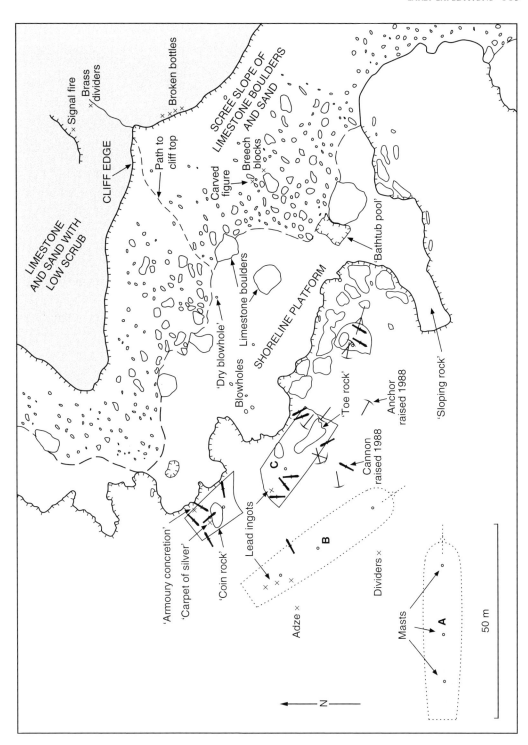

Jim Cruthers and Todge Campbell exploring the cave system below the shoreline platform (1954 expedition).

Photograph by the author, courtesy of West Australian Newspapers

However, the Peppers rode from Ramyard to our camp every day with water and often with a freshly killed kangaroo. Lurlie Pepper baked excellent camp-oven bread, and we caught scores of crayfish, speared many small sharks, and collected as many oysters as we wanted. So there was no need to go hungry; on the contrary, we ate very well. The water brought in by packhorse was insufficient for washing, so we bathed in seawater in an enclosed rock pool (bathtub pool; see Map 7), shoreward of the edge of the limestone platform. This pool is connected with the ocean through caverns under the platform, so it contains a lot of marine life, and water surges in with every wave. It provided us with many small sharks (John Stokes speared eight in one morning) and crayfish (Tom Pepper caught thirty-five in two hours in a net that he improvised from a piece of fencing wire and some string netting).

At the site, we undertook a systematic search for relics and for evidence of the activities of the shipwreck survivors. Most relics were found at the foot of the cliffs, where the shoreline platform

meets the scree slope of boulders, gravel and sand derived by erosion from the cliff face (see Map 7). Coins and other metal fragments were found wedged in crevices, in pockets below boulders, and in a cave system under the platform. Numerous objects that were formerly composed of iron were also found, in the form of expanded and fissured masses of dark brown iron oxide. Tom Pepper showed us where coins had once been thickly studded for about 30 metres along the shoreline platform ('reef') itself, but most of these had been picked up during the period 1927–39, and few remained.

Quite a lot of wooden wreckage was scattered in rocks at the foot of the cliff, in the form of eroded pieces of mast, planks from the ship's decks, and miscellaneous other fragments, most being wedged under boulders or lying out of reach of all but the highest storm waves. The largest and most conspicuous wooden object was a weathered piece of straight, round timber, about 7 metres long and 17 centimetres in diameter, which must once have formed

The author collecting coins on the shoreline platform at the Zuytdorp wrecksite (1954 expedition).

Photograph by John Campbell, courtesy of West Australian Newspapers

Yardarm from the Zuytdorp, held by Jim Cruthers and the author (1954 expedition).

Photograph by John Campbell, courtesy of West Australian Newspapers

part of a yardarm. Much of the wooden wreckage consisted of baltic pine, but some planks were of oak. Pine that was subject to frequent spray from waves had a thick 'beard' of salty wood fibre around a solid interior. More wooden wreckage, thought to be from the ship, was found about 500 metres south of the wrecksite.

Planks and other woodwork from the ship, together with more recent wooden debris, were collected by expedition members to

build a table and benches at our campsite. I was opposed to the use of *Zuytdorp* wreckage for this purpose, but the others regarded it as a practical solution to our lack of tables and chairs, these non-essential items having been left behind in the utility. Jim Cruthers recorded:[109]

The author and Jim Cruthers at the 1954 expedition campsite. The table and bench seats were made from wooden wreckage, largely derived from the Zuytdorp.

Photograph by John Campbell, courtesy of West Australian Newspapers

> It upset Phil more than a little to think that wood which might find a place in museums in many parts of the world was being splashed with tea and smeared with fat and butter. Once when Phil complained, John said jokingly 'the wood's lain down there for more than 240 years, exposed to sun, rain, wind, and sea; a bit of tea won't hurt it!' Obviously Phil was not convinced, but he saw that it was not much good arguing!

When we eventually packed up to leave camp, I carried most of the *Zuytdorp* timbers used in our camp back to the foot of the cliffs, washing some pieces that had been stained. This was observed with some hilarity by the others.

I had been interested in museums all my life, having had my own 'museum' set up in the spare room of our home in South Perth when I was still in primary school. It gave me a great deal of pleasure to learn about the objects in my collection and I proudly showed them to friends and visitors. In addition, the mineral display in the old Woodward Gallery at the WA Museum had played an important role in my childhood wish to become a geologist. Consequently, at the time of this expedition, I already had in mind the need for a display, at the museum, of the material found at the site. This was also to be my motivation, nine years later, in persuading Jim Henderson and John Cowen to pass their claim in the *Vergulde Draeck* wreck to the museum. They followed this advice, and their action was responsible for the WA Museum's first involvement in marine archaeology.

From the distribution of wreckage and coins at the site, we were able to predict confidently where the ship had come to rest, hard up against the edge of the shoreline platform. However, sea conditions were too rough to allow diving at the site during the whole of our stay. Each night, we would go to bed hearing the thump of waves on the shore, and every morning it would be the same when we woke. On one relatively calm day, John Stokes was able to enter the water in an embayment south of the wrecksite for a posed photo session. However, sea conditions were still much too dangerous for him to swim or dive in the area where we believed that the remains of the ship would eventually be found on the sea-floor. It was not until ten years later that the first successful dive was made at the site, by Tom Brady, Max Cramer and Graham Cramer.

On my first visit to the wrecksite in August 1954, while walking beside a creek on my way back to the Land Rover, I noted a number of barrel rungs scattered on the south slope of the creek. At the time, I thought little of this, believing that they must have come from a barrel that had been abandoned by Tom Pepper many years before. However, I remembered this during the expedition, and asked Pepper about it. When he responded that he had never left a barrel in the area, I realized that the rungs must be connected with survivors of the shipwreck. Pepper and I promptly went on horseback to the spot, about 1.2 kilometres north-east of the wrecksite. We found five barrel rungs scattered down the slope, above which was an open, relatively flat area surfaced with thin, sandy soil over limestone (capstone). In this open area stood a low cairn of stones, which had clearly been placed there long ago by human hands. In the surrounding clear area, we picked up a

number of fragments of clay pipes, including one with the name Apffenbergh moulded on the stem.[110] A brass plate from the butt of a musket was found in the bed of the creek, about 100 metres downstream from this site.

It seemed that this was a place where survivors of the shipwreck had obtained water, perhaps in gnamma holes or from the base of a little waterfall in the adjoining creek bed. Some survivors must also have camped there. Perhaps the mound of stones in

The author examining the barrel rungs that lay scattered down the slope below the no. 1 campsite of the Zuytdorp survivors (1954 expedition).

Photograph by John Campbell, courtesy of West Australian Newspapers

the clear area had supported the base of a pole, used to hold up a shelter of sailcloth. The site is marked as no. 1 on Map 5.

A small gnamma hole just south of the clear area contained about 15 litres of water in July 1995, but it was almost dry by mid-October. There are several similar gnamma holes nearby, but these are now largely filled with sand and hold little water. There is also a larger hole, about 2 metres long and 1 metre wide, in the limestone on the north side of the clear area, extending back into a low cave. Some rocks seem to have been excavated from this hole long ago, but it is now largely filled with sand. If this sand were to be excavated, the hole might hold significant amounts of water during winter and spring. Perhaps this hole and the smaller gnamma holes nearby were once used as sources of water by Aborigines, who may have guided the survivors to the spot.

After quickly examining the barrel-rung site, Tom Pepper and I rode back to the others with the exciting news of our discovery. Our arrival was later to be described by Jim Cruthers in the opening paragraph of his series of articles on the expedition:[111]

> We looked at Phil Playford, shocked. Trickles of blood ran down the calves of his legs and into his boots. He wore only a bushman's wide-brimmed hat, a pair of old khaki shorts, and boots. His bare legs were scratched and raw. But Playford was elated. He leant over the pommel of the saddle and shouted excitedly: 'We found where they've been. Over there—over there in that gully.' He stood in the stirrups and pointed to the heavy scrub country to the north-east. 'We found where they'd been looking for water. There are some rusty barrel rungs on the gully slope and nearby we found several pieces of clay pipe.'
>
> Five of us milled about, chattering excitedly, as Playford dismounted. Here was a find. We believed that the casks the iron rungs came from, and the clay pipes, were dropped by shipwrecked Dutch sailors from another age. To find them in such thick, rugged scrub country 242 years later was little short of a miracle.

This conveyed the excitement of the find very well, although the description of my legs was an exaggeration. Certainly, they had been scratched as a result of riding a horse through dense scrub

while wearing shorts (not a recommended practice), but they were scarcely 'raw'. However, more was to come. The following article in the *Daily News* (11 December 1954) showed a photograph of Tom Pepper and me at the place where the barrel rungs and clay pipes had been found. The photo apparently showed dense streaks of blood extending down into my boots, just as described in the previous article. However, most of the 'blood' had been painted onto the print used in the article; little can be seen on untouched prints of the same photo. But a little deception by journalists and photographers is not unknown in the newspaper world—and it added to the colour of an exciting story that attracted a lot of public attention.

The barrel rungs were remarkably well preserved. Although rusted, they were still quite strong, having only a relatively thin coating of rust. Because the rungs had been lying on limestone boulders, they dried out rapidly after rain, thereby minimizing the tendency to rust. Moreover, being situated on the south slope of

The author and Tom Pepper sieving soil while searching for relics at the no. 1 campsite of the Zuytdorp *survivors (1954 expedition).*

Photograph by John Campbell, courtesy of West Australian Newspapers

a gully, they were protected from salt-laden winds blowing from the ocean. The rungs were hand-forged, the individual marks left by hammer blows being clearly visible. One of them was bent, possibly as a result of impact when a water-laden cask was dropped on the rocks.

After finding this site, where survivors had probably camped and obtained water, I endeavoured to trace the route that they would have used in walking to and from the wrecksite. While following a kangaroo pad through the scrub about 150 metres south-west of this site, on a direct line to the wreck, I found two more barrel rungs lying beside the pad, together with several broken clay pipes. It seemed to me that the survivors might also have been following such a kangaroo pad, and it was conceivable that this pad might have remained in almost the same position since 1712. However, the large amount of material that was later recovered at this place, during the 1958 expedition, suggests that it must have been another campsite used by the survivors (site no. 2, Map 5). There is an uninterrupted view of the ocean from here, so the survivors would have been able to see any ships that might sail by, unlike the no. 1 site, 150 metres to the north-east, where the sea is obscured by the topography and dense scrub.

Of course, we do not know how dense the tea-tree thicket was when the ship was wrecked. Aborigines used to burn the bush regularly, and if this area had been burnt a short time before the wreck occurred, the tea-tree scrub may then have been quite low. Photographic comparisons show that tea-trees in the area today are on average about one-third higher than they were in 1954. Burnt stumps of older trees could often be seen in 1954, but they are rarely discernible today. I think it is likely that the last major fire burnt through this belt of tea-tree scrub about 100 years ago.

A third possible survivors' campsite, 850 metres north-east of no. 1, was identified by Robert and Dominic Lamera in 1981 (no. 3, Map 5; see also Chapter 5).

The broken glass that I observed scattered around the cliff top during my first visit in 1954 had been noted by Tom Pepper in 1927. Most of the glass came from square gin bottles, which probably testifies to a drinking spree by the wretched survivors. The path they must have used in ascending the cliff follows a relatively smooth slope that is easy to climb, whereas the cliffs north and south of the wrecksite are precipitous and difficult to climb. The survivors' path up the cliff was no doubt the same as the route taken by Tom Pepper on his first visit to the site in 1927 and by most visitors since then (see Map 7).

On the 1954 expedition, we also found two pairs of brass dividers near the top of the cliff (see Map 7). The brass arms were still well preserved, although the iron points had completely rusted away long ago. These dividers were probably carried ashore by the skipper or a steersman, to use in plotting their position on a map of the South Land. This find suggested that before the wreck broke up completely, it was possible for officers to gain access from the shore to a cabin where maps and navigation instruments were stored.

We also found clear evidence that the castaways lit one or more huge fires on the cliff top immediately above the wrecksite, at a place that is partly sheltered from northerly and north-westerly winds by a low cliff (see Map 7). A few centimetres under the sand, there was a layer of ashes, containing brass parts of chests and completely rusted iron objects. Some pieces of brass had clearly been melted in the intense heat of the blaze. We deduced that this must have been the site of an enormous signal fire, designed to attract the attention of a passing ship.

Tom Pepper showed me where the 'figurehead' (actually a carved woman's figure from the stern of the vessel) had originally been found, wedged under a rock beyond the reach of normal waves (see Map 7). It seemed clear to me that it must have been carried there by a survivor soon after the ship was wrecked, as it was in an excellent state of preservation despite having lain in the open for nearly 230 years. If it had been thrown there by waves, it could not have escaped severe damage.

Close to the place where the figure was found, behind a large boulder, Tom Pepper had also found about eight breech blocks of cannon (see Map 7) and a broken pair of cannonball callipers (having one of the arms missing and part of the graduated scale broken off). He collected the callipers and several of the breech blocks during the period 1927–39. However, like many other relics found by Pepper, the callipers were given away to a person visiting Murchison House Station. Through correspondence, I eventually succeeded in locating them, and they are now held in the WA Maritime Museum.[112] Other breech blocks were removed by Ernest and Ada Drage, whose family referred to them as 'jugs', but these have since been lost.

Jim Cruthers, in his *Daily News* article, said that the breech blocks, when originally found, 'formed a circle about 3 feet [1 metre] in diameter and were placed symmetrically with their tapering ends pointing inwards. In the centre of the circle was what appeared to be a navigation instrument—a sundial or an old type of sextant.' He went on to say, 'surely, we thought, this was a pointer. After all, it was set in the only patch of loose soil at the foot of the cliff. And with such precision.'

However, when I spoke to Tom Pepper about this during the 1958 expedition, he told me that the breech blocks were simply lying together in a group, without any particular orientation, and that the object we now know to have been cannonball callipers lay nearby. This seems a more likely, if less intriguing, description of how they were found. On digging beneath the patch of sand where Pepper's breech blocks had lain, members of the 1954 expedition

Breech block of a swivel cannon found during the 1954 expedition.

Photograph by John Campbell, courtesy of West Australian Newspapers

uncovered another one, completely buried, and better preserved than the others. It was certainly not part of any regular placement of objects. The broken end of the scale from the callipers was also found under the sand there, together with lumps of iron oxide (derived from iron objects), and quite a lot of charcoal, suggesting that another large bonfire had been lit at this locality. The belt buckle I had picked up on my first visit to the wrecksite, in July 1954, also came from this spot.

It is clear that the heavy breech blocks (each weighing about 13 kilograms) could not have been washed ashore. They must have been carried there, thus confirming that the survivors were able to climb on and off the wreck for some time.

Right up to the last days of the 1954 expedition, we held hopes that sea conditions would improve sufficiently for John Stokes to be able to dive at the site. However, this was not to be; the thundering surf continued unabated throughout our visit. Eventually, it was time to leave, much to our regret. Two trips had to be made from our camp to the utility in order to ferry equipment and personnel.

The expedition was voted as having been a great success by all of those involved. We got on well together and had a lot of fun, while making many exciting discoveries. The only major disappointment was that sea conditions had been unsuitable for diving. We all look back on that expedition as being among the most memorable experiences of our lives.

Since then, I have often wondered what a difference it would have made to my life if diving conditions had been favourable at the time of our expedition. Given a couple of days of calm seas, we would no doubt have discovered the *Zuytdorp*'s treasure, lying as a glistening mass of silver on the sea-floor. At that time, there was no legislation in Western Australia to protect historic wrecks, and members of the New Holland Syndicate would have been recognized as the owners of the treasure, unless the Netherlands Government had sought to intervene. However, in my own case, I feel sure that fate was on my side in preventing us from diving. Experience elsewhere shows that treasure commonly brings out the worst in people, leading to endless legal and personal disputation. As it was, we all remained friends after the expedition, and I continued my rewarding career as a geologist without interruption.

The *Daily News* expedition, 1958

I gave a lot of thought to the wreck during the three years after the 1954 expedition, and in 1957 took up the research work that led to positive identification of the wreck. As my research progressed, it became clear that another expedition was warranted. I believed that the remains of the ship would be found on the sea-floor adjoining the edge of the shoreline platform, and that what was needed was another expedition with better facilities, the principal objective being to dive on the wreck. This would be expensive, and so I spoke to Jim Cruthers in early 1958 to see whether West Australian Newspapers would again be interested in participating. At his suggestion, I prepared a detailed proposal, outlining the results of my recent research and what might be accomplished during an expedition, both underwater and on land. Cruthers regretted that he would be unable to participate himself, because of his impending move into Western Australia's pioneer television industry, but he successfully recommended the proposal to the company.

The original plan was that I would be the leader, but when the size, expense and complexity of the expedition increased, the company decided that Doug Burton, the Head Photographer of West Australian Newspapers, should be in charge, although I would be given responsibility for the on-site investigations. However, in practice, I had little or no authority in relation to decisions made during the expedition. The New Holland Syndicate agreement had expired on 31 January 1955, and West Australian Newspapers decided that it would claim ownership of anything found during the 1958 expedition.

Doug Burton had recently led a very successful expedition to photograph the first British atomic-bomb explosion in the Montebello Islands. The other members of the party were Hugh Edwards (journalist and diver), Jack Eaves (newspaper executive), Maurie Hammond (photographer and diver), Len McWhinney (diver), Lloyd Robinson (caving enthusiast), Ted Packer (pilot) and Ron Bywaters (tractor driver). Tom and Lurlie Pepper and their son Arthur joined us at the wrecksite, with Lurlie acting as cook. Hugh Edwards wrote a series of articles on the expedition for the *Daily News*.[113] He later became the author of several excellent books on wrecks, one of which includes an account of the *Zuytdorp* and the 1958 expedition.[114]

The expedition was well equipped, with four Land Rovers, two provided by West Australian Newspapers, one by Lloyd Robinson, and the other by the Peppers; a Chamberlain tractor loaned by Chamberlain Industries; a large ungainly trailer owned by Ted Packer, and dubbed 'the monstrosity'; and an Auster aircraft (a single-engine, high-wing, fabric-covered monoplane) owned by Ted Packer.

Several weeks prior to the expedition, Maurie Hammond and I flew over the wrecksite on a reconnaissance with Ted Packer in his Auster. The purpose was to view the wrecksite from the air and to gauge the prospects of putting in a suitable landing strip for the excursion. We thought that the aircraft would be useful, especially for spotting and general reconnaissance purposes. On the day that we flew over the site, the sea was relatively calm, boosting our hopes for successful diving during the expedition. But regrettably,

Ted Packer's Auster aircraft taking off at the airstrip constructed during the 1958 expedition.

Photograph by Maurie Hammond, courtesy of West Australian Newspapers

we were never to see such calm conditions during our three weeks' stay there. This reconnaissance supported my belief that a suitable airstrip could be prepared near the corner of the old fenceline, 2.5 kilometres east-north-east of the wrecksite (see Map 5).

The tractor was used primarily in preparing this airstrip. Two lengths of iron railway line, chained parallel to one another at right angles to the direction of the strip, were dragged behind the tractor. This simple device scraped off the low scrub, which we burnt, and the result was a rather rough surface, which really didn't look safe enough for a plane to land on. The strip was mainly over sand, but there were also patches of limestone, and these outcrops became more prominent as the surrounding sand was scraped and blown away. Nevertheless, Ted Packer said that it was fine to go ahead and land the Auster; indeed, that the strip was 'good enough for a Liberator'—a type of World War II bomber that he claimed to have flown. By then, all of us were aware of Ted's devil-may-care attitude and his tendency to tell tall stories, so we watched apprehensively as the Auster flew in to land for the first time. The narrow strip was oblique to the wind direction, so Ted had to angle his approach, and on touching down the plane bounded alarmingly over the rough surface. We let out a cheer, very relieved, when it came to a halt, undamaged, at the end of the strip. Most expedition members were not brave (or foolish) enough to fly with Ted Packer, but it didn't worry me, Hugh Edwards and Maurie Hammond. Ted was a highly skilled bush pilot who knew his plane well, and we enjoyed the adventure of going up with him, even if we didn't believe his tall stories!

Fortunately, there were no serious mishaps with the Auster. On the flight up from Perth, the plane was left overnight in a farmer's paddock near Northampton, and we were concerned that goats in the paddock might eat the fabric covering the fuselage. Luckily, they didn't. Another time, a twig tore part of the fabric, but the damage was easily repaired with a piece of sticky-tape.

In 1978, twenty years later, our airstrip would be reactivated for the WA Museum, by the owner of Murchison House Station, Prince Mukarram Jah. He agreed to restore and widen the old strip with a bulldozer. By then, it had almost disappeared through regrowth of the heath vegetation. Prince Jah told me that during this work, he found, and marvelled at, our primitive railway-line clearing device, which had remained there since 1958. The new

strip was somewhat smoother and wider than the original, and it was to be used for two years during the museum's operations at the wrecksite. However, despite the improved landing surface, museum staff tell stories of several hair-raising landings, especially when a cross-wind was blowing. There were no crashes, but several near misses.

The 1958 expedition got under way on 11 April, when one Land Rover, the tractor and the trailer left Perth, followed next day by two other Land Rovers and the plane. From the North West Coastal Highway, we followed the usual route through Eurardy and Bungabandi to Gee Gie, and from there to Billiecutherra Soak, where most of the party spent the night, while I drove on alone to Ramyard Shed in order to meet the Peppers.

Tom Pepper and I set off for the wrecksite early next morning, leaving Lurlie and Arthur at the intersection of the old fenceline, to direct the vehicles that would arrive later from Billiecutherra. I had

Daily News Land Rover driving through the belt of dense tea-tree scrub along the track to the wrecksite (1958 expedition).

Photograph by Maurie Hammond, courtesy of West Australian Newspapers decided that on reaching the end of the old fenceline, we should not follow the route of the previous expedition, which penetrated the tea-tree scrub 2 kilometres to the north, because some of the sandy slopes on that route would be unsuitable for the tractor. Further examination of the aerial photographs suggested that, instead, we should drive to the end of my original track of August 1954, to the spot where I had left the vehicle to walk to the coast, and from there head south across the nearby creek, and follow a spur between two creeks down to the wrecksite (see Map 5).

On Monday 14 April, Tom Pepper and I followed this plan of action, driving to the end of my original track, then heading south through the tea-tree scrub. The Land Rover was equipped with scrub bars based on my original design, and we were able to push over the scrub without any major problems. The creek was no impediment, and about half an hour after leaving my old stopping point, we reached the wrecksite and our 1954 campsite. Several members of the party soon followed us there. They went eagerly with Tom and me to the wrecksite, and Hugh Edwards, in his journal,[115] described their reaction in these terms:

> We were prepared for ruggedness, but this was on an immense scale. We had all seen photographs from the previous expedition, but had not imagined that the cliffs would be so high, the broken boulders and rock-falls so huge, or the surf so fierce. Down below, the white 25-foot section of baltic-pine spar is the only relic we can see from the wreck. It looks like a toothpick. The cliffs—which are rather like the crumbling earthy red walls one sees in some kinds of soil erosion, but on a gigantic scale—dropped straight down to sea level. At the foot were piles of huge red boulders, sometimes a little sand, a rocky step, and then the ocean. Except during a dozen days of the year a huge surf beats in on these rocks. Thirty and forty foot waves are not exceptional, and spray was blown high above the cliff top, wetting our watches like a gentle drizzle.
>
> On that first day at the wrecksite a huge surf was booming in; diving would have been suicidal. Tom Pepper said that it had been calm on Friday, but Shark Bay had had the tail-end of a cyclone on Saturday and that had stirred the sea up. We were very disappointed as we had picked that

time of the year as calmest after considerable research with weather authorities. The divers were rather quiet as we drove back over the hill. It is obviously going to be no picnic in there.

In fact, there was never any possibility of diving during the three weeks that the party spent at the site. Huge swells, generated far out in the Indian Ocean, continued to pound the cliffs on almost every day. On the few occasions when conditions ameliorated to some extent, it was clear that there would still be big risks in entering and emerging from the water, because of the treacherous surge of breaking waves at the edge of the shoreline platform. Five days after we had arrived, conditions were relatively calm, and Edwards and Hammond were willing to enter the water, even though they recognized that getting out would be a problem. However, it was eventually decided that the risks were too great. There was still a real danger of a 'king' wave coming in, which could easily be fatal for a diver swimming in the turbulent area where we knew that the wreck must lie.

Some thirty-four years later, in 1992, when I was at the wrecksite with my wife, Cynthia, and daughter Katherine ('Taffy'), I was to recall the king waves of those early expeditions. Katherine and I were skirting around the headland 100 metres south of the wrecksite when I heard the roar that heralded the arrival of a big wave. I shouted to her to hold on tightly to the rocks at the foot of the cliff, shortly before being hit by a wall of water. Both of us managed to avoid being swept away, but it was a hazardous situation. Indeed, it is amazing that no one has been killed during expeditions and casual visits to this extremely dangerous place.

During the 1958 expedition, we felt very frustrated at being unable to dive on the wreck, as this had been the main objective of our trip. However, our days were fully occupied in searching for relics at various sites identified during the 1954 expedition, and in scouring the surrounding gullies and scrub for additional sites. We collected quite a lot of interesting material at the old localities, but no new sites were found, despite systematic searching. We also used the tractor to plough the sand at several localities immediately behind the cliff top, where the survivors might have camped, and the same localities were traversed with a metal-detector, but nothing was found. Of course, present-day standards would

Lloyd Robinson and Hugh Edwards with keys found at the no. 2 campsite of the Zuytdorp survivors (1958 expedition).

Photograph by Maurie Hammond, courtesy of West Australian Newspapers

never permit ploughing to be undertaken in such an important and environmentally sensitive area. Fortunately, the area has now recovered fully, and nothing can be seen of the ground and vegetation disturbance caused by these activities.

The worst environmental damage in the vicinity of the wrecksite resulted from bulldozing in 1978 that was designed to improve access to the site for the WA Museum. It eventually resulted in a deep trench blowing out along the straight bulldozed line. This line has recently (1993, 1995) been rehabilitated by Mike McCarthy and his team.

The most interesting discoveries on the 1958 expedition were made at the second of the two localities where barrel rungs and clay pipes had been found during the 1954 expedition (site no. 2, Map 5), at a place where some survivors probably camped while maintaining a lookout for passing vessels. Soil at this site was sieved, and many fragments of clay pipes were found. Some pieces of slate, probably writing slate, were also picked up nearby. However, the most exciting discovery was that of two large iron keys, each about 15 centimetres long. They were heavily rusted, but one was quite well preserved. A similar key was later uncovered on the cliff top, although that one was in poor condition. When he picked up the first key, Lloyd Robinson sounded his 'moose-call' whoop, by then well known to us all, followed by the shout 'I've got the key to the treasure chest.'

These keys may have come from doors to the officers' cabins or other compartments that had been left locked to prevent looting while the wreck was still accessible from the shore. The keys were probably taken ashore by the skipper or an officer, but were discarded when the wreck disintegrated. Other keys were found at the site of the signal fire, and Dominic and Robert Lamera claim to have found two more at campsite no. 3.

After having been at the site for about ten days, without any prospect of entering the water, we concluded that it might have been possible to dive during the calmer days if we had had a boat anchored about 100 metres offshore, outside the belt of breaking waves. It was decided that Ted Packer and I should fly up to Shark Bay (Denham) to see whether the Fisheries Department's boat, the *Garbo*, might be made available for us to use in diving. Alternatively, we could seek to persuade a private fishing boat to assist us. We flew first to Shark Bay, where the Fisheries Department's officer-in-charge, Neil McLaughlan, advised that the *Garbo* was not available. From there, we flew on to South Passage, between Dirk Hartog Island and Steep Point, hoping to contact one of the large fishing boats operating there and arrange for the fishermen to meet us on the island for a discussion.

No one had previously landed an aircraft on Dirk Hartog Island, but I had carried out geological work there in 1955, and knew of a claypan, known locally as a 'birrida', that might serve as a suitable landing place, at the south end of the island. Ted Packer took my word for this, so we flew low over one of the boats and threw out a sealed bottle containing a note, inviting some of those on board to go over to the beach on the island after we had landed nearby. The note said that they should wave to us if this was OK. After seeing that they had collected the bottle and waved their agreement, we flew off to the birrida. Ted Packer was uncharacter-istically cautious about landing, suspecting that the clay surface might be too soft. He decided to test it by briefly touching the wheels on the surface, while maintaining sufficient air speed to keep the plane airborne. It bounced, so he agreed that the surface was hard enough to land on, and after again circling the birrida the plane touched down for an easy landing. We walked over to the beach to meet the fishermen. Although they were sympathetic to our proposal, they would lose valuable fishing time by helping us, and we could not offer financial compensation. So the proposal fell through, and we flew back to the wrecksite without having achieved any positive results.

On landing at our airstrip, we found that two visitors had arrived: the manager of Murchison House Station, Fred Blood, and another man, who had driven there in a Land Rover. Blood said that they had noticed a pall of smoke from a fire we had lit, and had come up to see what was going on. The fire was originally started to assist in clearing the airstrip, and it had been extended by Tom Pepper as a means of generating green feed for the sheep that he would be droving from Tamala to Murchison House later that year. Blood took me aside, complaining that he had not been advised about our expedition, and asserting that we had no right to use water from Ramyard Shed. I responded that the wrecksite was situated on the Tamala pastoral lease, and that his brother Cecil Blood, as manager of Tamala, had raised no objections to our plans and was happy with our use of water from Ramyard. Moreover, Cecil had given two of his employees, Tom and Arthur Pepper, time off to participate in the expedition. Fred Blood departed after telling me darkly that his brother was 'risking his job' by his actions. Tom Pepper later dismissed this threat and the other complaints as 'a lot of rot'.

We all became rather despondent about the sea conditions. It was especially frustrating for the divers to stand at the cliff top, watching and listening to the breakers crashing in, while believing that the wreck lay close at hand beneath the belt of foaming water. Hugh Edwards and I, who shared a tent, would often be wakened at night by the boom of the surf. Lurlie Pepper was rather superstitious, and maintained that we must be lying over a couple of dead Dutchmen who were disturbing our sleep. Maybe she was right!

Explosives had been brought along on the expedition, as it was felt that they might be useful in uncovering relics underwater or below boulders. The small amount of blasting done on the

Lurlie Pepper with her famed camp-oven bread (1958 expedition).

Photograph by the author

1954 expedition had yielded some significant coins at one locality. However, nothing that was seen during the 1958 expedition seemed to warrant excavation through explosives. Nevertheless, towards the end of the visit a decision was made, against my protests, to do some blasting 'for the hell of it'. As a result, several boulders were split open, and one very large boulder was rolled down-slope for several metres, and is now lying on the shoreline platform. However, a person visiting the site today would see little or no evidence of this blasting or that of other people who subsequently used explosives there. The WA Museum team, under Mike McCarthy, has done an excellent job in healing the scars left by a variety of activities at the site, as well as restoring vegetation behind the cliff top.

When the time came for the expedition to depart, it was decided, again contrary to my wishes, that the remaining wood from the ship, including the yardarm and pieces of mast, should be taken back to Perth. Doug Burton afterwards provided the Commonwealth Receiver of Wreck with a list of the relics that had been found, and advised that a museum would be set up at the offices of West Australian Newspapers Ltd, to house the material.[116]

Ted Packer (left) and Hugh Edwards with wooden wreckage of the Zuytdorp *(1958 expedition).*

Photograph by Maurie Hammond, courtesy of West Australian Newspapers

This museum never materialized, and the relics were not donated to any other museum. None of the people involved seems to know what happened to them. Even the very large items, such as the yardarm and pieces of mast, have apparently disappeared.

On several occasions during the 1960s, I urged staff of the WA Museum to seek this material from West Australian Newspapers, as I had no doubt that the company would have been quite willing to relinquish the relics at that time. However, nothing was done. A museum file records that the Director wrote a memo to Colin Jack-Hinton, Senior Curator in charge of maritime archaeology, on 1 October 1968, saying that I had informed him that 'Doug Burton, head of the photographic department of West Australian Newspapers, has a yardarm from the *Zuytdorp*.' The memo continued: 'Do we know anything about this? Should we make arrangements to collect it for display at Fremantle?' No response was recorded on the file, and Doug Burton informs me that he was never contacted on the matter. He left the yardarm lying beside the back fence of his home when he sold it more than twenty years ago, but it is no longer there and the present occupants know nothing about it. This lack of action by the museum in acquiring such important relics is surprising, especially when its outspoken public position, which I shared, was that all historic wrecks should be the property of the State.

The 1958 expedition did not yield a great deal of new information about the wreck and its survivors. It was unfortunate that the main objective of the trip, to dive at the site, was not accomplished because of continually rough sea conditions. This was simply bad luck, as at least one day might have been expected to provide suitable diving conditions at that time of the year.

Immediately after the 1958 expedition returned, I compiled the results of my historical research as a paper entitled 'The wreck of the *Zuytdorp*', which was published by the Historical Society in 1959. Since then, the society has reprinted the paper, in booklet form, many times, most recently in 1995.[117] The *Zuytdorp* was the first early Dutch shipwreck to be found and positively identified in Western Australia, and my research was the first to be published on any historic wreck in this state. The publicity associated with the *Zuytdorp* stimulated a great deal of interest in other Dutch wrecks, leading before long to the discovery of three more—the *Vergulde Draeck* and *Batavia* in 1963 and the *Zeewyk* in 1968.

Tom Brady, Max Cramer and others

Early in 1964, a keen skindiver from Geraldton, Tom Brady, visited me at my office at the Geological Survey. He told me in confidence that he was hoping to dive on the *Zuytdorp* in May of that year, with Max and Graham Cramer. They had already made a reconnaissance visit to the site, and had surmised that conditions suitable for diving were most likely to occur in mid- to late May. Brady said that they would keep me fully informed about their activities. In discussing what might be found, I said that the remains of the ship should lie in shallow water immediately in front of the shoreline platform, and that several anchors and cannon would almost certainly be preserved there. I expressed doubt that much of the ship's treasure of silver coins could have survived 250 years of pounding by waves in such shallow water, although it seemed possible that some coins might have been trapped, with other relics, in crevices and potholes on the sea-floor.

On 16 May 1964, Tom Brady and the Cramer brothers noted that the sea had become very calm at Geraldton, and they hoped that favourable conditions for diving might persist on the following day. After hurriedly packing their gear, they left Geraldton in the evening with two other local men, Tom Muir and Alf Morgan. Muir provided a four-wheel-drive vehicle, while Morgan, a bushman familiar with the area, acted as guide. Taking the track through Eurardy, they reached Gee Gie after midnight, managing to snatch a couple of hours of sleep there. They left before dawn, reaching the wrecksite in the early morning.

Conditions on that day were ideal, with virtually no swell running. Max Cramer described it as a 'freak day, the best in three years'.[118] The divers donned wetsuits and entered the water with snorkels, via the 'sloping rock' (see Map 7). Even though conditions were good, it required a great deal of courage for them to make this dive, knowing that their families were very apprehensive about the venture. Cramer later recorded the event in these terms:

> It is impossible to describe the excitement of that moment. We had already experienced something of it with the *Batavia* off the Abrolhos in 1963. But there was more build up to this dive—more worry, anticipation, and apprehension, because of the fearsome reputation of the place and because of persistent rumours that other divers planned a similar expedition. We badly wanted to be first, and now it was within our reach...
>
> I started to see the familiar signs of shipwreck. Straight lines and regular forms showed on the bottom, and my heart beat faster as I sighted one cannon then another. Then there was a bronze cannon worn away by sand so that it looked as though half the barrel had been cut away lengthways...
>
> We...were beginning to get pretty tired when I spotted some green shapes in a pothole...Down I went and found what at first looked for all the world like modern navy four-inch shell cases...I grabbed one [and found it was] a small bronze cannon a little over half a metre long, worn by sea and sand.

They also saw a number of anchors and many lead ingots, and managed to bring ashore three small eroded cannon before conditions deteriorated. 'The sea, which had been still and calm, broke into a short chop with long swell and the wind began to blow out of the north. The calm was over.' Tired, but elated, they drove back to Geraldton to break the news.

The success of these three men in completing the first dive on the *Zuytdorp* wreck was announced in the *Daily News* next day (18 May), in an article by Hugh Edwards, under the headline 'Divers see famous wreck'.[119] I was reported as saying that their feat was 'wonderful news', as indeed it was. Tom Brady, Max Cramer and Graham Cramer deserve much credit for their courage and skill in diving for the first time in these dangerous waters.

A short time later, one of the three small guns was brought to Perth, and I examined it with interest before it was taken back to Geraldton. The gun was not a breech loader, as I had expected, but a small muzzle-loading swivel cannon that had been strongly eroded after having rolled around on the sea-floor during the past 250 years.

In 1994, Tom Brady told me that he had not been particularly enthusiastic about diving again on the *Zuytdorp* wreck after that first dive, as he did not regard it as an especially interesting wreck, and diving there was dangerous in the extreme. Nonetheless, he continued to visit the wrecksite each May, and completed four further dives during the next four years, one of them with Max Cramer.

Brady had promised one of his friends, Eric Barker, a Fisheries Department employee, that he would take him to the site for a dive. An opportunity arose when Barker rang one day in February 1967 to say that north-easterly winds had blown continuously for twelve or thirteen days, and consequently conditions for diving on 'the Z wreck' should now be ideal. A team consisting of Tom Brady, Neil McLaughlan, Eric Barker and Gordon Hancock set out on the evening of 17 February, driving through the night to the site, which they reached at about 6 o'clock next morning. They entered the water straight away, spending about five hours exploring the wreck before conditions deteriorated.

Many of the cannon and lead ingots that had been visible in May 1964 were now covered by thick sand. However, it was during this dive that Neil McLaughlan claims to have first seen

masses of silver coins, lying stacked together on their sides, in the vicinity of what is now known as 'coin rock' (see Map 7). He told me that his attention was drawn to the site by a polished and eroded bronze cannon projecting from the side of a mound on the bottom. He found that the sea-floor at this locality was covered with masses of coins, closely packed and cemented together, forming what became known to WA Museum personnel as the 'carpet of silver'. The divers managed to recover some of the coins to prove their discovery, before conditions forced them to leave the water.

Tom Brady and Max Cramer later reported that they had seen no sign of the glistening carpet of silver on their 1964 dive. This is surprising, as diving conditions on that occasion were ideal, allowing them to examine much of the wreck. Moreover, the eroded bronze cannon, described by Cramer as looking as though it had been cut lengthways, was situated immediately beside the carpet of silver—it was this cannon that first attracted McLaughlan's attention to the coin deposit in 1967. When it was recovered later by museum divers and Kalbarri fisherman

John Allchin, it was found to contain masses of coins cemented inside the barrel. This bronze cannon is now on display at the Geraldton Museum.

Members of the Brady group were sworn to secrecy, and it seems that no information about the treasure discovery leaked out before Brady and others returned to the site three months later, in May 1967. Again, they were able to dive and to confirm the presence of a strongly cemented conglomerate of many thousands of silver coins. It must have been a fantastic sight. The sea-floor was mantled by a broad, glistening carpet of closely packed coins, polished brightly by drifting sand, beside a small cave lined with layers of coins. Brady described the deposit as having been rather like a pour of coin-filled concrete. He concluded that it represented the contents of about four or five chests. However, the *Zuytdorp*'s treasure would have occupied many more chests—probably at least ten—carried in the captain's cabin at the stern of the ship. These chests were very strongly constructed, and some must have held together for several decades after the superstructure of the wreck collapsed around them. Lime, derived from seawater, precipitated between stacks of coins in the chests, cementing them together to survive more than 250 years in this extremely turbulent environment.

Brady's group continued to maintain close secrecy, with the intention of returning to investigate the coin deposit more thoroughly a year later. Brady and Max Cramer did indeed dive again on the wreck, on 8 May 1968, as reported on the following day in the *Geraldton Guardian*. Once more, no mention was made of the silver coinage, although Brady afterwards stated that they were planning to submit a full report and map to the WA Museum.

When I discussed this with him in 1994, Brady said that he felt badly about not telling either me or Hugh Edwards of the discovery, as he had previously undertaken to keep us both informed. He said that they had been anxious to prevent any information on the matter being conveyed to Alan Robinson, and felt that the more people who knew about their find, the greater was the chance that word would leak out.

But the group's secrecy proved to be of no avail. On 9 May 1968, Alan Robinson announced that a party of divers, under his leadership, would undertake an ambitious program of work on the *Zuytdorp*, to begin later that month.[120] Brady responded through statements to the *Geraldton Guardian* (9 May) and *West Australian* (10 May).[121] He said that a claim for ownership of the *Zuytdorp* wreck had been lodged with the Commonwealth Receiver of Wreck in 1964, advising him of the first dive and the recovery of three cannon. Brady stated that this claim for wreck ownership had been made on behalf of Max Cramer, Graham Cramer and Tom Brady, naming Tom Pepper as a joint discoverer.

However, this statement was not accurate: the claim for ownership had been submitted by Max Cramer in the names of Max Cramer and Phil Playford. I knew nothing of this until 1994, when the Commonwealth Archives sent me a copy of Cramer's handwritten submission, dated 30 May 1964, which reads as follows:

> Dear Sir,
>
> Since declaring the brass cannon at your office I have made contact with Phil Playford of Perth and have learned that till now [neither] he nor his party have laid any claim to the wreck of the *Zuytdorp*, mainly because until our dive no one was certain that a wreck existed. As both him and I are interested in its historical background and we are hoping one day that action will be taken to keep looters away from such I hereby make claim to all rights that may exist or be brought into claim, legal ownership of all relics, for the historical benefit in the name of myself and Phil Playford of Perth.
>
> Hoping that this will at least be kept as a record of the first dive on what has been established as the wreck of the *Zuytdorp*.
>
> Yours faithfully
> [signed] Max Cramer

I had indeed discussed the need to protect the *Zuytdorp* wreck with Cramer in 1964, but had stated my view that this wreck, like that of the *Vergulde Draeck*, should be vested in the WA Museum on behalf of the people of Western Australia. I had no idea that as a result of this conversation, a claim would be lodged using my name.

On 13 May 1968, four days after Brady's report appeared in the *Geraldton Guardian*, Cramer wrote again to the Receiver of Wreck, asking whether his earlier claim had been received, and if not whether a new one could now be registered in the names of himself, Tom Brady, Graham Cramer and Tom Pepper. The Commonwealth Department of Shipping and Transport responded that the earlier submission was on file and a copy could be made available if requested.[122]

In the *Geraldton Guardian* report on 9 May, Brady said that his group had conducted four successful dives on the wreck in the past four years, and that it was their practice to visit the site every May. He added, 'as a matter of fact, Max Cramer and I were diving on the wreck yesterday.' The article stated that members of the Brady group 'believe they know the location of the most probable area in which the treasure could be located', and that 'over the years they have sent all information and location charts of their work to the W.A. Museum.' However, Brady's group at that time knew precisely where the treasure was located, had recovered coinage, and had not advised the museum of their activities.

When Robinson did succeed in diving, he immediately announced to the press that he had found several tonnes of silver coins on the sea-floor, worth millions of dollars.[123] Nine days later, Brady wrote to the Director of the WA Museum, disclosing that his party had first located the silver deposit in February 1967, and had dived there again twice, in May 1967 and May 1968. He also furnished the museum with an accurate map showing the location of the coinage on the sea-floor.[124]

The museum authorities were not favourably impressed by this admission, as Brady and his colleagues had contravened provisions of the *Museum Act* in removing material from the wreck without permission. However, he and Cramer were granted a meeting with the WA Museum Board on 3 July 1968, at which Brady justified what had happened by saying that 'the discovery was so small and uninteresting that we did not make any panic…it is such a small deposit…and the sale of it would be of no real gain.'[125] This statement contrasted with that of Robinson, who had claimed that tonnes of silver, worth millions of dollars, was preserved on the sea-floor.

At that time, the museum authorities had no way of assessing whether either of these conflicting accounts could be accepted, and it would later be shown that neither was valid. The deposit was much larger than Brady had reported, while Robinson's estimate was grossly exaggerated.

Alan Robinson

Ellis Alfred Robinson, generally known as Alan Robinson, features prominently in the story of the *Zuytdorp* wreck, just as he does in accounts of the *Vergulde Draeck* and *Tryall*. Robinson was a controversial figure, who was condemned by many for his violence and irresponsible behaviour, but supported by others as an adventurer who was a victim of the bureaucracy. Before discussing Robinson's role in relation to the *Zuytdorp*, it is appropriate to review his involvement in the *Vergulde Draeck* discovery and his consequent relationships with the WA Museum.

I first met Alan Robinson in April 1963, when he and Jim Henderson came into my office at the Geological Survey to discuss their discovery of a wreck that might be that of the *Vergulde Draeck*. Robinson was then thirty-five years old—a strong, stocky man with a disarmingly direct manner. He spoke well, and overall I was quite favourably impressed, although I do remember thinking that he had a rather pugnacious expression.

During the few weeks after their discovery, the group led by Jim Henderson managed to salvage a good deal of material from the wreck, including coins and a cannon, all of which was consistent with the hypothesis that this was the wreck of the *Vergulde Draeck*. I accompanied them to the site on several diving expeditions, although I could only snorkel over the wreck, as an ear problem prevented me from scuba diving.

I was not initially aware that during this period Alan Robinson was becoming more and more resentful about the way things had turned out. His resentment stemmed from the fact that some six years previously, he had claimed to have found the *Vergulde Draeck* wreck near Ledge Point,[126] but, as he had afterwards been unable to relocate it, many people believed that his claimed 'discovery' was either a hoax or the misidentification of a natural feature in the reef. Now that a wreck had definitely been found and identified, Robinson maintained that it was his wreck that had been rediscovered. He became dangerously obsessed with the issue, believing that Jim Henderson was attempting to 'steal' the wreck and gain all the credit. However, from the published description of his earlier 'discovery', said to show a row of cannon still in position and pointing skyward, it seemed clear to me and others who were involved that it could not be the same as the newly discovered wreck. Indeed, we were highly sceptical about his claim to have found any such wreck.

Prior to this, Alan Robinson, Jim Henderson, John Cowen and their families had been close friends, but that friendship ceased not long after the wreck was discovered. All of them would suffer, in one way or another, from 'the curse of the Gilt Dragon'. I had been unaware of any trouble brewing within this group until one day, when I was at the wrecksite with Henderson, Cowen and others, Robinson suddenly arrived on the scene in another boat, dived into the water, and launched a frenzied physical assault on Henderson. Robinson shouted that Henderson had stolen his wreck and was interfering with other men's wives. I was shocked by this violent incident, as Robinson had apparently run amuck without any valid reason. It seemed clear to me that the 'theft' accusation was nonsense, and Henderson denied the other claim.

Some six years later, Henderson reported the assault in the *Sunday Independent*,[127] which led Robinson to mount a libel action against him and the owners, editor and printer of the paper. I was called as a witness for the defence in the case. Mr Justice Virtue ruled in Robinson's favour, stating that the article was not a truthful statement of the matters that it purported to report. He condemned it as a slanted and distorted account by an interested party, admittedly designed to discredit Robinson. The judge said that it portrayed Robinson quite unfairly as a person without any claim to have either found the wreck himself or shared in its discovery with Graeme Henderson and others. It seemed to the judge that the assault had been prompted by a personal dispute between Robinson and Henderson. However, he said that Robinson's deliberate and dangerous action could not be justified, and that this would be taken into account in assessing damages. Accordingly, the damages awarded to Robinson amounted to the relatively small sum of $2,000.[128]

I felt at the time that this was not a fair verdict, as it amounted to a reward for Robinson's vicious assault on Henderson, and the judge's statement gave undue credence to Robinson's claim to have discovered the wreck long before it was found by Graeme Henderson and his party. It is ironic to note that the $2,000 damages awarded to Robinson in this case were greater than the fine of $400 that he had to pay later on being convicted of fabricating coins from the *Vergulde Draeck* and selling them as genuine articles.

Not long afterwards, Robinson was reported to be blasting at the wrecksite in order to recover coinage. I was present at an incident when a Fisheries Department patrol boat investigating the illegal use of explosives chased Robinson in his small boat from the wrecksite to the beach. The Fisheries Inspector fired a .303 rifle across the bows of Robinson's boat, but to no avail. Robinson landed and ran over the sandhills, apparently carrying explosives and no doubt intent on hiding the evidence, but we were not game enough to pursue him!

During this period, I became increasingly concerned that the wreck was being plundered by Robinson, and perhaps others, for its silver and artefacts, without regard to its historical and archaeological importance. I felt that the best way of preventing this would be for the WA Museum to accept responsibility for work on the wreck, and that legislation should be introduced to bring this about. As a newly appointed Honorary Research Associate of the WA Museum (a position that I have since held for more than thirty years), I urged the Director, David Ride, to take action on this. As a first step, I suggested to the Hendersons and John Cowen that they formally pass over their rights, as discoverers of the wreck, to the museum. This they did through a legal assignment, on 24 December 1963. That assignment marked the beginning of the museum's involvement in wreck investigations, which led eventually to establishment of the WA Maritime Museum, with Graeme Henderson as its Director.[129]

When Henderson and Cowen made their assignment, I suggested to Ride that they be invited to survey the wreck and recover material on behalf of the museum, pointing out that this was urgently required, as the wreck was in serious jeopardy through Robinson's activities.

Soon afterwards, I was surprised to learn that the museum authorities were negotiating with Robinson on a proposal for him to work the *Vergulde Draeck* wreck as the museum's sole salvage agent. I also learned that during those negotiations, staff of the museum had accompanied Robinson on a visit to the wreck, in Robinson's boat, and that Henderson and Cowen were told nothing about it. On learning of this, I expressed my strong concern to both the Director and the Chairman of Trustees, maintaining that such actions were not in the museum's best interests, and that they would be ill advised to enter into any arrangement with Robinson.

Moreover, as Henderson and Cowen had just granted the museum their rights to the wreck and donated the relics they had recovered, it would be unfair to them if the museum granted salvage rights to Robinson. Exactly what transpired as a result of this advice is not recorded in any documents that I have seen. The key museum file on the discovery of the *Vergulde Draeck*, arguably the most important file relating to the history of marine archaeology in Western Australia, cannot be found.

In December 1964, the WA Museum assumed ownership and control of the *Vergulde Draeck* wreck, and other historic wrecks (pre-1900) on the Western Australian coast, through the *Museum Amendment Act* of 1964. This legislation was revised in 1969, and it was finally consolidated as a separate Act, the *Maritime Archaeology Act*, in 1973. Under this legislation, the control of all historic wrecks on the coast of Western Australia was vested in the WA Museum.[130]

In July 1979, in response to an action brought by Alan Robinson, the High Court of Australia ruled that the Western Australian *Maritime Archaeology Act* was invalid, because the State did not hold jurisdiction over offshore areas. However, this outcome had been foreseen by the Commonwealth Government when Robinson first initiated his action, and consequently the Federal Parliament had passed the *Historic Shipwrecks Act* of 1976, which allowed for Commonwealth possession and control of historic shipwrecks around the Australian coast. Agreement had also been reached with the government of the Netherlands for ownership of VOC wrecks in Australian waters to be transferred to the Commonwealth. The Commonwealth had in turn agreed to pass control of historic shipwrecks along the Western Australian coast to the WA Museum. As soon as the High Court gave its ruling on the State Act, the Commonwealth *Historic Shipwrecks Act* was proclaimed, and administrative arrangements were put in place to allow control of Western Australian wrecks to remain with the WA Museum.[131]

When the Commonwealth wreck legislation was introduced into the House of Representatives, it received strong support from both the government and opposition parties.[132] The Attorney General, Mr Ellicott, stated that 'everybody will agree that it has been a most constructive debate' and that 'a great deal of credit must go to Western Australia for having the foresight to preserve these historic relics.' Kim Beazley, Member for Fremantle, stated that there was

> no doubt about who is the plunderer whose activities have made the Western Australian and Commonwealth laws to protect the historic shipwrecks necessary. The legislation currently before the National Parliament is the culmination of many years of advocacy by Dr Phillip Playford and James Henderson [and] his son Graeme, who is now the Assistant Curator of Maritime Archaeology at the Western Australian Museum, and the dedicated work of the Maritime Archaeology Department at the Western Australian Museum.

It is important to note that Robinson's actions had been the driving force for change in successive pieces of legislation, even though it had never been his intention to initiate or improve the legislation; quite the contrary.

When the State's 1964 legislation was about to be proclaimed, the Museum Director, Dr David Ride, set up a Historical Materials Advisory Committee to advise on the WA Museum's role and functions in wreck research. I was invited to become one of its members, and the first meeting was held in December 1964.

In August 1965, Robinson put a proposal to the museum that he prepare a site plan of the *Vergulde Draeck* wreck, and a parallel proposal by John Cowen and George Brenzi was submitted at the same time. Both submissions were considered at a meeting of the Historical Materials Advisory Committee on 4 October 1965, which was attended by ten persons. The first motion, for Robinson to be appointed, was moved and seconded by H.G. Roberts and G.W. Robinson (no relation to Alan). Two or three other people supported the motion, while I spoke against it, and most of the others were moderately opposed or neutral. On being put to the vote, the motion was lost by a narrow margin. Jack Sue and I then moved that John Cowen and George Brenzi be appointed, and this motion was carried.

A contract was finalized in December 1965 for Cowen to be responsible for the preparation of a plan and model of the wrecksite. The contract, signed for the WA Museum Board by its Chairman, Sir Thomas Meagher, provided that Cowen would receive payment of £400 ($800) for carrying out this task, and went on to state:

> In the event of the Board deciding to recover relics from the
> site the contractors shall be given a first option to enter into
> a contract with the Board upon and subject to the terms and
> conditions as may then be agreed between the parties.

Cowen and Brenzi fulfilled their side of the contract, producing an
excellent plan and model of the site, for which they were paid the
designated amount—but this, Cowen informs me, was less than
the costs that they had incurred. He said that they were expecting
their reward to come through the forthcoming contract to recover
relics. However, the museum did not complete its side of the
agreement; it never offered them the option of entering into such
a contract.

In 1972, Cowen wrote to the WA Museum Director, pointing
this out, and received the response that an officer of the Crown
Law Department had advised: 'I do not believe there is liability
in the Museum arising out of the survey agreement of November/
December 1965.' No explanation was given for this opinion.
Cowen did not immediately seek his own legal advice on the
matter, and by the time he did so, in September 1981, the statute
of limitations had come into play. Cowen received legal advice
that 'There is no doubt that after 1968 up until 1974 you did
have a cause of action and that the Board breached the contract
with you in respect of your right of action'—but it was now too
late to do anything about it.[133] This has been a continuing source
of discontent to Cowen, recently exacerbated by the fact that he
was not recognized by the 1994 Select Committee on Ancient
Shipwrecks as having been a primary discoverer of the *Vergulde
Draeck* wreck (see Chapter 1).

The decision by the Historical Materials Advisory Committee
in favour of Cowen and Brenzi had been regarded as controversial
by some museum staff, and no further meetings of the committee
were called for twelve months. When it next met, on 20 October
1966, David Ride informed members that Colin Jack-Hinton had
been appointed to lead the Division of Human Studies and that his
responsibilities would extend to the investigation of Dutch wrecks
on the Western Australian coast. Ride said that the committee
would now 'be in abeyance pending Dr Jack-Hinton's decision
regarding advice and assistance from outside sources'. In practice,
the committee had been abolished. This meant that for the next

three years, the activities of the WA Museum in relation to Dutch wrecks were no longer subject to independent scrutiny. It was not until 1969, when Jack-Hinton resigned, that a meeting was called of a reconstituted committee.

Robinson did not take kindly to the decision of the Historical Materials Advisory Committee in favour of Cowen and Brenzi. On 6 December 1965, he advised the Acting Director of the WA Museum, Ray George, that he had been 'forced to take action', by planting sixty explosive units under rocks at the wrecksite. George recorded:[134]

> He then drew a diagram showing gelignite, detonators, battery, and wires leading out of a container. The wires were attached to a balloon. He said that anybody removing the rock that holds down any of these units would release the balloon, thus pulling the wires and thereby setting off the charges. He would go back to the area today and prevent anybody from going into the area and we could look forward to damage to boats or gear associated with anybody trying to work on the wreck site…[and] that this wasn't the end, it was only the beginning…I made no comment. He said that I would be responsible for any accident that occurred in the future. He shook hands and left.

In fact, it seems clear that the booby trap described by Robinson did not exist; it was a typical example of the tactics that he used to intimidate people. However, in spite of this and other evidence of Robinson's dangerous instability, he was employed on a part-time basis by the WA Museum on several occasions during 1967.

Robinson first signalled his interest in the *Zuytdorp* wreck when he wrote a letter to the Director of the WA Museum, dated 30 April 1968, advising that he wished to take a group of divers and support personnel to the wrecksite, to determine if the wreck could be worked using moorings, a flying fox, and derricks mounted on the shore. Colin Jack-Hinton, who was in charge of the museum's wreck program, assessed the proposal, and was unconvinced that it would succeed. However, he saw no harm in recommending that the museum authorize the project as a feasibility survey. Robinson was advised accordingly, and was asked to prepare a sketch map of the site and to collect, on behalf of the museum, any loose material that might be of interest.

Robinson's announcement of the project received extensive coverage in the *West Australian* of 9 May 1968, complete with a diagram showing the planned derricks, flying fox and mooring. Robinson said that his group was hoping later to secure a contract from the museum to work the wreck.

The other members of Robinson's party were Dr Naoom Haimson (diver and medical officer), Clive Daw, Bill Noonan, Terry Palmer, Joe Varris, Bob Johnson, Leith Goodall, Ned Harrold and Fred Hunton. The party left Perth on 11 May and travelled via Murchison House to the wrecksite, arriving there after dark on 12 May. I am indebted to Naoom Haimson, who kept a daily diary during the expedition, for providing information used in the following account.[135]

Expedition members were pleased to note that strong easterlies were blowing during the first night, which suggested that the sea could be calm next day. In the morning, there was still a moderate surf running, but they decided to go in anyway. Haimson was the first to enter the water, by way of the sloping rock. The method that he and the others adopted was to wait until a breaker rushed up the slope, then use the backwash to carry them out as far as possible, before diving to the bottom to hang on to a rock while the next breaker swept overhead. The ensuing backwash was then used to carry them out beyond the breaker line. I have seen a film taken on this expedition, and it is astounding to see how these divers were able to enter the water under such rough conditions.

The divers had intended using a rope between a buoy and the shore as a safety line, the buoy having been put in place from a crayfish boat on the previous day. However, it was swept in towards the shore during the night, so this part of their plan did not succeed. After getting out beyond the breakers, they swam north and approached the wreck from the ocean side, managing to observe some anchors and several cannon when the waves were not too high. Haimson became nearly exhausted, but he succeeded in getting ashore by surfing up the sloping rock. Robinson, Daw and Varris continued searching until midday, when the wind turned around to the south-west and the seas rose, forcing them to leave the water. Robinson and Daw emerged without difficulty, but

Varris was caught in a cross-current when half-way up the sloping rock. He was washed north, off the rock, losing his flippers. It was a perilous situation, but fortunately the next wave threw him into a position where he could be grabbed by the others and pulled to safety. Varris sustained only cuts and bruises, but it was a salutary lesson of what could happen at this treacherous place.

For the next four days, south-westerly winds blew strongly, and the associated rough sea conditions made it impossible to dive. The group spent the time combing the base of the cliffs and other land sites, finding a few fragments of coins and other bits and pieces. On 18 May, the wind turned around to the east again, and it seemed likely that conditions would become suitable for diving. However, after watching the sea for some time, it was decided that the swell was still too high. They spent a couple of hours searching for relics on the platform, before all but Naoom Haimson and Bob Johnson climbed back up the cliff.

As Haimson and Johnson sat at the foot of the cliff, knowing that the party was due to depart next day, and becoming more and more frustrated, they managed to convince themselves that the waves were abating. Haimson entered the water in the usual way, down the sloping rock, but soon realized that conditions were far too rough and that he had made a dangerous mistake. After signalling Johnson to stay on land, Haimson attempted to surf up the slope, but before he could get out of the water he was caught by a cross-wave, just as Varris had been. He was swept north, thrown against the platform, and carried into the undercut below. His mask and flippers were torn off and carried out to sea, and Johnson thought that Haimson had gone with them. However, as a wave receded, he was relieved to see Haimson emerge from the undercut and crawl up over the lip of the platform, before passing out. By the time that Haimson regained consciousness, the others had brought down his medical kit and a stretcher. All were very concerned, suspecting that he had sustained a serious back injury. Robinson gave him a morphine injection, under Haimson's guidance, and they then undertook the difficult task of getting him up the cliff by stretcher.

It later transpired that Haimson was not seriously injured; he had broken a few ribs, torn some muscles, and suffered cuts and bruises. Over the next few weeks, he recovered and soon resumed diving—but never again on the *Zuytdorp*.

The party left the wrecksite next day, travelling to Kalbarri to spend the night there. Robinson remained in Kalbarri while the others returned to Perth, and he arranged for a crayfisherman, Keith Dalgleish, to take him to the wrecksite in his boat *Psyche* on the following day, 21 May 1968. Diving conditions were good, and Robinson, using scuba gear, soon saw 'the glint of silver', and observed thousands of coins covering the sea-floor. He described his find as

> the biggest single mass of bullion I ever hope to see. Coins were in conglomerate form by the ton and everything I touched showed silver. I removed a few dozen and then returned to the boat, on the last ounce of air in the bottle.[136]

Next day, Robinson announced his dramatic find to the press,[137] stating that 'there are coins and bullion worth millions of dollars'. He said that he had informed the WA Museum of the discovery and would await a reply before deciding on his next move. He also appealed to the State Government to take action

Part of the 'carpet of silver', beside 'coin rock', May 1978: stacked masses of coins, mainly schellings and double stuivers, mantling the sea-floor and the walls of a small cave.

Photograph by Jeremy Green, courtesy of the WA Maritime Museum

to prevent pilfering from the wreck. Haimson told me that other members of the party were somewhat incredulous when they heard of Robinson's claim: 'of course no one believed him, [but] later expeditions by the Museum proved him right.'

Robinson was exhilarated by the publicity his announcement generated. He probably felt that this discovery marked the pinnacle of his treasure-hunting career, and he seemed determined to demonstrate publicly that he was a responsible citizen who had the best interests of the people of Western Australia at heart. Indeed, up to that time, Robinson had behaved correctly in relation to this wreck, in stark contrast to his earlier conduct with the *Vergulde Draeck*. He had sought permission from the museum authorities to undertake the *Zuytdorp* project, kept them informed of the results, and provided them with relics that he recovered at the site. The map he produced of the wreck was quite good, considering the limited amount of time that he and his party had been able to spend there, but it was notably deficient in failing to show the location of the treasure.[138]

Robinson's solicitors wrote to the WA Museum on 7 June 1968, stating that he was willing to undertake salvage operations at his own cost, in exchange for retaining 80 per cent of all materials recovered from the wreck. The museum would receive the remaining 20 per cent, plus any items of special historical interest.[139] Colin Jack-Hinton advised the Museum Director that Robinson's proposal included the construction of a caisson around the wreck, costing more than $250,000, which would be raised from investors; and archaeological excavations, to be supervised by the museum. Jack-Hinton said that this proposal had

> many attractions, in that the State Government would get some financial returns, whilst the Museum would receive historical material and have the opportunity to conduct a standard excavation under good conditions. If the project failed Government would lose nothing.[140]

A counter-proposal was received from Tom Brady, dated 11 June,[141] in which he again stated that the silver deposit was 'quite small', but that his group would be prepared to undertake salvage operations at their own expense if they could keep all the silver recovered, except for 'historical pieces' that the museum considered 'necessary for research'. Brady stated further that 'There is not much show of winning much silver as we see it, but [it] could be a reasonable reward for the effort that will be used in recovering same.'

Jack-Hinton reported on 14 June that of these two proposals, he preferred Robinson's, 'in that there is a greater chance thereby of Government making some profit, and there is likely to be a total excavation of the site.'[142] The massive environmental damage that would have resulted from Robinson's project, involving bulldozing of the cliff and platform at the wrecksite, was not mentioned, although it was acknowledged that failure of the caisson could cover the site with debris.

Robinson soon became infuriated because the WA Museum Board did not take immediate action to grant him a contract and instead seemed prepared to give consideration to the Brady group's counter-proposal. In a meeting with Jack-Hinton on 28 June, he expressed his view that the only way to get action from the board would be to expose it to the public for its treatment of him and its attitude towards wrecks. Jack-Hinton stated:

> My demeanour towards him, despite his tantrums and apparently pathological lack of control (which I have experienced repeatedly over the past eighteen months) was one of amiability and sympathetic humour which I hoped would relieve his disturbed state, as it has in the past.[143]

The WA Museum Board granted Robinson and his group an interview on 4 July, just as it had done for Brady and Cramer the day before.[144] Robinson was quite restrained at this meeting, without his usual threats and bluster, simply outlining his group's plans to construct a groyne around the site in order to facilitate the recovery of relics. Sir Thomas Meagher responded that 'there will be no panic or rash decisions made by the Board and our decision will come when we have seen it from all angles.' After Robinson and his group had departed, the board decided:

> In view of the conflicting statements made by the persons in attendance at the Special Board Meetings of 3rd and 4th July 1968, concerning (a) the feasibility of operations at the site, (b) the vulnerability of the site to pillage, (c) the reliability

of the other teams, (d) the quantity of material, bullion, and other relics at the site, the Board resolved that it could not proceed to a decision at this time which it could say would benefit the people of Western Australia.

This 'do nothing' decision further infuriated Robinson. Less than a week later, he made a press statement, published in the *West Australian* on 10 July 1968,[145] issuing an ultimatum that if there was not a favourable response to his proposal by Friday 12 July, the syndicate would 'go ahead with the project whether or not the Museum Board gave its approval'. He said that members of his group were aware that they risked heavy fines or imprisonment if they removed material from the wreck without approval, but that they 'thought the risk was justified to get some action on the matter'. Robinson announced that he had also written to the Premier, David Brand, about his group's intentions, and that his group would start work within hours of the declared deadline.

Premier Brand responded next day in the *West Australian*, with 'a stern warning' that members of Robinson's syndicate would not be allowed to take the law into their own hands. When Robinson's deadline to the WA Museum Board arrived a day later, Robinson announced that his group would not break any laws, but would still go to the wrecksite that weekend in order to undertake preparatory studies. On Saturday 13 July, the Museum Director, David Ride, stated in the *West Australian* that although Robinson's group had been given permission to take material from the wreck during its May expedition, that permission no longer applied, and the board could not agree to the wreck being worked under the terms that had been suggested by the group.[146]

Finally, on 17 July 1968, Jack-Hinton recorded in an internal memo:

> The situation now, it seems to me, is one where Robinson must never ever be allowed any sort of contract or any sort of work with the Museum again. I have tried to cooperate with him and overcome the trying Museum/Robinson relations which existed when I came here. Now so far as I am concerned he is in the category of a crank, albeit a dangerous one, if not a criminal one, and I propose to treat him as such.[147]

This was the final chapter in the chequered history of the WA Museum's attempts to work with Robinson. The surprising thing is that it took the museum authorities so long to reach this conclusion.

The next wreck to attract Robinson's attention was the *Tryall*. He joined an expedition, led by Eric Christiansen, which succeeded in locating the wreck of this ship at Tryal Rocks, in May 1969.[148] A year later, Robinson faced a serious assault charge, unrelated to his wreck activities, but he promptly left the state for Darwin and no action was taken to seek his extradition.

Several months later, in June 1971, there was a press report of a 'mystery trawler' operating in the Geraldton, Houtman Abrolhos and Shark Bay areas,[149] and on 10 July it was announced that this trawler, the *Four Aces*, had been abandoned in Shark Bay.[150] It later transpired that Robinson had brought the trawler from Queensland, with a small crew, and that it carried firearms, gelignite, detonators and fuse wire. There is only sketchy evidence regarding the vessel's movements. However, it seems likely that Robinson used it to carry out blasting operations on the *Tryall*, although he was eventually acquitted of a charge of doing so.[151] Moreover, the *Four Aces* seems to have been used by Robinson to dive on the *Zuytdorp* wreck during May or June that year.

We know nothing definite about this dive, but there is one important clue pointing to the fact that it took place. On 16 September 1979, the WA Museum was notified that a cannon had been found by four boys, near the end of the jetty at Denham (Shark Bay), and Jeremy Green was sent to investigate.[152] He found the gun to be a very well-preserved bronze muzzle loader, 0.87 metres long and with a bore of 5 centimetres, and bearing the insignia of the Zeeland (Middelburg) Chamber of the VOC. Green secured the cannon on behalf of the museum, and it is now on display at the WA Maritime Museum in Fremantle. The museum later had replicas made and presented to the four boys.

Green observed that the gun seemed to be of the same type as the small eroded swivel guns that had been found at the *Zuytdorp* wrecksite by Tom Brady and the Cramer brothers. He did not think that it could have lain at the foot of the jetty for very long, noting that there was still some concretion (lime encrustation) adhering to it. A lot of relics at the *Zuytdorp* site are embedded in the same type of material.[153] Green was also told that in 1971 Robinson's

Part of the barrel of a swivel gun from the Zuytdorp, showing the insignia of the Chamber of Zeeland (Middelburg) of the VOC. The gun was found at Denham, having been thrown overboard from the Four Aces by Alan Robinson.

Photograph by Pat Baker, courtesy of the WA Maritime Museum

boat, the *Four Aces*, had been tied up very close to the spot where the gun was found.

Reports of the discovery of the cannon were published in the *Geraldton Guardian* on 20 September and the *West Australian* on 25 September 1979. In the *Sunday Times* of 7 October, there was a comment by Robinson that when he was 'jumped' by police at Shark Bay in 1971, his crew members had 'panicked', throwing overboard two cannon that he had salvaged from the *Zuytdorp*, together with 'half a bucket' of pieces of eight, some musket shot, and other artefacts. He asserted that he had conducted 'a legal salvage operation' on the *Zuytdorp* and that he would shortly be presenting a bill for recovery of the material to the Western Australian Government.[154]

If there had indeed been a second gun thrown overboard, it has never been found; nor have the other relics mentioned by

Robinson. However, dredging occurred at the end of the jetty during the period between 1971 and 1979, and it is possible that some material from Robinson's boat was lost as a result.

Robinson described this 1971 dive on the *Zuytdorp* in his book *In Australia treasure is not for the finder*, but he does not mention any material being recovered.[155] He claimed that he was almost drowned there, and was saved only through the efforts of his son Geoffrey. However, there is little in this book that can be accepted at face value: in many cases where something is mentioned that can be checked independently, Robinson's version has proved to be inaccurate—often wildly so.

Robinson's violent characteristics were later to be illustrated in a series of court cases, culminating in a charge in Sydney, against him and his then de facto wife, of conspiring to murder (with acid and explosives) a woman from an earlier de facto relationship. Robinson's trial was terminated through his death, apparently by suicide, on 2 November 1983, while the jury was deliberating on the case.[156] The jury was then directed by the judge not to deliver its verdict on Robinson, but it acquitted his de facto wife of the charge, and it is clear that it would similarly have acquitted Robinson, had he survived.

Robinson's death in custody brought a dramatic end to a life that had been colourful, violent and unstable. His mental attitude at the time of his death can probably be gauged from an article in the *Sunday Independent*, five years before,[157] in which Robinson told how 'wrecks have wrecked my life', stating:

> I have been publicly humiliated and disgraced...My diving has cost me everything a person could hope for in life. I've lost my family, my livelihood, I've been bankrupted and lost my friends, and I've forgotten how to enjoy life.
>
> I've been through so much that life has lost its charm. I've forgotten how to smile, how to be sociable, how to relax. What am I looking for out of life?...Maybe it's just recognition after all these years.

Robinson was to die, apparently in the depths of despair, without ever achieving the recognition that he craved and, to some extent, deserved. Even in 1994, eleven years after his death, the Select Committee on Ancient Shipwrecks denied him formal recognition as one of the discoverers of the *Vergulde Draeck* and *Tryall* wrecks, despite the fact that he is known to have played a significant role in both discoveries.

Robinson will be remembered as a highly controversial figure, who played a prominent role in the discovery and publicizing of early wrecks on our coast.[158] His destructive actions were responsible, albeit inadvertently, for much of the State and Commonwealth legislation that was enacted to protect our historic wrecks. Robinson had a certain charisma, and even today some people maintain that he was basically a 'good bloke' who was persecuted by bureaucrats, despite all the evidence of his psychopathic mentality and tendency to extreme violence. Certainly, it cannot be denied that he was a man of courage, with a lot of ability as a diver and organizer.

Dr Naoom Haimson has described Alan Robinson to me in these terms:[159]

> For many years he was my diving buddy. I was probably the only friend he had whom he didn't eventually cross. Also for 10 years I was his doctor. I knew him better than any one. In the water I trusted him implicitly. On land I was privy to his innermost secrets, fears, and hopes [and] I was aware of most of his crimes [and] deceptions. His book was, of course, a farrago of half truths, lies, and pure fiction. As his mental illness became worse, he began to have more problems [in] distinguishing which was which.
>
> Despite all this, I feel that he has not received the recognition that he deserved. Both the *Tryall* and *Zuytdorp* expeditions would never have taken place without his organization and drive. He provided the logistics and the money (where he got it from is another matter), and he *did* things where others just sat around and talked.
>
> He [also] did many very bad things, more than people know about, but he is dead [now]. Let him rest in peace, probably the only peace he ever knew.

5. ARCHAEOLOGISTS, ARSONISTS AND LOOTERS

ACTIVITIES SINCE 1971

Early work by the WA Museum

Alan Robinson's announced discovery in 1968, of masses of silver coins on the sea-floor, placed the public spotlight on the *Zuytdorp* wreck. Many people were understandably sceptical about his claims, and it was clearly necessary for the WA Museum, as the responsible government agency, to do something about it.

A party, including David Ride, the Museum Director, visited the site on 15 and 16 July 1968, together with a member of the Perth Criminal Investigation Branch (CIB). Following the visit, the Chairman of the WA Museum Board was advised that the museum planned to proceed towards 'large-scale recovery', after preparing a detailed chart of the sea-floor and the wreck itself. Ride also asserted that there had been no thefts of Crown property from the wreck to date, and that material removed by skindivers in the past had been delivered to the museum. He expressed confidence that the CIB would ensure the future security of the wreck and prosecute any violation of the law 'with the utmost rigour'.[160]

In fact, there had already been several violations of the law in relation to the *Zuytdorp*, and many more have occurred since then, but only one prosecution has ever been launched. Simon Jones, scuba instructor, was convicted on 8 May 1986 of having taken a small bronze cannon from the *Zuytdorp* wreck, and thirty-one musket balls and two coins from the *Batavia* wreck. He was placed on a good-behaviour bond for twelve months.[161] Jones's transgressions were minor in comparison with those of other people who have looted the *Zuytdorp* wreck, while escaping scot-free. It is clear that the police cannot stop the plundering of wrecks in remote localities. The only way to prevent the theft of historically important material is for the museum to recover that material before it is looted.

After rejecting Robinson's application to conduct salvage operations on the wreck, the WA Museum Board decided, on the basis of legal advice, that no future arrangement would allow a contractor to keep any relics. This meant that the counter-proposal from Brady's group was not acceptable, either, as it involved them retaining the silver coinage. However, Brady had indicated at the interview with the board, on 3 July 1968, that his group would be prepared to negotiate on this matter. He wrote several letters to the Museum Director over the next two years, requesting a formal response to his proposal, but to no avail.

On 24 January 1970, the Director received a letter from fisherman John Allchin, saying that he would agree to salvage material from the *Zuytdorp* wreck, on behalf of the museum, if he could retain 25 per cent of all coins recovered. Allchin suggested that he be granted rights to dive and collect material during January and February, and that the Brady group be given rights for the rest of the year.[162]

It took the museum authorities eleven months to decide on Allchin's proposal. On 30 December 1970, the Acting Director wrote to him, advising that he would be allowed to dive on the wreck and remove artefacts on behalf of the museum in January–February 1971. Brady also received a letter granting him equivalent rights for April–May–June 1971, two and a half years after he had first written seeking permission.[163] These approvals were given subject to stringent conditions: that a museum staff member would accompany them, if required; the museum would be advised in advance of any expedition to the site; separate authority would be needed for each expedition; no object would be removed before a photograph had been taken of it in situ; no explosives would be used; the Museum Director would be advised of each item recovered; those items would be delivered to the museum; and the divers would not retain any of the material raised. It is hard to imagine how either Allchin or Brady would have been prepared to dive under such conditions at this dangerous place, given that it would be at his own expense and with no reward in prospect other than 'thank you'.

The first dive on the wreck by museum personnel took place on 31 January 1971. The museum's Harry Bingham, Geoff Kimpton and Colin Powell were taken from Kalbarri to the wrecksite by Ernie Crocas in his own boat, accompanied by Neil Trudgeon, who had photographed the site for television on the previous day. They arrived at the wrecksite at about 6 a.m., and were met there, in accordance with a prior arrangement, by John Allchin in his boat. As diving conditions were good, they decided to dive immediately, and were able to spend about nine hours in the water before deteriorating conditions forced them to leave and return to Kalbarri.[164] Next day, sea conditions proved to be unsuitable for diving.

The divers had recovered a great deal of interesting material, including over 3,300 coins: mainly schellings and double stuivers, together with some pieces of eight and ducatons. Other items included navigation dividers, part of the ship's bell, the eroded bronze cannon referred to earlier—about 1.5 metres long, with its muzzle partly filled with coins and other objects—and miscellaneous pieces of brass, copper, lead, timber, rope and pottery. Kimpton described the sight of the glistening carpet of silver on the sea-floor as 'unbelievable'. He estimated it to be about 3 metres long and 1.5–2 metres wide, located just north of a small cave lined with coins. The divers dug out big lumps of the coin conglomerate, carrying them out to the boats. Kimpton said that he passed the largest lump to a deckhand, who promptly dropped it overboard. This prize piece sank to the bottom, never to be seen by museum staff again.

Prior to this successful dive, the museum's attitude towards the wreck had been rather negative, especially as navy experts had advised that diving conditions were so dangerous that the wreck was unworkable. But Bingham and Kimpton had now shown that skilled divers with the right equipment could effect a proper investigation. However, further work would not eventuate for many years, as other historic wrecks received higher priorities in the museum program, and both Bingham and Kimpton resigned to take up positions elsewhere. Kimpton was later to return to the museum and play a major role, with Mike McCarthy, in the *Zuytdorp* project (see p. 188).

The abalone divers

Serious consideration was first given to the establishment of an abalone fishery along the Zuytdorp Cliffs, north and south of the wrecksite, during the late 1960s. It got under way in the 1970s, and a network of rough tracks was soon established along the cliffs, to service the industry. Joe Cremers claims to have been the first person to investigate the abalone potential, in 1968. He began commercial abalone gathering in the area a few years later, and continued working there on a seasonal basis until 1993. Cremers was followed by Dominic Lamera and Ken Tester in 1975, and soon afterwards by Ray Mickelberg and Alan Wilson. These men were the principal operators during the late 1970s, but several others later became involved in the industry.

In the early days, most abalone gathering was done by scouring the shoreline platforms, which were thickly encrusted with many thousands of the shellfish. However, the biggest abalone were found in deep holes within and over the edge of the platforms, where it was necessary to dive for them. Most such diving was done using snorkels, although hookah systems were also used.

Today, as relatively few abalone remain on top of the platforms in the more accessible areas, diving is the principal means of obtaining them. The abalone divers are highly skilled, as indeed they have to be when operating in such a hazardous area. They work in pairs, for safety reasons, and no serious injuries have been reported.

Joe Cremers told me that among the Kalbarri fishermen at that time, 'everyone had a go at the wreck', meaning that there was a lot of pilfering of coins and other relics. He said that many times he has seen the water along the cliffs 'as flat as a pancake', when anyone could have safely swum and recovered artefacts at the wrecksite. On one such occasion in about 1980, when the museum's watchkeeper was at the site (see p. 173), Cremers dived there, describing the silver accumulation as a 'fantastic sight'. He said that he did not recover any relics himself.

Dominic Lamera began abalone gathering in the area during 1975. He told me that he made his first dive on the wreck the year before, and was impressed by the glistening 'river of silver', as he called it, about 2–2.5 metres long and 30–40 centimetres thick. Since then, he has dived many times at the site, and has also scoured the surrounding countryside, seeking signs of the *Zuytdorp* survivors. In late 1980, Lamera built a hut beside my old track to the wreck, using it as the base for his abalone operations, which are still continuing.

Ray Mickelberg and Alan Wilson started commercial abalone gathering in the area not long after Lamera, during the mid-1970s. Ray Mickelberg was later joined by his two brothers, Brian and Peter, and his cousin Terry Parkes. The Mickelbergs also set up a factory in Kalbarri, processing both abalone and crayfish, and

Dominic Lamera, in 1996, standing in front of the squatter's hut that he built in 1980.

Photograph by the author

exporting the products overseas. They put in three airstrips along the Zuytdorp Cliffs (two of which are shown on Map 6, the third being further south) and used their own plane, a Cessna 185, and a helicopter to travel from Kalbarri to the abalone grounds and to transport the abalone back. They were not authorized to use the museum's airstrip at the *Zuytdorp* wrecksite.

Ray Mickelberg told me that this airborne system gave them a lot of flexibility in their operations, despite the high costs involved. They were able to collect, process and export the abalone, thereby keeping all the profits. The last year that they operated in the area was 1980, when they sold the factory in Kalbarri.

The Mickelberg brothers would later gain notoriety as the perpetrators of the 1982 Perth Mint swindle, being convicted in March 1983 of obtaining gold bullion worth $653,000, by passing worthless cheques. Two of the brothers, Ray and Brian, were also convicted in June 1984 of faking a large gold nugget, the 'Yellow Rose of Texas', and selling it (as a genuine nugget) to Alan Bond for $350,000. For that offence, Ray Mickelberg was sentenced to a maximum of five years in prison, and Brian Mickelberg up to three years, but these sentences were later virtually halved, on appeal. For the mint swindle, the sentences originally handed down were up to twenty years for Ray, sixteen years for Peter, and twelve years for Brian. Brian was later acquitted, on appeal (and died in an aircraft crash in 1986), but Ray and Peter spent eight and six years in prison before being released. These sentences seem severe considering the fact that their crimes did not involve personal injury to anyone. Moreover, in two books on the subject, author Avon Lovell has cast doubt on the validity of the mint-swindle convictions.[165]

I asked Ray Mickelberg if he had ever dived on the *Zuytdorp* wreck, and he replied that he had done so only once, when museum divers were there. I later noted that press reports in May 1983 described how police had located a walled-in cellar underneath Mickelberg's home, and, on smashing their way into it, had found gold and silver bullion worth more than $86,000, various documents, underwater gear, and a box of 'old Dutch coins'. It was subsequently demonstrated that the gold and silver bullion was not derived from the mint swindle, but was Mickelberg's own property.[166] The police recorded that there were forty-seven coins and pieces of coins in the box, and that these had been identified by Stan Wilson, honorary numismatist at the WA Museum, as having come from the *Zuytdorp*. This material— including fifteen schellings, seven double stuivers and seven pieces of eight—was given to the museum for safekeeping. When I asked Ray Mickelberg about the coins, he said that he had purchased them from a fisherman in Kalbarri, but would not identify the person.

Ray Mickelberg's wife, Sheryl, told a reporter that Ray had bought the gold and silver found in the raid 'for tax purposes'.[167] She said further:

> Nobody seems to understand that those three men [Ray Mickelberg and his brothers, Peter and Brian] made a lot of money out of abalone fishing. In the early days they could take as much abalone as they liked. Then they built a processing factory at Kalbarri and after three or four years sold it for $400,000. A lot of that money was invested and a lot was lost.
>
> As long as I have known Ray he has bought gold and silver and he has hidden things. This secrecy and his tendency to hide things has been his downfall. I have told him that by hiding things he has made himself look bad.

These remarks may have initiated a story that circulated in Kalbarri soon afterwards, about the whereabouts of the gold derived from the Perth Mint swindle. A press report of 31 October 1984[168] stated:

> There is no doubt in the minds of some people in Kalbarri that the gold is somewhere up at the Zuytdorp Cliffs, possibly under water, 50 km to the north of Kalbarri…'My theory [according to one fisherman] is that there is an Aladdin's cave up there with the gold inside…They [the Mickelbergs] were up there all the time, they knew the area better than anybody.'
>
> The seas are so rough around the *Zuytdorp* wreck, said to still contain priceless coins, that it is possible to dive on the wreck only a few days every year. The use of a helicopter for abalone diving in the area was a stroke of genius.

This report shows that although the Mickelbergs had sold their business in Kalbarri in 1980 and had ceased abalone diving along the Zuytdorp Cliffs at that time, some people considered it possible that they had returned in 1982 to hide gold from the mint.

In fact, the theory that the stolen gold was planted along the Zuytdorp Cliffs seems highly unlikely, because most of the gold was eventually returned, via reporter Alison Fan of TVW Channel 7, in 1989. No convincing explanation has been given as to why or how this was done. Indeed, like so much of the Mickelberg saga, the return of this stolen gold was quite bizarre. First of all, a small gold bar, undoubtedly one of those involved in the swindle, was delivered to Alison Fan by post on 11 July, when both Ray and Peter Mickelberg were still in gaol. Three months later, a few days after Peter Mickelberg was released on parole and Ray was still behind bars, the bulk of the missing gold was placed near the gates of Channel 7, in the form of small globules formed by pouring molten gold into water. Presumably, a trusted accomplice was involved, but it is hard to visualize how that person could have first recovered the gold from a hiding place along the Zuytdorp Cliffs.

Note to reprinted edition (2006).
Following the publication of this work in 1996, the Mickelbergs successfully appealed their convictions, casting considerable doubt on the police evidence tendered at their trial.

Archaeological work, 1976–80

In May 1976, Jeremy Green (Curator of Maritime Archaeology at the WA Museum) wrote a memorandum regarding the possibility of more work being done at the *Zuytdorp* wrecksite, pointing out that museum personnel had made many visits there over the years, but had achieved only one successful dive, in 1971.[169] He felt that there were two ways of attempting to dive there: either by driving up and camping on the spot while waiting for suitable conditions, or by arranging for a local fisherman to report suitable weather, then travelling as quickly as possible to the site, overland or by boat. He concluded that the first option was not viable, because the time spent at the site might extend to many months, but that the second could be tried. However, he thought it unlikely that divers could reach the site within twenty-four hours of hearing of favourable conditions, by which time those conditions would probably have passed.

In Green's opinion, other options were to: (1) contract a local fisherman to recover material; (2) employ a watchkeeper at the site to report on sea conditions, and reactivate the 1958 airstrip so that divers could get there quickly; (3) work the site intensively from a barge or land base, using some artificial method of reducing the swell, such as a groyne or 'bubble curtain'; or (4) leave the site alone. Green noted that it was commonly claimed that diving on the *Zuytdorp* wreck could be attempted on only one or two days a year, but he believed that a more realistic estimate would be thirty days a year. The only feasible options, in his opinion, were (2) and (3), and (2) was clearly the most practicable. He estimated that about ten full days spent diving on the site would suffice to recover the major part of the material, so that the wreck could then be regarded as completely excavated from a practical point of view.

Jeremy Green and Graeme Henderson succeeded in diving at the site in June and November 1977, observing a large concentration of coins, and indications that some small-scale looting had taken place since the 1971 museum dive. Henderson told me later that the mass of coins covered an area 'about the plan view of a large car'. As a result of these dives and of Green's report, the museum decided to expedite excavation of the wreck, intending especially to remove the silver coinage that formed such an obvious target for looters.

In April 1978, Green spoke to Prince Mukarram Jah, owner of Murchison House Station, who generously agreed to assist the museum with the *Zuytdorp* project, at his own cost. Soon afterwards, Jah personally bulldozed a track to the wrecksite (see Map 5), graded the airstrip that had originally been established on the 1958 expedition, and designed, erected and financed a flying fox. The flying fox comprised a massive iron tetrapod on top of the cliff, a steel cable extending down to two large anchors laid out to sea, and a cage suspended on runners from the cable, which was to be used to facilitate divers and equipment entering and leaving the water and relics being brought ashore. Unfortunately, it never worked (see p. 173).

Jah is the eighth Nizam of Hyderabad. His forebears ruled the independent State of Hyderabad before it was forcibly incorporated into India in 1948. The Nizam princes and their ruling upper class had always been Muslim, whereas most of the population were Hindu. The seventh Nizam, Jah's grandfather, was generally acknowledged to have been the richest man in the world. He was also renowned as an eccentric miser, who is said to have boasted that his personal expenses never exceeded seven shillings and sixpence (75 cents) a day.[170] Nevertheless, he was often very generous to favoured people. Hyderabad, under the Nizam's rule, became one of the most prosperous parts of British India, having good schools, hospitals and universities, and large-scale irrigation projects.

Jah has a keen interest in the *Zuytdorp* wreck, and he was especially interested to learn from me that in 1704 the ship had been involved, at Surat, in clashes with forces of Aurangzeb, the great Mogul emperor of India (see Chapter 2). His family had originally been brought from Samarkand to India by Aurangzeb in 1687, together with 30,000 horsemen who were used to conquer southern India. Aurangzeb made Jah's ancestor the military governor of Hyderabad, based in Golconda. The dynasty that he founded ruled the princedom for more than 250 years, up to the time of Indian independence. Each prince was known as the Nizam of Hyderabad, *nizam* being the Persian word for military governor. Jah is thus the current head of a dynasty that has continued unbroken from the time of India's great Mogul empire.

Jah uses Murchison House Station as a retreat (some say as a 'hobby farm'), commonly spending several months of the year there, while returning periodically to his palace in India. Access to the station is forbidden without prior authority. Gates are locked at most entry points, and a sign on the track between the wrecksite and Gee Gie Outcamp warns that spikes have been laid, so that persons attempting to drive along it risk having their tyres punctured.

Murchison House Station has changed a lot since I first visited it in 1954. Sheep numbers have fallen drastically, and the property now supports large numbers of feral goats. Most of the internal fencing has collapsed, and a noxious weed, the star thistle, has spread over wide areas. In addition, historic buildings, notably the imposing shearing shed and the little outcamp at Gee Gie, are in urgent need of repairs.

Jah is keenly interested in heavy earth-moving machinery, having on Murchison House several bulldozers, graders, and even a tank, which he enjoys driving around, clearing new roads and renovating old ones. This interest stems from the time when he trained as an engineer at Sandhurst.

The airstrip at the wrecksite, newly graded by Jah, was used for the first time by museum staff on 12 May 1978. A party led by Jeremy Green landed on the strip and made a successful six-hour dive on the wreck. Others who participated on this trip were Jimmy Stewart, Colin Powell, Scott Sledge and Bob Richards. The conditions were the best that museum personnel had experienced, and, on inspecting the coin deposit, Green noted that looting had occurred since he was there with Henderson in the previous November. The divers managed to excavate several thousand silver coins, together with a three-wick gimbal oil lamp, another small lamp, part of a cartridge container, a knife handle, and a number of round-headed brass nails, all in very good condition. A large copper cauldron was also found lying loose where it had been dropped recently, no doubt by the person who had been illicitly extracting coins. Green estimated that the area that had been looted represented about 25 per cent of the museum's excavation.[171]

Dr Ian Crawford, Green's supervisor, stated in an internal museum report that about 12,000 coins had now been recovered by museum divers, representing approximately 10 per cent of the coins in the deposit.[172] Crawford went on to say:

> the disturbing element in his [Green's] report is that there has been further tampering with the wrecksite, and some coins [have been] removed since June 1977. We had believed that our security would be effective during this period, and it is disappointing to find that it has not fully protected the site.

It was accordingly decided that a watchkeeper should be installed in a caravan near the wrecksite, and this was done in June 1978.

In his report, Green estimated that once the flying fox was operational, it would be possible to extract all the coins and lead ingots in sixteen days of diving time. He guessed that this would involve about forty days on the site, in ten trips over two years. However, when the flying fox was installed, the anchors dragged, causing the cable to chafe on the rocky sea-floor. When Jimmy Stewart was about to descend using this gear for the first time, it was prudently decided to send down the cage filled with rocks, in order to ensure that everything was secure. The cable promptly broke where it had chafed on the sea-floor, sending the cage plummeting to the bottom of the cliff. If it had carried the diver, he would no doubt have been killed or seriously injured. The tetrapod was therefore abandoned, and rusted away for thirteen years before it was removed by McCarthy and his team during their rehabilitation of the site in July 1991. The anchors, supplied by Jah, still remain on the sea-floor.

As a result of the failure of the flying fox, a major element of Green's plan for working the wreck was never operational. Nevertheless, the museum was at that time much better equipped at the site than ever before, with a useable airstrip and a watch-keeper installed in a caravan, having radio communication with Perth and Murchison House Homestead. The divers were called up several times when sea conditions seemed suitable, only to find on each occasion that it was too rough to dive, or conditions for diving were only marginal and nothing could be salvaged.

Meanwhile, the airstrip deteriorated as wind blew away patches of sand, exposing bare rock below. Jeremy Green, Geoff Kimpton, Mike McCarthy, Bob Richards, Scott Sledge and Colin Powell flew to the site on 30 October 1979, using two planes, the second of which almost crashed on landing. As a result, the pilot said that he would never attempt to land there again unless the strip was upgraded. They found that conditions for diving were poor, but nevertheless Green and Kimpton went in, leaving McCarthy on shore to keep watch, as the safety man. When conditions deteriorated further, Green tried to come ashore in the little bay south of the sloping rock, but he got into trouble because of the strong backwash, losing his flippers and being cut about on the rocks. It was a perilous situation, but McCarthy dived in, helping Green to scramble out on the south side of the little bay. Kimpton was also lucky to get out safely.

As a result of this untoward incident, and other problems, Green became very pessimistic about further work on the wreck, writing in an internal memorandum on 7 October 1980 that 'the particular problems with the *Zuytdorp* site seem almost insur-mountable.'[173] He said that the two occasions when they had been able to dive and recover material, in 1971 and 1978, were probably 'freak occurrences', and that over the past two years there had been no suitable conditions. He believed that this situation could easily continue for several years.

Consequently, Green concluded that it was pointless to contemplate any further work unless the airstrip was improved, and that until that was done the watchkeeper should be withdrawn, and replaced by use of the Commonwealth airborne coastal surveillance system. He suggested six alternatives that could be considered by the museum for the future: (1) abandoning the site permanently; (2) contracting the work to outsiders; (3) continuing with the existing basic approach; (4) constructing a groyne; (5) approaching the site from the sea; and (6) salvaging without divers—for example, using a grab.

Later on the same day that he submitted this report, Green learned that the situation was even worse than he thought: an arsonist had destroyed the watchkeeper's caravan and equipment.

Burning of the WA Museum caravan

The watchkeeper, a twenty-nine-year-old New Zealander named Ian Field, left the caravan at 5.45 a.m. on Monday 7 October 1980, to drive to Kalbarri.[174] He had arranged by radio, a week before, to have his vehicle serviced on that day. After calling at Murchison House Homestead, and speaking to the manager there, he drove on to Kalbarri.

Field spent the night at the Kalbarri Hotel and did his usual shopping in the morning, before leaving to return to the wrecksite, calling briefly at Murchison House Homestead at about 10 a.m. While passing through the gate on the barrier fence, he noted that another vehicle had crossed his tracks of the previous day. He deduced that it had driven there from the highway, via the barrier fence and the access road to the abandoned site of the Kalbarri no. 1 oil-exploration well. The new vehicle wheel tracks passed through the gate and headed towards the wrecksite, and there was no sign of return tracks. As Field continued towards the campsite, he noticed that a sign warning people not to enter the reserve around the wrecksite had been removed by someone in the vehicle ahead. About 200 metres from the caravan, his dog started growling, with its hair bristling, and Field experienced a sick feeling of apprehension as he drove on. Turning the last corner of the track, he beheld the smoking ruins of his burnt-out caravan.

Someone had poured several jerrycans of petrol through the windows of the caravan and over equipment that had been stored

The burnt-out caravan of the WA Museum (9 October 1980).

Photograph by Ian Field, courtesy of the WA Maritime Museum

outside, including some belonging to Channel 9 television studios, before lighting the fire. The emptied jerrycans had been neatly stacked, with their lids open, in essentially the same position that they had been left by Field. He estimated that the fire had probably been lit four or five hours previously. There was nothing to suggest that the caravan had been broken into, and its door was still locked. The only items that appeared to have been stolen were a generator and the compressor for a hookah unit, both of which had been stored in the open. Field lost all his personal possessions in the conflagration.

Field found signs that his outdoor barbecue had been used to cook a meal, and he had the frightening feeling that the perpetrators were still lurking nearby; he told me he could 'almost smell them'. Consequently, he took a firm grasp on his rifle while looking around. On going down to the wrecksite, he found footprints in the sand at the foot of the cliffs, indicating that the persons concerned had visited there before departing. From these footprints and those at other localities, he concluded that two men were probably involved, although he could not be certain that there were more than one.

Field afterwards realized that the reason he could see no evidence that the vehicle had returned along the usual access track was that it had left the area by the other route, travelling south-south-east on an oil-exploration track from near the airstrip to the barrier fence. He later concluded that the vehicle and its occupants might well have been hiding west of the gate on this fence when he drove through it that day, waiting until he had passed, before heading on to the highway.

Field found that the radio aerial had been cut down, and the radio in the caravan had been destroyed in the fire. However, by using the transceiver in his vehicle, he managed to communicate with Jeremy Green in Perth, letting him know the dramatic news. It occurred to Field that the arsonists might have been listening to this conversation, so he was careful what he said. After taking photographs of the scene, he drove to Kalbarri that evening. Next day, he returned to the site, accompanied by the curator of the Geraldton Museum, Greg Wallace, a detective from the Geraldton CIB, and a constable from Kalbarri. They inspected the scene of the fire and surrounding areas, without finding any significant new evidence. As they arrived at the wrecksite, a wave obliterated the footprints in the sand, but Field had photographed them on the previous day. The police departed, and Field and Wallace spent the night at the camp of the abalone fisherman Dominic Lamera, about 6 kilometres north of the wrecksite. Field had become quite friendly with Lamera, and felt free to use his camp, even though Lamera was away at the time, having left the day before Field went to Kalbarri.

Next morning, Field and Wallace completed a detailed inventory[175] of what had been lost in the fire, before returning to Kalbarri. Lamera told me recently that half of his own gear was destroyed in the caravan fire, but this claim is not supported by the inventory, which lists nothing of Lamera's as having been lost.

It seems clear that the burning of the caravan was a carefully planned and executed operation. It was not a case of spontaneous vandalism. There were no signs of beer cans or anything else to suggest drunken behaviour or hooliganism, and the petrol jerrycans were neatly stacked after their contents had been used to light the fire. The arsonists must have known that Field was going to Kalbarri to stay overnight and that Lamera had left his nearby camp. The operation was timed to match Field's movements. The perpetrators drove to the site after Field had passed through the barrier fence on his way to Kalbarri, and left via a route that he would not be using on his return.

I have examined the CIB file of the investigation into this matter. The police were of the opinion that the vehicle used by the arsonists was a short-wheel-base Land Rover. Brief enquiries seeking to determine who was responsible produced no positive leads. No suspects were interviewed, and the investigation was closed.[176]

In my opinion, the burning of the caravan must have been carried out with the objective of driving away the watchkeeper, leaving the treasure of the *Zuytdorp* virtually unprotected. The operation was completed in a proficient manner by one or more persons who had prior knowledge of the area and of Field's planned itinerary. I have discussed the matter with several people who are familiar with what happened, and different opinions have been expressed regarding the identity of the principal arsonist. I have my own ideas on the matter, but there is no proof.

The part-time watchkeeper

As a result of the fire and the other factors listed in Green's report of 7 October 1980, the WA Museum Board resolved to discontinue the post of full-time watchkeeper at the site. Green's original plan was that surveillance of the wrecksite be taken over by the Australian Coastal Surveillance Centre as part of its regular aerial patrols of the coast north of Geraldton. However, aerial patrols between Geraldton and Karratha ceased in December 1980, soon after the fire, so this method of surveillance was no longer an option. Instead, it was decided to employ the abalone diver Dominic Lamera as a part-time warden, with the intention that he would 'keep an eye on things' when collecting abalone in the area.[177] He retained this position from 1980 to 1994, initially as a paid officer, and then in an honorary capacity.

Immediately after the fire, in November–December 1980, Lamera constructed a small squatter's hut not far from the remains of the caravan, and he has since used this as his base when working in the area. For some years, he spent about five to six months annually collecting abalone, in spells of about one week each throughout the year. However, this was reduced to three months a year, from October to December, when abalone quotas were introduced by the Fisheries Department. His son, Robert, normally worked with him.

In appointing Lamera as a part-time warden, the WA Museum trustees had no idea that he would later admit to having recovered large numbers of coins and other artefacts from the wreck, without authority. This fact came to light when Lamera disclosed this information to the museum through a Commonwealth amnesty, in 1993–94, under which people who had unlawfully recovered shipwreck material could declare and retain their finds, without being liable to prosecution. Lamera declared the largest and most valuable collection known to have been taken from the *Zuytdorp*. It includes many well-preserved ducatons and pieces of eight, part of the ship's bell, and a decorative silver buckle. He informed the museum authorities that this material had been recovered in 1974, six years prior to his appointment as warden at the wrecksite.

The collection that Lamera declared includes 54 ducatons, 123 pieces of eight, 13 schellings, 12 double stuivers, and several half ducatons, pieces of four, and pieces of two. Most of these coins are in excellent condition; indeed, the ducatons are generally much superior to those held by the museum. Lamera reported that his material came from close to the edge of the platform, opposite coin rock.[178] Material recovered by museum divers shows that the vast majority of coins in that area consisted of schellings and double stuivers, but Lamera declared only 25 of those coins. Furthermore, he claims to have removed only a small amount of material from the carpet of silver, which must have contained more than 100,000 schellings and double stuivers, and several thousand of the other coins. Lamera told me that he regarded schellings and double stuivers as 'rubbish', because they are so common, and that he has given away most of those he recovered.

Looting of the *Zuytdorp* treasure

The carpet of silver, which once formed most of the *Zuytdorp* treasure remaining on the sea-floor, was extensively looted some time between 1980, when the caravan was burnt, and 1986, when museum divers made their next successful dive at the site (see p. 189). In 1978, it had been estimated that 90 per cent of the

deposit was still intact, but by 1986 very little remained. Although patches of coins were preserved in potholes and crevices on the sea-floor, the area once occupied by the glistening carpet of silver was now almost bare. It seems probable that the silver was looted by the same person or persons who burnt the museum caravan.

Mike McCarthy and Geoff Kimpton have recently expressed the opinion that a diver using a few well-placed explosive charges could easily have removed the carpet of silver in one or two days, given good diving conditions. McCarthy told me that from his knowledge of the attitudes of many divers outside the museum, he could understand, but not condone, their desire to explore

wrecks and to remove coins and other relics without permission. He said that every keen diver in Western Australia yearned to explore the Dutch wrecks, and that a dive on the *Zuytdorp*, the most difficult of all, is to a diver what climbing Mount Everest is to a mountaineer:

Stacked schellings from the 'carpet of silver'.

Photograph by Pat Baker, courtesy of the WA Maritime Museum

> Every diver I have ever known always felt that what they find is theirs. If the Museum was leaving a carpet of silver at a divers' Everest and someone was there on a good day and was keen to dive anyway, he would feel he was an idiot if he didn't go in and get it. Only in recent years have people realized the value of wrecks from educational and cultural points of view.
>
> If I was a hypothetical diver who was working along these cliffs, with a basic dislike for bureaucracy and a jaundiced view of any Government group; if I had the equipment and rapid access in and out of the area, and I knew that the Museum wasn't coming and that there was a big packet

of silver lying there; if I had a good day at the site and there
was no one to be seen; if I had been that person, there is no
doubt that I would have gone in and got it.

This seems to be a realistic assessment of what happened to
the *Zuytdorp* silver, although the identity of the person or persons
responsible is unproved. Although some people may not regard
such an action as a serious crime, it must be recognized that it
amounts to the theft of extremely valuable historic material owned
by the people of Australia, and that conviction would probably
result in a substantial gaol sentence.

What happened to the coinage after it was stripped from
the wreck? There is no evidence to suggest that large numbers
of the coins have yet been sold to collectors, as such sales would
probably have become widely known. The common schellings and
double stuivers and other worn coins may well have been melted
down for their silver content. Another, more intriguing, possibility
is that whoever stole the silver has concealed it somewhere in
the vicinity of the wrecksite or elsewhere along the Zuytdorp
Cliffs, and several people have suggested to me that this is what
happened. Abalone divers know of many holes in the shoreline
platforms where a large cache of coins could be hidden, but it is
perhaps more likely that the treasure would be buried somewhere
in the hinterland of the cliffs. Maybe we will never know the
answer to this mystery.

Prince Jah told me that a few days after the museum caravan
was burnt, when he was staying at Murchison House Homestead, he
received telephone calls from a man asking for assistance in working
the wreck, pointing out that the museum had now withdrawn
from the area. Jah said that he advised the caller that he must seek
permission from the museum authorities before doing anything at
the wrecksite. Although the person did not give his name, Jah had
the impression that he may have been Alan Robinson.

It is possible, but in my opinion unlikely, that Robinson was
implicated in the burning of the museum caravan. Certainly, he had
a motive: in common with a number of other divers, he disliked
the museum and had a strong interest in recovering the *Zuytdorp*
silver. However, at that time Robinson was running a successful
business in Karratha, and probably did not have the means of
monitoring the movements of the watchkeeper and going quickly

to the site when an appropriate opportunity arose. Moreover, his de facto wife had just left him and moved to Victoria, and he was embroiled in legal argument with the Commonwealth regarding compensation for the loss of his 'rights' to the *Vergulde Draeck* wreck. Then, on 24 December 1980, he was arrested on two charges of disposing of relics from a historic wreck (the *Vergulde Draeck*), without a permit. After being released on bail, he departed for Victoria, and soon after arriving there was arrested on a charge of assaulting his estranged de facto wife. Although Robinson was acquitted of that charge, he continued to be involved in various legal actions, leading up to his eventual death in police custody on 2 November 1983.

Even if Robinson was one of the arsonists who destroyed the caravan, I think it is unlikely that he was responsible for stripping the wreck of its silver, as there was little time for him to have done so in the brief period between the caravan fire and the legal actions in which he was involved soon afterwards.

The coin register of the WA Maritime Museum, as updated to November 1991, shows that 13,210 coins, weighing about 60 kilograms, were recovered from the *Zuytdorp* by museum divers. It is expected that about 1,000 more coins will be added to this list when their conservation is complete. If this total represents about 10 per cent of the coins in the original deposit, more than half a tonne of silver coins must have been preserved on the sea-floor, out of about 3 tonnes on the ship when it was wrecked. The majority of the coins recovered by museum divers are schellings (5,726) and double stuivers (6,644); others include ducatons (48), half ducatons (6), pieces of eight (eight reals) (483), pieces of four (140), pieces of two (159), pieces of one (2) and *rijksdaalders* (2). Most of the schellings and double stuivers came from the carpet of silver, but many of the ducatons and pieces of eight were from a smaller coin accumulation, the 'armoury concretion', closer to the edge of the platform, in the vicinity of which Lamera claims to have obtained most of his coins.[179]

As the museum's collection is probably reasonably representative of the coinage carried on the ship, the theft of a large percentage of the treasure—perhaps as much as 80 or 90 per cent—by looters may not be of major importance, from a purely archaeological point of view. On the other hand, the silver deposit is known to have contained many other relics, very well preserved,

and these must have been taken from the site along with the coins. The loss of these relics is archaeologically far more important than that of the coins.

From a financial viewpoint, how significant was the theft of so much silver? There can be no doubt that the coins had a high monetary value, especially in 1980, the year when silver reached its peak price and the caravan was destroyed. If the weight of coinage removed was about half a tonne, its silver value in early 1980 would have been as much as $500,000, equivalent to about $1,200,000 in 1995 dollars, assuming that the coins were predominantly schellings and double stuivers (58.3 per cent fine silver), with lesser numbers of ducatons and pieces of eight (94 per cent and 93 per cent fine silver). However, the same amount of silver would realize only $78,000 today, because the silver price is now much lower. Of course, the value of the coins to collectors would be far greater—probably more than $1,000,000 on the open market. Two schellings from the *Zuytdorp* were sold at auction for $340; this compares with their silver value of about $1.20.

Five years of indecision, 1981–85

The WA Museum's spate of activity on the *Zuytdorp* in the late 1970s was followed by a period of little or no action during the early 1980s. This inaction became a matter of concern to the Australia/Netherlands Committee on Old Dutch Shipwrecks (ANCODS), which had been set up to monitor progress in implementing the wreck agreement between the two countries. Under the terms of this agreement, the Netherlands Government granted ownership of early Dutch shipwrecks on the Australian coast to the Commonwealth Government, in exchange for a share of the historic material to be recovered through marine-archaeological investigations of those wrecks.

The ANCODS committee discussed the *Zuytdorp* at its meeting in August 1983, arriving at the following resolution:

> Believing its obligations will not be fulfilled until the matter of the recovery of material from the *Zuytdorp* has been resolved, the Committee requested the Director of the Western Australian Museum to furnish a report on the

Opposite: The main types of coins found at the wrecksite. Top two rows: ducatons of the Dutch Republic and Spanish Netherlands; third row: pieces of eight; fourth row: pieces of four and two; fifth row: schellings of the province of Zeeland, minted in 1711; bottom row, first two coins: schellings of the province of Utrecht; last four coins: double stuivers of the province of Zeeland, minted in 1711.

Photograph by the author

various options available for a full maritime archaeology and/
or salvage recovery of the *Zuytdorp* material and the costs of
these options.

In response to this resolution, Jeremy Green prepared a
memorandum to Ian Crawford, dated 20 February 1984,[180] setting
out what he considered to be the best options for working the
site. He pointed out that there had already been several near-fatal
accidents, and expressed the opinion that normal diving would
be impracticable without some method of modifying the sea conditions: building a breakwater, sinking a block-ship out to sea,
or utilizing a 'bubble curtain'. However, he felt that these options
would probably be too expensive in relation to the expected returns.
Green stated that the only other way to dive would be to have a five-
to six-person team based at the site for at least two years, waiting
for flat-calm conditions. He was opposed to the employment
of contractors to work the site, and felt that the option of using
underwater television equipment on a crane or gantry, together
with a grab or dredge, was potentially the most attractive method,
even though the necessary technology had yet to be developed. He
seriously questioned the ethics of conducting salvage excavation
of the site, as this 'would inevitably lead to damage of artefacts
and material. It would be preferable to leave the site for the future
[when] adequate technology and funds may be available.'

Crawford responded to this memorandum, in a report to the
Museum Director, John Bannister, on 26 April 1984, pointing out
that ANCODS was pressing for work to be done on the site, and that
unless Green could persuade that body otherwise, the museum was
committed to carrying out an excavation.[181] Crawford felt that there
was some urgency in removing the silver, but that the work must
not be destructive of artefacts or structures. He also felt that this
work should extend beyond the silver area, if practicable, so that a
normal excavation could take place and the site could be properly
documented. In response to Green's point on the ethics of conducting
a salvage operation, Crawford said that the site was at risk from
abalone divers and crayfishermen who had opportunities for looting
the silver, 'so that if we leave the site pending the development of
new technologies…little of the site may be left by the time these
are available.' Crawford recommended that an expert committee be
convened to explore the options available for excavation of the site.

Bannister responded by establishing an advisory committee to consider the matter, consisting of Dr W. Andrew (Public Works Department), Dr J.D. Penrose (Western Australian Institute of Technology), Associate Professor R. Silvester (The University of Western Australia), Captain J. Woodcock (Marine Surveyor), J.N. Green, Dr I.M. Crawford, and me.

Crawford and Green prepared a report, dated 16 July 1984, setting out options for consideration by the committee at its first meeting. Their options were to: (1) use a breakwater, block-ship, bubble curtain or floating raft to provide protection to divers from the waves; (2) use a flying fox, crane or helicopter to enter and leave the water; (3) operate from the sea by boat; (4) upgrade the airstrip, use a watchkeeper, and operate from the land on calm days; (5) use contractors to do the work; (6) use a high-powered suction dredge or grab, guided by an underwater television camera; and (7) use a dragline to recover material without using divers.[182]

The committee met four times between 19 July 1984 and 31 May 1985, and also made a visit to the *Zuytdorp* wrecksite.[183] One member advocated the construction of a breakwater, although it would involve bulldozing the cliff at the wrecksite, and result in other adverse environmental effects. Another recommended an innovative new proposal, for a 'slurry-filled-sausage breakwater' to be installed to protect the excavation site. This would involve the placing of large flexible membrane units ('sausages') on the sea-floor, which would then be pumped full of cement slurry.

Because of these divergent views, the committee made little progress in achieving a consensus. Bannister and I were unable to attend the committee's final meeting, on 31 May 1985, but Crawford as chairman communicated my views that (1) the breakwater proposal would involve unacceptable levels of damage to the environment of this historic site, (2) all other construction options would prove to be too expensive, and (3) the museum would be forced to come back to the conventional diving option. Outside the committee, Bannister and I agreed on these points, and we also concurred that the option of using contract divers should be considered if museum staff were unwilling to work the site.

The various options were considered by ANCODS at its meeting on 18–20 September 1985. It was resolved that the land-based diving option should be adopted, and that in the event of the museum being unable to undertake the project with its own staff, private contractors should be authorized to do so on behalf of the museum, in return for a proportion of any silver recovered, or its cash value. The ANCODS committee considered that the work should be undertaken as a matter of urgency 'in view of the temptation for looting still presented by the probable presence of a considerable quantity of silver at the site.' The expression 'probable presence' indicated that the committee was fully aware that the silver might have been pillaged during the five years that had elapsed since museum staff had last dived at the site.

The ANCODS resolution meant that the museum was being asked again to pursue the land-based diving option, using either its own staff or outside contractors. Soon afterwards, Bannister held a meeting with the marine archaeology staff, inviting their response to the ANCODS resolution. He stated that if they did not wish to undertake the *Zuytdorp* project themselves, he would seek contractors to do the work.

Mike McCarthy and Geoff Kimpton discussed the matter together and concluded that the site could probably be worked adequately using conventional diving methods. Indeed, they were enthusiastic about taking up the challenge. McCarthy advised Bannister that he and Kimpton, with appropriate support staff when needed, would be prepared to undertake the task, provided that Green agreed.

After further discussion, it was decided to adopt the McCarthy–Kimpton plan, and McCarthy was designated as leader of the *Zuytdorp* team. He and Kimpton were joined periodically by Jon Carpenter (diver and conservator) and Pat Baker (diver and photographer), with assistance from others as required.[184]

Archaeological research since 1986

I was delighted to learn of the museum's plans to resume work on the *Zuytdorp*, and readily agreed to a request from Mike McCarthy to join his team as its historical adviser. In late 1986, I recommenced my historical research, seeking from the Netherlands and Jakarta copies of original documents relating to the ship and its voyages, and obtaining information on all known visits to the wrecksite and its surrounds, from 1927 to the present. I later undertook a thorough study of all relevant museum files.

McCarthy and Kimpton formed an effective partnership in exploring the wreck and recovering artefacts. McCarthy is a skilful diver and good organizer who 'gets things done', and he has a special ability to gain cooperation from people with diverse backgrounds. Kimpton, a very experienced and courageous diver, was responsible for the major part of the diving activities. McCarthy acknowledges that the *Zuytdorp* project could never have succeeded without the diving skills, stamina and enthusiasm of Kimpton, who recovered most relics from the wreck, and was prepared to operate under difficult sea conditions. They were jointly responsible for preparing the plan of the wrecksite.

McCarthy and Kimpton began the new project with reconnaissance dives on the wreck, on 27 April and 3 May 1986. Kimpton told me that as soon as he dived at the site, he recognized that the carpet of silver had almost vanished. Most of the coins and accompanying artefacts must have been pillaged during the seven years that had elapsed since museum personnel last dived on the wreck.

After returning to Perth, McCarthy drew up plans for his team's investigation of the *Zuytdorp*, involving considerably more than the recommended minimum requirement of a salvage operation to remove the silver.[185] The principal features of this plan became: (1) examination of the wreck itself, concentrating on the preparation of a site plan, removal of visible coins, and the excavation and recovery of significant artefacts; (2) archival research; (3) examination of the survivors' campsites and other material remains; (4) search for evidence of movements of the survivors away from the wrecksite; (5) examination of the artefacts recovered; (6) compilation of all written, visual and oral material on the wreck; (7) cataloguing of all 'declared' material that may be disclosed through an amnesty; (8) restoration of the *Zuytdorp* land site; and (9) publication, in written and video format, of the results obtained. Most of these tasks have since been completed or are in progress.

The next dives on the site by Kimpton and McCarthy were accomplished on 2, 13 and 14 March 1987, under conditions that were far from ideal. They concentrated their efforts on an accumulation of relics in the armoury concretion between coin rock and the platform. This concretion was about 15–45 centimetres thick, originally forming a strongly cemented layer in a hole on the rocky sea-floor, about 1 metre in diameter and 4 metres from the edge of the platform. Debris from the wreck, including items that may once have been stored in the ship's armoury, had packed into this hole soon after the ship was wrecked, and the mass of debris was rapidly cemented together by the growth of lime-secreting organisms, principally coralline algae and serpulid worms, and lime cement. Items recovered included many coins, together with a variety of artefacts, the most interesting of which were a sword handle and scabbard. Surprisingly, some leather and wood were still preserved in the scabbard.

McCarthy, as the leader of the project, was often loath to approve diving when he felt that conditions could be too dangerous. However, Kimpton, as the more experienced diver, and one who was comfortable with white-water conditions because of his background as a teenage 'surfie', would press McCarthy to approve diving even when conditions may have seemed hazardous. McCarthy went against his better judgment on several occasions, in allowing diving to proceed. He noted in his journal on 12 March 1987:

> [I was] continuously troubled by Geoff's desire to do everything his way on this trip. He is unable to compromise and bullies his way through. Again we are successful, however, due to his tenacity.

Such problems continued on subsequent trips, but McCarthy's respect for Kimpton's judgment and ability grew with each dive. On one occasion, on 1 June 1987, he wrote:

> Geoff has been absolutely incredible and must at all times be credited [for] his strength, endurance, ability, and common sense. Our differences, partly due to lack of understanding, [are] now resolved.

On a later dive, on 2 February 1988, McCarthy again recorded his growing admiration of Kimpton's ability, tinged with continued anxiety about safety:

> Geoff continued working [on the bottom], having wedged himself in with a crowbar, and recovered three full bags of material—coins, brass, firearm side plates, a shot dispenser, a comb, wood, glass, and ceramics. He is a real 'crab', and

difficult to dislodge by wave or human force. All credit again
to Geoff, and it is clear as indicated before that there are few
if any men [to] my knowledge who could or would even
attempt such feats.

There is a very fine line between brilliant success and
savage recrimination to be borne in the case of death or
injury at this site. Geoff takes me to the very edge of that
line, though to date we have not crossed it. Such are the
responsibilities which bear heavily [on me] in the light of
Geoff's single-minded attention to the job, which has been
his hallmark in all his endeavours—*Batavia* timbers, *Xantho*
engine and hull, *Zuytdorp*, etc.

Of course, McCarthy well knew that there had been some
opposition within the museum, on safety grounds, to his plans for
diving on the *Zuytdorp*, and that he would be held culpable if there
were a serious accident at the site. Diving on this wreck is always
hazardous, and McCarthy and Kimpton were fortunate not to
receive any significant injuries during their dives, especially as sea
conditions were never ideal when they were at the site. They always
yearned to be there during the one or two days each year when the
sea is completely calm, but regrettably this never came about.

McCarthy dived again at the site on 8 May 1987, and decided
then that on the next dive, some of the estimated fifty to sixty lead
ingots known to be present at the wrecksite should be raised. This
happened on 31 May, when he and Kimpton used airbags to lift
several ingots, towing them out into deeper water for later recovery.
As a result of this successful operation, McCarthy decided that they
should also seek to raise an anchor and a cannon. The ingots were
taken on board the *Jolly Roger*, a boat from Kalbarri skippered by
Andrew Young, on 2 June.[186] On the following day, there was a low
swell, but they decided to dive again from the boat, even though
McCarthy recorded that there was 'white water breaking over
Geoff'. They succeeded in raising more lead ingots, bringing the
total raised to sixteen, of which the largest is 78 centimetres long,
27 centimetres wide, weighs 140.68 kilograms, and is inscribed
with the date 1702. The total weight of all sixteen ingots is more
than a tonne. During the dive, they also found a group of fifteen
brass dividers resting in a hole on the sea-floor, and a large wooden
pulley sheave.

Lead ballast ingots on the sea-floor at the Zuytdorp wrecksite (June 1977).

Photograph by Jeremy Green, courtesy of the WA Maritime Museum

The conditions on this dive were such that they could not have got in and out of the water from the land; the use of a boat was essential. It was therefore decided that future diving should always be done from a boat, as this would be safer, especially when deteriorating conditions made it necessary for them to leave the water. McCarthy arranged for Alison and Bic Glass to act as the museum's observers in Kalbarri, with the idea that they would call him whenever sea and weather conditions seemed suitable for diving. McCarthy would then get his team together and drive from Perth to Kalbarri, towing a fast work boat that could be used to reach the wrecksite.

On 1 February 1988, a call from Alison Glass indicated that conditions were suitable, so McCarthy, Kimpton and Baker immediately drove up from Perth. Next day, they went to the site in the museum's boat, departing from Kalbarri at 7.10 a.m. and arriving at the wrecksite at 8.40 a.m. There was a low swell running, but it seemed that conditions would be suitable to begin work on raising an anchor and a cannon that had previously been targeted for removal. However, on entering the water they

Mike McCarthy jumping into the water at the wrecksite (May 1987).

Photograph by Pat Baker, courtesy of the WA Maritime Museum

were surprised to find that most of the site was covered by sand, estimated to be about 2 metres thick.

Two days later, they returned to the site by boat, and Kimpton and Baker were again surprised: in this relatively short time, sand about a metre thick had been swept away from the site. The cannon that had earlier been chosen for recovery, about 10 metres south-west of 'toe rock', was now exposed. It was cemented to the sea-floor by lime concretion, and Kimpton used a 10-tonne hydraulic jack to dislodge it. They successfully lifted the gun, using airbags, and towed it about 400 metres offshore, in water 15 metres deep, where it was placed on the sandy bottom.

They returned on 12 February, to find that the sand around the cannon had been swept away completely, and it was now resting on bare rock. However, conditions were not suitable to take the gun on board, as there was a moderate swell running.[187] It was not until 21 February that they were able to haul the cannon aboard the museum's boat *Henrietta*.

This well-preserved iron cannon is 2.59 metres long, with a bore of 11.2 centimetres. During treatment to conserve the gun, it was found to have been loaded, with the cannonball still lying in place. Both the ball, weighing 3.556 kilograms, and the charge were readily removed and have since been conserved. The presence of a broad-arrow symbol stamped on the gun's upper surface shows that it is of British origin, having no doubt been purchased from England by the VOC.

Further dives were made on 5 and 6 March 1988, during which McCarthy and Kimpton worked on the site plan and recovered many relics from the armoury concretion. The most remarkable of these is a beautifully preserved wine glass, made of clear, colourless glass, engraved with a wreath of leaves around its rim and decorated elsewhere with floral and pictorial motifs, including a building with towers and flagstaffs.[188] It seems incredible that such a fragile object could have survived for 275 years in shallow water subject to extremely violent wave action. It must originally have been held in place in the wreck by a mass of debris that was rapidly cemented together by the growth of lime concretion, thus protecting the glass from breakage and erosion.

During the next dive, on 15 March 1988, Kimpton used the jack to dislodge an anchor lying about 10 metres south-south-east of toe rock. He lifted it with airbags, then towed it out into deep water, where it was placed on the bottom. Next day, the anchor was taken on board the *Henrietta*. After cleaning and stabilization, it will be placed on display, as the largest anchor to have been recovered from any Dutch wreck on the Western Australian coast.

McCarthy and Kimpton did not dive on the wreck again until four years later, on 17 March 1992, travelling to the site by boat from Kalbarri. They worked on the armoury concretion and also recovered a number of lead ingots. However, the most interesting discovery was that of a bronze adze-like object, north of the location where the cluster of dividers, probably originally in a box, had been found. The adze and dividers were situated further from the shore than any other objects that have been found. They were probably tipped out of the upper cargo soon after the ship first struck the sea-floor and heeled over, swivelling around parallel to the coast (see Map 7).

Fourteen months later, on 14 May 1993, McCarthy and Kimpton dived again, and decided, for the first time, to use explosives in working the armoury concretion. A short length of

Wine glass recovered from the Zuytdorp *wreck by Geoff Kimpton (March 1988).*

Photograph by Pat Baker, courtesy of the WA Maritime Museum

gelignite was used, being placed about 1 metre away from the concretion itself. This method proved to be very effective in breaking up the concretion, and the divers recovered many large pieces for treatment in the conservation laboratory of the WA Maritime Museum. It was concluded that this means of excavation caused less damage to artefacts than the traditional method of chipping away with a geological pick. However, diving conditions were far

Geoff Kimpton freeing an anchor on the sea-floor (March 1988).

Photograph by Jon Carpenter, courtesy of the WA Maritime Museum

from ideal on this day, with a low swell, and it proved impossible for McCarthy and Kimpton to collect the smaller material that had been broken away, before having to leave the site.

Three years later, on 3 April 1996, museum staff resumed diving on the wreck, experiencing the best sea conditions of the past ten years. Mike McCarthy, Geoff Kimpton and Ian Godfrey recovered many relics, especially coins, and Jon Carpenter took an excellent underwater videotape of the wreck. The divers noted that large numbers of coins are still present in potholes and crevices on the sea-floor between coin rock and the edge of the platform. There can be little doubt that if this visible silver, probably worth thousands of dollars, is not recovered by the museum, it will eventually be taken illegally, as unprotected 'treasure' acts as a lure to divers. Legal deterrents have proved ineffective in protecting the wreck, as it has been virtually impossible to apprehend pillagers, some of whom have been identified through the recent amnesty but are immune from prosecution. Moreover, anyone taking material illegally can always hope that another amnesty will allow them to gain legal rights to their ill-gotten gains. Consequently, I believe it is imperative that the WA Maritime Museum be adequately funded

and encouraged to complete its marine-archaeological and salvage work on the wreck, thereby removing the incentive for further looting.

An anchor from the Zuytdorp (recovered March 1988).

Photograph by Jeremy Green, courtesy of the WA Maritime Museum

McCarthy recognized at the outset of the *Zuytdorp* project that there was also a need for archaeological investigations of associated land sites. These included relevant Aboriginal sites, both close to and remote from the wrecksite, in the belief that these might provide evidence of interaction between Aborigines and the survivors. The localities remote from the wrecksite are discussed in Chapter 6, which deals with hypotheses regarding the fate of the survivors.

A lot of excavation had already taken place at land sites near the wreck before professional archaeologists could examine them. Significant sites linked with the survivors had been identified, on the 1954 expedition, at the foot of the cliffs (the breech-blocks locality), the top of the cliffs (where a large fire, probably a signal fire, had been lit), and at two localities about 1 kilometre inland, where the survivors had probably camped and found water (see site nos 1 and 2, Map 5). Each of these sites had been partly excavated during the 1954 and 1958 expeditions, and the results were reported in my

1959 Historical Society publication. Since then, there have been unauthorized excavations carried out, by unknown persons, at several of these sites, without recorded results.

A third possible campsite of the survivors was found in 1981 by Robert Lamera, when he noted part of the stem of a clay pipe lying on the track half a kilometre east-north-east of his father's hut (see site no. 3, Map 5). This site has not yet been archaeologically examined, but an area of about 20 square metres was raked and dug by Dominic and Robert Lamera, who also used metal-detectors to seek metallic objects. This work was not authorized by the WA Museum, although Dominic Lamera subsequently advised museum personnel of his find. He showed me many fragments of clay pipes, including well-preserved bowls, that he and his son collected there, and I brought them to Perth for Mike McCarthy to examine. Lamera told me that they also found parts of two large keys and an iron ring at the site. The clay pipes are identical to some that had been found at campsite no. 1.

It is hard to deduce why survivors would have selected this site as a camp, as it is now situated in the midst of dense tea-tree scrub, and is 2 kilometres from the wrecksite. Perhaps the vegetation pattern was different in 1712, and the camp was then located beyond the eastern margin of the tea-tree thicket. Alternatively, the coastal belt might have been burnt not long before by Aborigines, and the new growth of tea-trees was still low.

In 1987, Fiona Weaver and Mike McCarthy made detailed archaeological examinations of the sites at the cliff top (the signal-fire site) and cliff base (the breech-block site),[189] and reported their results to the WA Maritime Museum. Both sites had been severely altered by earlier excavations, so systematic archaeological work was now of limited value. However, Weaver commented that both sites 'have evidence to support the descriptions of Playford regarding the presence of "fireplaces" and the range of artefacts which he described as present during his expeditions.' The most significant new discovery was that of a copper token, of French origin, at the signal-fire site. This may have been a personal possession of one of the survivors.

In the same year, an archaeological survey was conducted by Kate Morse, assisted by McCarthy, of accumulations of shells that museum staff had noted beside the cliff top near the *Zuytdorp* wrecksite.[190] The purpose of this work was to determine whether such deposits represented Aboriginal kitchen middens, or refuse left by survivors of the shipwreck, or combinations of both. The investigation indicated not only that they were Aboriginal middens, but that they pre-dated the *Zuytdorp* wreck. A shell from a midden 200 metres south-east of the wrecksite gave a radiocarbon dating of 4,000 years.

It was concluded, from Morse's work, that the Aboriginal people had ceased gathering shellfish in this area long before the *Zuytdorp* was wrecked. The reason for this has not been established, but one possibility is that there was a fatal episode of food poisoning among Aborigines after eating shellfish, which then became taboo as a food source. However, survivors of the *Zuytdorp* would have had no such aversion to shellfish. They no doubt gathered them to supplement food supplies from the wreck, although Morse found no evidence of shell accumulations that could be definitely linked with the survivors.

The only human skeletal material that has been found at the wrecksite consists of a thighbone, located by Dominic Lamera about 8 metres north of the northern corner of bathtub pool, in 1988. It was wedged, with other wreck-derived debris, in a fissure on the shoreline platform. No bones have been found on the sea-floor, and no burial sites are known on land.

The bodies of scores of crew members must have been cast ashore immediately after the *Zuytdorp* was wrecked, along with tonnes of wreckage and cargo. There was nowhere at the cliff base where bodies could be buried, and the survivors, in their traumatized state, would not have had the energy, or inclination, to carry them to the cliff top and beyond for burial. If the bodies were allowed to decay in the open, the resulting stench would surely have been unbearable, especially when the survivors were attempting to salvage material from the wreck. Consequently, they may have decided to cremate the bodies, using timber from the ship. If this was the case, the general lack of skeletal material at the base of the cliffs is not surprising.

Some survivors may have died at their campsites not long after coming ashore, as a result of injuries sustained during their escape from the wreck. Their shipmates would probably have buried them in sand somewhere behind the cliffs. The bones of these people may well remain there today, but their burial sites have yet to be identified.

The Fate of
the Survivors

THE principal remaining mystery surrounding the wreck of the *Zuytdorp* concerns the fate of its survivors. We know that a number of people escaped from the wreck and lived nearby for some time, but none ever returned to civilization to tell their story. There are three main hypotheses to explain what eventually happened to them: they may have lingered and died near the coast, unsuccessfully attempted to sail a boat to Batavia, or joined the Aborigines.[191]

Circumstances of the wreck

It is known that the ship's complement, on departure from the Cape, consisted of 200 persons, of whom an estimated 80 to 90 were newcomers. More than half had been with the ship for the 10 months since it left Zeeland. They had survived the disastrous passage to the Cape, and no doubt believed that the worst of the voyage was now behind them. Little did they realize what lay ahead.

The voyage over the Indian Ocean to the coast of Western Australia probably occupied only five to six weeks, and it is likely that few of the ship's complement would have died during this period. By way of comparison, only one person was lost on the *Belvliet* during its nine-week voyage from the Cape to Batavia. Consequently, it is reasonable to surmise that nearly 200 people were still on board the *Zuytdorp* when it sailed within sight of the coast of Western Australia, around the first week of June 1712.

The ship approached the coast near latitude 27° south, in accordance with the VOC sailing instructions for that time of the year. I believe it probably encountered an early winter storm and was running under short sail before a westerly or south-westerly gale, when the forbidding cliffs suddenly loomed into view through a curtain of rain and spray, accompanied by the terrifying thunder of surf. If this scenario is correct, there was little that could be done. The big square-rigged ships of that time were unable to tack effectively when driven before a gale, so the *Zuytdorp* could not have avoided disaster as it was driven relentlessly towards the cliffs.

Archaeological evidence on the sea-floor, obtained by Mike McCarthy and Geoff Kimpton, suggests that the ship may have first struck bottom about 45–50 metres from the edge of the shoreline platform. It then swivelled around, parallel to the coast, with its stern to the north-west and bows to the south-east (see Map 7). The ship's position soon after it first ran aground is indicated by those relics that were found furthest from the shore: an adze-like brass object and a group of fifteen dividers, which presumably were tipped overboard as the ship heeled over. The adze location is shown fairly reliably on the site map, but the position of the dividers, a similar distance offshore, could be plotted only approximately, because of rough sea conditions when they were found.

After first striking the bottom and swivelling around, the ship must have been driven sideways towards the shore, with its hull crashing on the rocky sea-bed and surf sweeping the lurching and steeply sloping decks. Cannon must have broken free at that time, rolling along the decks and crushing people and woodwork. One or more masts probably snapped and came crashing down in a tangle of rigging and sails. The bottom of the ship was torn out, flooding the holds and leaving lead ballast behind on the sea-floor. Although most of the hull would have remained more or less intact at that time, the ship was still too far—about 25 metres—from the platform to allow anyone to reach land alive through the maelstrom of swirling surf. Those who were not swept overboard or drowned below the decks would have clung to the rigging or woodwork, as the flooded ship, heeled over on its side and swept by waves, was progressively pushed closer towards the shore.

Eventually, it seems likely that the relentless pounding broke the hull into three major pieces, which were driven separately into very shallow water, 1–2 metres deep, beside the platform. This fragmentation of the hull is suggested by the spread of cannon, anchors, coins and other relics on the sea-floor in a belt 75 metres long, compared with the ship's length of 45 metres. The stern section came to rest over coin rock, the central section over toe rock, and the smaller bow section against collapsed blocks of platform in the little bay between toe rock and sloping rock. The chests of silver coins, carried in the captain's cabin below the poop deck, eventually fell to the bottom among the wreckage beside coin rock, while the eight anchors carried in the forward part of the ship ended up around toe rock and in the little bay immediately south of there.

The wrecksite, looking south-west from the top of the cliff, showing 'toe rock' (where central section of the wreck lies) on the left and 'coin rock' (where stern section lies) on the right (see Map 7).

Photograph by the author

The distribution of anchors and cannon on the sea-floor indicates that the stern and central sections of the *Zuytdorp* must have been driven against the edge of the platform, or very close to it, allowing some of the people who had survived on those sections to scramble ashore using the tangled rigging and stubs of masts extending over the platform. However, if anyone had remained on the small bow section, they would have found it impossible to reach land, because of the jumbled mass of wave-swept rocks between the bow and the edge of the platform.

How many survived?

It is not possible to make a reliable estimate of the number of people who survived the wreck. Of the nearly 200 people who were on board when the vessel first struck, most must have drowned or otherwise been killed during the horrific period when the ship was being driven sideways towards the platform. Perhaps fewer than fifty remained alive when the stern and central sections of the wreck, still lurching about and progressively breaking up, were forced against the platform margin. It is hard to judge how much time elapsed between the ship first striking bottom and the wreck reaching its final resting place. If there was a big swell running, it might have been only an hour or two.

Among those who had survived to that time, several would have perished or been seriously injured while attempting to scramble ashore from the wreck over the wave-swept and debris-strewn platform. Some were no doubt swept into the hole on the platform opposite the stern section of the wreck. Others probably died soon afterwards, as a result of injuries sustained in scrambling ashore. People without adequate footwear would have had their feet lacerated by the sharp rocks and shells on the platform surface. My guess is that no more than thirty people, some injured and all in a state of shock, were able to climb the cliff and survey the scene of devastation below. The wretched castaways would have been soaking wet, chilled to the bone by cold winter winds, and without shelter. They would behold a forbidding line of precipitous cliffs extending north and south as far as the eye could see, while behind them lay a belt of bare, windswept limestone and sand, followed by dense scrub: a singularly desolate scene. Some survivors no doubt tried to drown their despair with liquor that had been cast ashore, as witnessed by the debris of broken bottles remaining scattered along the cliff top more than 240 years later.

The castaways found themselves in a fearful predicament. How could they possibly escape from this dreadful place? Was life worth living if they could not? The following sections explore three possible explanations of their eventual fate.

Death near the wrecksite?

One of the first priorities of any officers who survived, after the initial period of trauma had passed, would have been to determine the geographic location of the wrecksite, so they could decide what to do next. Perhaps the skipper or a steersman was among the survivors, and was eventually able to climb back onto the stern section of the wreck to salvage navigation instruments and maps. That this did occur is suggested by the fact that two pairs of dividers, used in scaling positions on maps, were found behind the edge of the cliff above the wrecksite, and a graduated set square, for marking out courses on maps, was picked up near the base of the cliff. No trace was found of any back-staff that may have been brought ashore to determine the latitude, but, being made of wood, such an instrument could not have lasted for more than a few years.

After determining the latitude—about 27°11′ south—the officer concerned would have known that the wreck was close to the position where VOC ships were authorized to approach the Land of the Eendracht at that time of the year. The castaways could see a long way out to sea from their cliff-top vantage point, so they would have had a good chance of seeing passing ships. With the objective of attracting the attention of such ships, they apparently hauled large amounts of wooden wreckage to the cliff top, ready to ignite as a huge bonfire when a ship sailed into view.

The survivors may also have concluded that a cannon would be effective in signalling a passing ship, especially if fired while the bonfire was blazing. None of the large iron cannon could be carried ashore, as they were much too heavy, but the survivors may have hoped to recover one of the smaller bronze swivel guns that were mounted on the poop deck. It seems clear that this deck, the highest part of the ship, was still accessible from the shore at that time, as the survivors managed to carry off about eight breech blocks belonging to those swivel guns. These bronze objects, each weighing about 13 kilograms, were placed together in a bare area among boulders at the foot of the cliff. The survivors probably intended that several breech blocks would be loaded and made ready to use in a swivel gun, allowing it to be fired rapidly to attract attention.[192]

However, they did not succeed in carrying off any of the guns. The stern section may have broken up before this could be achieved, or it may have proved physically impossible to man-handle a gun from the wreck to the shore. The breech blocks were then abandoned, to be found 215 years later by Tom Pepper.

As the castaways were unable to secure a cannon, they could only employ bonfires in trying to attract attention from a passing ship, and clear evidence was found that they did indeed ignite such fires. At least one huge bonfire was lit immediately above the wreck in a small area that is partly sheltered from north-west winds by a small cliff (see Map 7). Excavation of this site during the 1954 expedition disclosed a layer of charcoal and ashes about 10–30 centimetres below the ground surface. This layer also contained metallic material—brass hinges, ornate brass clasps, other parts of chests, completely rusted iron objects, including barrel rungs, and some globular pieces of brass that had evidently been melted by the intense heat of the blaze. It seems likely that this material remained from a signal fire designed to attract attention from one or more ships seen by the survivors. They probably threw all available wood onto the bonfire, including chests and barrels, in a desperate attempt to be seen. Further fires may have been lit on several occasions at this spot as successive ships sailed by. Similar evidence suggests that another big fire was lit in the small bare area where the breech blocks were found, near the base of the cliff. However, that fire may possibly have been lit for cremation purposes, rather than as a signal to a passing ship.

During the few weeks following the wreck, as many as seven ships could have passed this stretch of the coast. The first of these may have been the *Kockenge*, which departed from the Cape with the *Zuytdorp* on 22 April but, being a slower vessel, was left behind next day. The *Kockenge* reached Batavia on 4 July, and it may well have passed the wrecksite within a week of the *Zuytdorp* being lost there. Other ships that might have sailed along this stretch of coast in June–July 1712 include four that left the Cape on 9 May—the *Belvliet* (arrived Batavia 18 July), *Oostersteyn* (arrived 8 July), *Zuyderbeeck* (arrived 17 July) and *Popkensburg* (arrived 22 July)— and two, the *Corsloot* and *Oude Zyp*, that left the Cape on 20 May and arrived in Batavia on 28 July.[193]

It is possible, if not likely, that the *Zuytdorp* castaways saw several of these vessels. They may have lit a signal fire on each occasion, only to watch the ship sail by without acknowledgment. The wretched survivors, in their despair, probably guessed that the crews of those vessels believed the fires to be those of native inhabitants of the South Land, as the VOC navigators often commented on the number of fires seen on this coast. Nevertheless, they would have hoped that some of those crew members, on learning of the non-arrival of the *Zuytdorp* in Batavia, might link the bonfires with the missing ship, and alert the authorities accordingly. There is no record that anyone did so, and in any case no action was ever taken to search for the *Zuytdorp* or its survivors.

The authorities in both Batavia and the Netherlands probably decided that it would be a hopeless task to search for the ship, as they had no knowledge of where it had been wrecked. Earlier search expeditions, for the *Vergulde Draeck* and *Ridderschap van Holland*, had failed to find the wrecks of those vessels or any survivors, and the authorities would have had no wish to repeat such fruitless and costly exercises.

Of course, the castaways of the *Zuytdorp* would have had no way of knowing this. Some may have been aware that Willem de Vlamingh's expedition, fifteen years before, had been made to search for the *Ridderschap van Holland*, the last vessel to disappear on a voyage from the Cape to Batavia. They may have thought that a search vessel would similarly be sent to look for the *Zuytdorp*, especially if their signal fires had been observed and reported. Consequently, they may have lingered for many months near the wrecksite in the vain hope that a search vessel would eventually appear.

In this connection, the question arises as to what the survivors would have done if they had succeeded in attracting the attention of a search vessel. How could they have been taken on board from this very exposed coast? It is difficult to be sure of what they might have had in mind. However, there is a small beach about

600 metres south of the wrecksite, fronted by a gently sloping rocky sea-floor. The castaways may have thought that a small boat could land at this site during a spell of calm conditions, take people on board, and return safely to the ship.

In hypothesizing on what might have happened to the survivors, it is important to note that the report of a wreck that was received in Perth in 1834 from Aborigines living somewhere near Shark Bay (see Chapter 3) indicated that survivors had lived in five 'houses'—two large and three small—constructed from timber and canvas and situated on the open coast.[194] As discussed earlier, I am confident that this report referred to the *Zuytdorp*, and it seems likely that the castaways would indeed have constructed tents, or 'houses', from sails and timber wreckage. The three places where numerous relics of the survivors were found (see Map 5) may have been sites of some of the tents. At the closest of these sites to the wreck, the survivors would have had unobstructed views of the sea, so that lookouts could be maintained for passing ships.

Food should not have been a major problem for the castaways for at least several weeks. Barrels of food and drink must have been thrown ashore from the wreck, and it may also have been possible to gain direct access to provision stores on board before the wreck broke up completely. Abundant shellfish, especially oysters and abalone, could also be collected on the shoreline platform, and the survivors may have been able to catch fish and shoot wildlife, such as kangaroos, with muskets salvaged from the wreck, provided that they could also salvage enough useable gunpowder and musket balls.

Water supplies would not initially have been a great problem. The ship was wrecked in early winter, and rainfall during the following two to three months would probably have yielded enough water for the people to survive. They could collect runoff from the sails used to cover their shelters, and store it in barrels. They may also have obtained water from gnamma holes in the limestone and from the little creeks that flow briefly after heavy rain. However, the water situation would have become critical during spring, once the rains ceased.

With the onset of the hot, dry summer, the castaways would undoubtedly have perished if they chose to remain near the wrecksite. It is possible that they would nevertheless have lingered there, still hoping that their signal fires had been recognized and that a rescue vessel would be despatched. But if they did decide to remain at the wrecksite, all would have eventually died of thirst, as permanent water does not exist there. The nearest water is at the Aboriginal soak named Billiecutherra, 13 kilometres to the south-east, while there are several other small soaks 15–20 kilometres inland. However, it is unlikely that the survivors could have found any of these without assistance from Aborigines.

The chart of the Western Australian coast carried by the *Zuytdorp* would have been based on that prepared by Willem de Vlamingh in 1696–97. His map clearly shows where he obtained drinking water near Red Bluff (Roode Houk), about 65 kilometres south of the *Zuytdorp* wrecksite, at the southern end of Gantheaume Bay. If the skipper or another officer of the *Zuytdorp* had survived, he may have known that water could be obtained there. The castaways might therefore have set out to walk to Gantheaume Bay before water supplies at the wrecksite became exhausted.

On the other hand, Vlamingh's map also showed a large embayment (Shark Bay) about 60 kilometres to the north, and although Vlamingh did not report any fresh water there, they may have thought that it was a likely place for water to occur. Consequently, some survivors could have decided to walk north, especially if they were guided there by Aborigines.

There has been some speculation that a low wall on the shoreline of Epineux Bay (Crayfish Bay), 110 kilometres north of the wrecksite, could have been built by survivors of the *Zuytdorp*.[195] It is roughly constructed of limestone boulders, and its original purpose is unknown. The wall is said to have already been there when the first pastoralists arrived. However, there is no positive evidence to link it with the *Zuytdorp* survivors, and it could possibly have been associated with early whaling activities in the area, which pre-dated the arrival of the pastoralists.

Escape by boat?

There are five well-documented cases of castaways succeeding in sailing small boats from the Western Australian coast to Java during the seventeenth and eighteenth centuries. The first was the voyage of two boats from the English ship *Tryall*, which was wrecked near the Montebello Islands in 1622.[196] They were sailed successfully to Batavia with forty-seven survivors, including the skipper, John Brookes. The second voyage was in 1629, when Francisco Pelsaert and forty-eight others sailed the longboat of the *Batavia* from the Houtman Abrolhos to Batavia.[197] The third was in 1656, when the understeersman and six other crew members of the *Vergulde Draeck* sailed one of the ship's boats from near Ledge Point to Batavia.[198] Then there was the epic journey of Abraham Leeman and thirteen other sailors who attempted to sail a small boat from near Ledge Point to Batavia in 1658. Their boat was destroyed on the south coast of Java, but Leeman and three others eventually managed to reach the VOC base at Japara.[199] The fifth case, and in some respects the most remarkable, was that of the *Zeewyk* survivors, who constructed a small ship on Gun Island and sailed it successfully to Batavia in 1728.[200]

Only one definite case is known of survivors of a VOC shipwreck disappearing while attempting to sail an open boat from Western Australia to Java. This was in 1727, when the upper-steersman and eleven other survivors from the *Zeewyk* left Gun Island in the ship's longboat, intending to reach Batavia, but were never heard of again. It is also known that survivors of the *Vergulde Draeck* were trying to extricate a small boat that was largely buried in sand when the other ship's boat left for Batavia. However, if they did manage to salvage this damaged boat and make it seaworthy, they did not succeed in completing the voyage. Of course, there is no way of determining whether other unsuccessful attempts to sail small boats to Batavia were made by survivors from VOC vessels whose fate was unknown after leaving the Cape—the *Zuytdorp*, *Ridderschap van Holland*, *Fortuyn* and *Aagtekerke*.

The location and circumstances of the wreck of the *Zuytdorp* make it most unlikely that a ship's boat could have been brought ashore intact or in a repairable state. Moreover, even if one was recovered, the chances of launching it successfully from the shoreline platform at the wrecksite would have been remote. It thus seems improbable that the survivors tried to sail one of the ship's boats from the wrecksite to Batavia.

However, the castaways could conceivably have considered building a boat from wreckage of the *Zuytdorp*, just as the *Zeewyk* survivors did, sixteen years later. Much would depend on the special skills of those who survived and the tools that could be salvaged from the wreck. At least one carpenter with boat-building skills and the necessary tools of trade would be needed. They would also have had to find a suitable place to build and launch a boat, and to complete its construction before their water supplies were exhausted.

It may have been possible for the survivors to construct a boat at the small beach about 600 metres south of the wrecksite, and launch it there during a relatively calm period. We have no way of determining whether they attempted to do this, although in my opinion it is unlikely, because of the practical difficulties involved. In any case, if they were able to build and launch a boat, they did not succeed in reaching Java.

Union with Aborigines?

The most intriguing hypothesis regarding the fate of the survivors is that some joined the Aborigines, cohabiting with them, producing offspring, and living out their lives as members of the local tribe. If so, they could perhaps have been Australia's first permanent European inhabitants, seventy-six years before the British colonized the east coast at Sydney Cove. However, this honour could earlier have belonged to the two *Batavia* mutineers (1629) or the survivors of the *Vergulde Draeck* (1656), provided that these people lived long enough to be considered as 'settlers'.

Behaviour of Aborigines towards the survivors

There can be no doubt that local Aborigines would have known of the *Zuytdorp* wreck, either just as it occurred or soon afterwards. Indeed, some may have witnessed the ship being driven ashore and the survivors scrambling off the wreck and climbing the cliff. Ever since the voyage of Dirk Hartog, nearly 100 years before, the Aborigines of this area must have been used to seeing Dutch ships sailing along the coast, but this was the first time that one of them had been cast ashore. Even if none of the Aborigines saw the actual event, they must soon have learned of it, as smoke from the survivors' fires would have drawn them to the site.

The *Zuytdorp* was wrecked just north of the boundary between territories of the Malgana Tribe of Shark Bay and the

Nanda Tribe (also spelled Nhanda and Nhanta by linguists) of the lower Murchison River (see Map 8).[201] I was told by elderly Aborigines, during the late 1950s, that this boundary extended approximately through Gee Gie, 25 kilometres south-east of the wreck. Consequently, the blacks who arrived at the site would have been members of the Malgana Tribe: an important factor in ascertaining where the survivors might have gone after leaving the wrecksite.

The appearance of naked blacks, armed with spears, probably added to the trauma of the desperate survivors. The blacks themselves must also have been astounded by the abrupt arrival of these strange white people. The story of a wreck and its survivors that reached Perth in 1834, almost certainly referring to the *Zuytdorp*,[202] illustrates what a sensational impact the event had on the local Aboriginal population. News of the wreck no doubt spread far and wide among neighbouring tribes, and the story was still well known more than 120 years later.

Newly arrived whites were commonly regarded with awe by Aborigines, who often believed they were spirits of the dead who should be given assistance if needed.[203] The Aborigines of the area between Cape Cuvier and North West Cape, 300–600 kilometres north of the *Zuytdorp* wrecksite, were very kind to survivors of the barque *Stefano*, wrecked in 1875. Only two men were eventually rescued, but, without assistance from the blacks, none could have survived. Their story gives a fascinating insight into the generous attitudes of Aborigines who had previously experienced only minimal contact with Europeans.[204]

The Aborigines who met the *Zuytdorp* survivors in 1712 would no doubt have heard from their parents and grandparents about Wouter Loos and Jan Pelgrom, the two *Batavia* mutineers who were marooned, not far away, in 1629. The Aborigines' attitude towards the newly arrived survivors must have been influenced by their knowledge of those two men. I believe that the place where the mutineers were put ashore is the small cove beside Red Bluff, near the present town of Kalbarri, only 65 kilometres south of the *Zuytdorp* wrecksite. However, some authors have maintained that the Hutt River, 60 kilometres south of Kalbarri, is the place where they were landed.[205] The issue is reviewed in the appendix.

The Aborigines of the area around the *Zuytdorp* wrecksite are unlikely to have behaved aggressively, as long as the castaways

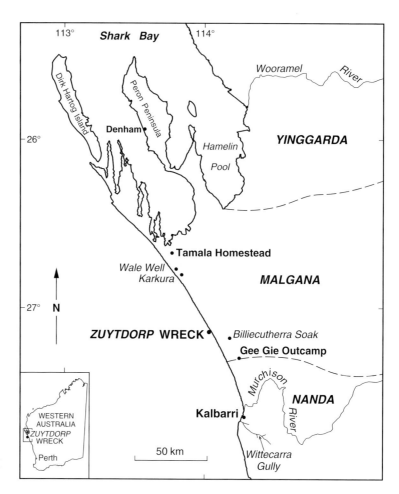

Map 8.
Territories of the
Nanda, Malgana and
Yinggarda Aborigines

did not shoot or otherwise provoke them, and provided that the
Aborigines had not been adversely affected by the behaviour of
Wouter Loos and Jan Pelgrom many years earlier. Good relations
may soon have been established with the Aborigines, who probably
made many visits to the survivors' campsites, in order to satisfy
their curiosity about these strange people. Indeed, the 1834
report from 'Wayl men' in this area indicated that the survivors
made friends with the Aborigines, giving them food ('biscuit') and
receiving spears and shields in return.

Initially, the survivors might not have felt any great need for
assistance from Aborigines. They may have had enough water and

food for their immediate needs, and would have been most intent on attracting the attention of a passing ship in order to escape. On the other hand, one of their probable campsites, 1.2 kilometres north-east of the wrecksite (site no. 1, Map 5), was situated near at least one good gnamma hole, which would have been difficult for them to find without Aboriginal assistance, suggesting that the castaways may have obtained help from the blacks at an early stage. Moreover, soon after the winter rains ceased, the whites would have had to find a permanent source of water if they were to survive, and assistance from Aborigines would probably have been necessary to achieve this.

Assuming that friendly relations were established between the two groups, the Aborigines would no doubt have been pleased to guide the whites to water at a nearby soak, such as Billiecutherra, and to show them how to obtain food in this seemingly inhospitable country. From Billiecutherra, they could follow a chain of Aboriginal soaks extending north to Shark Bay, eventually reaching a waterhole known to the Aborigines as Wale, which was the site of the largest encampment of Malgana people in this area. Wale Well is situated in a large interdunal depression, 10 kilometres south of Tamala Homestead and 50 kilometres north of the *Zuytdorp* wrecksite. I believe that the 'Wayl men' of the 1834 wreck report almost certainly came from this area.

Tamala Station, which includes the Wale area, was first taken up as a pastoral lease in 1865.[206] The native waterhole there was probably developed soon afterwards as a watering point for sheep, the Aborigines being driven away. I was told by an elderly Aborigine that most of the blacks on Tamala 'cleared out' soon after the pastoralists arrived, no doubt following shooting incidents. I expect that it would have been possible to learn a great deal about the *Zuytdorp* and its survivors from the Wale Aborigines at that time.

The name 'Wale' in the Malgana language refers to a white rock, termed calcrete by geologists, that forms the floor of the depression where the well is situated. When I first visited there in 1954, the ground was strewn with scores of grindstones and other artefacts, together with large bailer shells used as water-carriers by Aborigines. Many shells of smaller marine snails that were used as food are still scattered around the site. The grindstones are composed of a wide variety of rock types, the most common being Tumblagooda Sandstone from the Murchison River area, 100 kilometres to the south-south-east; garnet granulite and dolerite from the Northampton Block, 140 kilometres to the south-east; and quartzite from the Badgeradda Range, 170 kilometres to the east. Some are very large: one of Tumblagooda Sandstone weighs about 8 kilograms. This heavy grindstone must have been carried for about 100 kilometres from its source in the gorge of the Murchison River.[207] Visible artefacts have since been removed from the site, and are included in the collection of the Centre for Archaeology at The University of Western Australia. Wale is a designated Aboriginal site, which may not be disturbed without authority.

Some 4 kilometres south-east of Wale is an Aboriginal burial ground known as Karkura, in a sand ridge that has now been largely blown away after losing its vegetation cover through over-grazing. In the four decades since I first visited the site, the strong prevailing southerly winds have exposed scores of Aboriginal skeletons. A skeleton usually lasts for only a few years after it has been exhumed, and until very recently there were often five to ten visible at any one time. The bodies, some of very tall men, were originally buried in an upright crouching position, with the knees drawn up and the face looking west, towards the setting sun. They are mute testimony to the large population of Aborigines who once lived in this area.

The last full-blood Malgana men, Ginger McDonald and Ben Carlo, died more than twenty years ago. It is sad to reflect that before white settlement, the Tamala area supported many Aboriginal people—perhaps as many as 200—and their hunter-gatherer way of life had no adverse effects on the environment. That contrasts with the situation today: only a handful of whites now live on the station, the Malgana Aborigines have gone, and overgrazing by sheep has resulted in severe environmental degradation.

Wale was clearly an extremely important place to the Malgana people, and for many years I had felt that this site was worth careful investigation for evidence that it was visited by survivors of the *Zuytdorp*. Consequently, I organized a visit to Wale in April 1990, with Mike McCarthy, Tony Cockbain (a geologist friend of mine) and Bob Sheppard (a metal-detector expert). We took four metal-detectors and spent a day on a reconnaissance archaeological examination of the site. Within about two hours of starting the search, Tony Cockbain, then a novice at metal-detecting, located a beautifully preserved tobacco-box lid, 10 centimetres below the surface and within 20 metres of the well. This lid, made of thin brass, is inscribed with the name Leyden, together with an idealized depiction of the town. It is virtually identical to a tobacco-box lid from the wreck of the *Zeewyk* (1727), and there can be no doubt that it came from the *Zuytdorp*.[208]

The only question is whether it was taken to Wale by a survivor or an Aborigine. I think it was probably a survivor who carried it there, soon after the ship foundered, as it is almost undamaged, other than having been separated from its base. If the tobacco-box had been carried around by Aborigines for some time, the thin brass of the lid would presumably have been more dented.

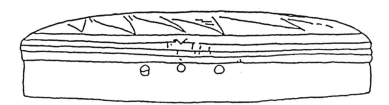

Brass tobacco-box lid found in April 1990 at Wale Well, probably carried there by a survivor of the Zuytdorp.

Drawing by the author

Subsequent systematic metal-detecting of the whole site, and detailed archaeological investigations of a small area by Professor Sandra Bowdler,[209] have not uncovered any further relics of definite Dutch origin, although some brass buttons found there could possibly be Dutch. Nevertheless, the part of the site that has been thoroughly examined archaeologically is very small. Wale and other waterholes in the area clearly warrant more comprehensive archaeological investigations in attempting to find evidence of movements of the *Zuytdorp* survivors.

Another piece of evidence to link the wreck with the Malgana people comes from a report published in the *Inquirer and Commercial News*[210] on 12 May 1869:

> A curiosity has been received from Mr Charles Gill, manager for Mr C von Bibra, from the aborigines at Shark's Bay, of which the wood cut below is a facsimile. It is evidently a coin of the reign of Charles II, about 209 years old, and must have been struck 50 years after Shark's Bay was discovered. The coin is silver, weighing about 1 ounce 2 dwt. The native who found it is named War-du-ma-rah—another curiosity. It was picked up about 20 miles south of Shark's Bay, at a well named Woonah-ra-car-rah.

I sent a copy of the article and wood-cut illustration of the coin to Dr H. Enno van Gelder of The Hague, an expert on early Dutch coins. He advised that the coin was not British, as claimed in the article, but a silver ducaton of the Spanish Netherlands, minted at the Brabant Mint in Antwerp in 1660, during the reign of Philip IV. The coin could not have been very well preserved, so the person making the wood-cut interpreted it as British and inserted the appropriate coat of arms.[211] However, the inscription that was shown proves its true nature. The coin was identical to ducatons of the Spanish Netherlands that have since been found at the wrecksite.

The two full-blood Malgana Aborigines who still lived at Tamala during the 1950s told me that they had never heard of Woonah-ra-car-rah; nor had elderly European station people whom I consulted. The well was probably situated about 20 miles (32 kilometres) south of Tamala—'Shark's Bay' was used in a broad sense in those days—and may have been in the vicinity of Womerangee Hill.

It was probably one of the many small sand soaks once used by Aborigines in this area, but which are now unknown. The coin may well have been carried to the soak by a survivor, although it could equally have been taken there by an Aborigine.

It is hard to know how much material was removed from the wrecksite by Aborigines over the years, but it seems likely that a lot would have been taken away, including metallic objects, coins and glass. Indeed, it is surprising that so much material still remained there when Tom Pepper first visited the site. For example, there was still plenty of broken glass and a number of solid barrel rungs, yet glass would surely have been valued by Aborigines for cutting purposes, and the iron of barrel rungs could have been used to make various implements. It is hard to understand why all of these materials were not removed, if some of the survivors mixed with Aborigines and showed them how to use them. One possibility is that Aborigines, like Lurlie Pepper, were superstitiously frightened of the ghostly woman's figure that lay for more than 200 years at the wrecksite, believing that it embodied the spirits of the people who had died at that site.

European characteristics of Aborigines

The principal evidence that the survivors lived and interbred with Aborigines is from reports that the native people in this general area showed mixed-race physical characteristics. The well-known explorer A.C. Gregory, who visited the Murchison River area in 1848,[212] reported in 1885[213] that he had met a tribe there

> whose characters differed considerably from the average Australian. Their colour was neither black nor copper, but that peculiar yellow which prevails with a mixture of European blood; their stature was good, with strong limbs, and remarkably heavy and solid about the lower jaw...But though these and many other traces of their origin exist, it is singular that no trace of knowledge of the arts of civilized people remains; there is nothing in their weapons, erection of dwellings, or ornamentation of their persons or belongings which is not common to the greater part of the Australian tribes.

Gregory went on to link these supposed European characteristics with the two mutineers who had been marooned by Pelsaert in this area in 1629. Of course, he was unaware of the potentially much larger number of castaways who had come ashore nearby from the wreck of the *Zuytdorp*.

Gregory was a highly respected explorer with extensive experience of Aborigines throughout Australia, and his observations should be given considerable weight. On the other hand, it seems surprising that he made no reference in the journal of his 1848 expedition to any unusual features of the Aborigines in this area. The thirty-seven year delay in making his report may cast some doubt on its veracity.

The other well-known person to link characteristics of Aborigines in this area with Dutch castaways was Daisy Bates, who lived among Aborigines in Western Australia and South Australia for some forty years. She learned a great deal about those people, although her writings have generally not been well received among anthropologists. In her book *The passing of the Aborigines*,[214] she claimed to have

> found traces of types distinctly Dutch. When Pelsart marooned two white criminals on the mainland of Australia in 1627 [sic], these Dutchmen had probably been allowed to live with the natives, and it may be that they and their progeny journeyed far along the river-highways, for I found these types as far out as the headwaters of the Gascoyne and the Murchison. There was no mistaking the flat heavy Dutch face, curly fair hair, and heavy stocky build.

Daisy Bates said no more regarding this claim in her book, but she gave a far more imaginative and provocative account in the *Sydney Morning Herald* of 28 March 1925.[215] Her description of the way in which the Aborigines may have reacted to the two marooned criminals from the *Batavia* was as follows:

> In fear and trembling…some older men among the watchers, holding the green branches of amity in their hands, finally approached the Dutchmen, and friendly overtures were received and returned. Sign language is universal among humans, and so by signs the newcomers were greeted, given

food and drink and a place apart amongst the elders in the camp, in the full belief that the white-skinned men were the returned spirits of their own dead…[But] the coming of these criminals brought evil only to the natives. They [the Dutchmen] would soon grasp the fact that their persons were sacred for some reason, and from the first they would abuse the hospitality of the Aborigines. Ignorant as they were of the social organisation, system of relationship, tabus, etc., all of which made for camp morality, the men, whose frightful lust had made them castaways in a strange land, raped the girl children of their preservers, broke down every tabu, ate and drank to repletion of the food and drink supplied to them, and followed unchecked the law of their own vile passions only…Their sojourn brought only evil and ruin to the natives…and the suggestion may be hazarded that the many changes in the four class divisions of the northern and central areas were due to the unchecked and unrestrained lusts of these Dutch criminals…Mothers and daughters, sisters, daughters-in-law, every young girl became the victim.

When a group broke through its class restrictions, and when, as in the Dutchmen's case, no punishment could be inflicted, the moral law of that group disappeared, it became a promiscuous mob, with no restraints upon the lusts of its young men and women. Wherever the writer found these virile female Dutch types in the mobs of derelicts that haunt white settlement, the group was living in promiscuity…Men had their own daughters, sisters, mothers, and even grandmothers as wives, but they clung to the white settlements for protection.

Laverton is in a line direct east from Geraldton and many Dutch types were found among the women there, also at Peak Hill, Meekatharra, and other centres where the mobs foregather. A fair-haired male Aborigine was never met with…It is probable that all the male half-castes were killed in those far-off days; they may have shown some individuality or initiative or some character foreign to the natives, and so, while the women were allowed to live, the men were killed. There is no fair-haired 'tribe' in Western Australia, but throughout all the area between the heads of the four rivers mentioned [the Murchison, Gascoyne, Ashburton and

Fortescue] and the border, Dutch-built, fair-haired women and children will be met with amongst the derelict mobs. The type will persist until the last fair-haired woman dies.

It is difficult to understand how Daisy Bates concluded that such depravity could be linked to the two Dutch criminals, and that they would have been immune from retribution for their actions. There are numerous examples of Aborigines attacking Europeans soon after first contact was made; for example, the spearing of George Grey in the Kimberley District in 1837,[216] and of Governor Fitzgerald near Champion Bay, in 1848.[217] The two marooned Dutchmen would probably have been killed promptly if they seriously offended the Aborigines. Moreover, given the licentious characteristics they had both displayed on the Houtman Abrolhos, it seems likely that they would have transgressed Aboriginal law not long after first making contact.

Another intriguing report appeared in the *Perth Gazette* of 9 August 1861,[218] as follows:

From Champion Bay we hear that a tribe of natives have made their appearance at the easternmost sheep stations upon the north branch of the Irwin River, who differ considerably from the aborigines previously known, in being fairer complexioned, with long light coloured hair flowing down upon their shoulders, fine robust figures, and handsome features; their arms are spears, ten feet in length, with three barbs cut out of the solid wood, [and] long meros with which they throw the spear underhanded. A gentleman, who some months since explored the country to a distance of 100 miles north-east of the Irwin, informs us that he found these natives residing there; they were very friendly and gave through a native interpreter, servicable information as to the country in their neighbourhood.

Of course, it is impossible to ascertain just how reliable that report was. Moreover, it did not suggest directly that these Aborigines could have been descended from Dutch castaways.

If credence can be given to this 1861 report and to those of A.C. Gregory and Daisy Bates, it is feasible that a pronounced genetic legacy of this type could have persisted if a significant number of men (say ten to twenty) from the *Zuytdorp* had joined the Aborigines in 1712. Of course, it would also be necessary for their descendants to have spread out for more than 300 kilometres from the wrecksite, which is quite possible. It is less probable that the observed European characteristics could have been inherited solely from the two Dutchmen of the *Batavia,* who were marooned in 1629, as they are likely to have produced fewer offspring, and any resulting European characteristics would be less likely to have persisted in a recognizable form through many more generations.

The Walga Rock ship painting

The 'different' Aborigines described in the 1861 report were said to live in the area about 100 miles (160 kilometres) north-east of the Irwin River. This is not far from Walga Rock (also known as Walgana Rock), near Cue, where a small white painting of a sailing ship is to be seen in a gallery of Aboriginal rock art. The gallery is in an undercut cave at the foot of the prominent granite outcrop that forms Walga Rock. The ship painting has been ascribed by some to a hoax, and by others to a Dutch castaway or the descendant of a castaway. [219]

The painting depicts a sailing ship with two masts, square gun ports, stays and shrouds. A structure shown extending above the deck near the centre may represent shrouds over the stub of a broken third mast, although some people have interpreted it as a smoke stack. Underneath the ship are four or five rows of what appears to be regularly executed script, each word beginning with a characteristic upward flourish. However, closer examination shows that this is not really a form of writing, but consists of a regular pattern of symbols with no apparent meaning. I expect that it was probably designed to imitate writing.

The first description and photograph of the Walga Rock ship painting were published in the *Weekend Mail* supplement to the *Daily News* of 1 October 1955, which stated that the painting had already been in existence 'when John Meehan, founder of Austin Downs Station on which Walga Rock stands, came to the district about 1890', and that 'Meehan learnt from Afghan camel drivers who had been through the area earlier that the ship painting had

Ship painting in the Aboriginal cave gallery at Walga Rock, showing square gun ports, two masts with shrouds and cross-stays, and a vertical structure between the masts that may represent the stub of a broken third mast covered by shrouds. Lines of pseudo-writing are shown below the ship.

Photograph by the author

been there on their first visit and that none of them had painted it.' Subsequent articles by Ross Elliott, published in the *Daily News* during 1968, prompted several elderly people who had seen the painting many years before to come forward, confirming that it was already there before the turn of the century. One of the *Daily News* articles and another in *Walkabout* claimed that an Aboriginal girl with fair hair had done the painting, and that by doing so she had desecrated this sacred place, and had consequently been killed and her body buried nearby.

The ship painting has the appearance of being significantly more recent than traditional Aboriginal paintings in the cave gallery; indeed, it is drawn over some older paintings. However, if the statements attributed to John Meehan and others are valid, and there seems to be no good reason to believe otherwise, the ship painting must have been painted before 1900. Moreover, a comparison between close-up photographs taken in 1955 and 1994 shows that most of the painting, apart from the thick line outlining the hull, has deteriorated very little over the thirty-nine year period, and this is consistent with the view that it is very old. The 1955 newspaper report stated that part of the painting, presumably the outline of the hull, had recently been touched up with chalk. If so, this chalk has washed away since then, thereby explaining the apparent deterioration of that part of the painting, leaving the rest almost unaltered.

Two principal colours, red and white, have been used in the traditional Aboriginal paintings in the cave gallery. The red pigment is ochre derived from the Aboriginal mine at Wilgiemia, 50 kilometres north-north-east of Walga Rock. At this site, Aborigines dug out a large cavern to extract ochre (*wilgie*), which was traded over large areas of western and central Australia. Wilgiemia represents the largest known mining operation by Aboriginal people in Australia prior to European settlement, and the enterprise of Dutch castaways from the *Zuytdorp* could conceivably have played a role in its development.

Visual examination of the white pigments used in various paintings in the gallery at Walga Rock suggested to me that the same white substance had been used in painting both the ship and the traditional Aboriginal designs, but scientific confirmation was required. Analysis of minute pieces of the white pigment by the Western Australian Chemistry Centre, using X-ray-diffraction and electron-microscope techniques, provided this confirmation.[220] The pigment is now in the form of calcium phosphate, derived by weathering of bird excrement of the same type that still accumulates in the cave below roosting ledges of birds of prey. Fresh excrement must have been used in painting both the ship and the traditional Aboriginal designs, but rainwater flowing over the rock surface and the paintings has gradually leached out uric acid and other soluble material from the excrement, converting the residue to insoluble calcium phosphate, which is very durable.

There is not enough evidence to prove who painted this enigmatic ship, but it does seem clear that it was done before 1900. The artist may have been an illiterate person, black or white, who was for some reason seeking to depict a sailing ship and European writing. Alternatively, the painting could be an elaborate hoax.

The hoax hypothesis is supported by the fact that there are some similarities between the ship painting and an illustration of the *Batavia* wreck that was published in the Christmas edition of the *Western Mail* in 1897. This illustration had been reproduced from an engraving of the *Batavia* wreck in the book *Ongeluckige voyagie*, first published in 1647. An English translation of that book, by Willem Siebenhaar, was printed by the *Western Mail*, together with the illustration, which shows the ship with its mainmast collapsed and crossed stays (ropes) between the two remaining masts, in much the same way that they are shown on the Walga Rock painting. The *Western Mail* Christmas edition was popular throughout Western Australia, and copies of the 1897 issue would certainly have circulated in Cue, then a thriving gold centre. It is possible that a prospector visiting Walga Rock thought it would be amusing to paint a ship based on the illustration of the *Batavia* wreck, using bird excrement as the pigment, just as Aborigines had done with some of their paintings at this locality. The hoaxer may have been idly seeking to fool others into believing that a *Batavia* survivor had visited Walga Rock, using pseudo-writing as an added element in his deception.

Another possibility is that the painting was done by someone, such as an Afghan camel driver, who had come to this country in a sailing ship and was seeking to illustrate that ship, without intending any deception. However, this seems unlikely, as the square gun ports suggest an older ship than one that would have brought such a person to Australia in the late nineteenth century. Moreover, there would seem no reason for him to have included pseudo-writing in the painting.

The most intriguing hypothesis is that the Walga Rock painting is connected with a survivor of either the *Zuytdorp* or the *Batavia*. Walga Rock is some 350 kilometres east of the *Zuytdorp* wrecksite, near the source of the Sanford River, a tributary of the Murchison, which was one of the major 'river highways' of Aborigines. The river may at some time have been followed by survivors of the wreck and their descendants in moving among the various Aboriginal people. There seems to be a reasonable possibility that this ship painting and the associated pseudo-writing were painted by a son or daughter of a survivor of the *Zuytdorp* or *Batavia*, who was seeking to imitate a drawing and writing done by that survivor when recounting the story of his dramatic arrival in the Great South Land. Alternatively, it could be the work of an illiterate survivor himself, although such a person would have had little reason to imitate writing.

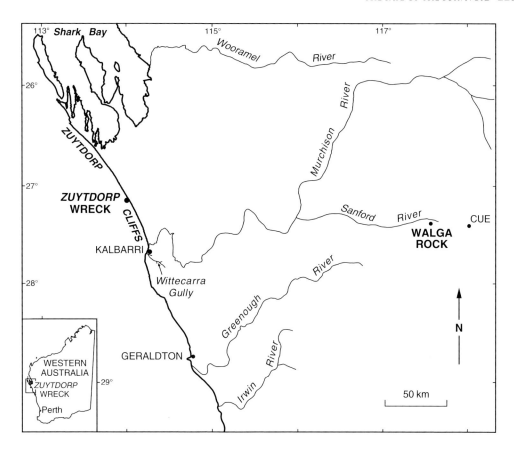

Aboriginal language and customs

In a recent publication, Rupert Gerritsen claims to have found evidence that Dutch castaways from the wrecks of the *Batavia*, *Vergulde Draeck*, *Zuytdorp* and *Zeewyk*, and from ships' boats of the *Goede Hoop* and *Sardam*, were assimilated into Aboriginal tribes over a wide area extending from the Swan River to Exmouth Gulf.[221] One of his principal arguments is that the language and customs of the Nanda Aborigines were significantly modified as a result of the influence of Dutch castaways.

However, linguists Juliette Blevins and Doug Marmion, who have studied the Nanda language in detail, can find no evidence to support Gerritsen's claims of Dutch influence on that language.[222] They have given me a detailed rebuttal of his arguments (in a manuscript to be submitted for publication), concluding that

Map 9.
The location of Walga Rock in relation to the wrecksite

'Gerritsen's hypothesis and etymologies are based on misunder-standings, mistranscription, and lack of knowledge of Australian Aboriginal language structure and history...there is no evidence of Dutch influence in Nhanda [Nanda].'[223]

Gerritsen maintains that the *Zuytdorp* survivors must have travelled north to the Kennedy Range and on to the area around Exmouth Gulf and the Ashburton River. He bases this primarily on 'anomalous sounds mapping'. However, Blevins and Marmion found no linguistic basis for this assertion. They show that the so-called 'anomalous sounds' are not at all anomalous in Aboriginal languages.

Thus, although survivors of the *Zuytdorp* and other Dutch shipwrecks could conceivably have introduced some words to the Aboriginal vocabulary, there is no valid evidence to indicate that they did so. On the other hand, after colonization, the Nanda language absorbed adaptations of many English words, for animals and objects that had not previously been known to Aborigines. A number of examples are given by Blevins and Marmion.

I have had some personal experience of making first contact with nomadic Aborigines. In 1964, I was a member of an expedi-tion to the Gibson Desert and south-eastern Great Sandy Desert that was seeking to find some of the last remaining nomadic Aborigines in Australia who were still following their traditional hunter-gatherer lifestyles, unaffected by European ways.[224] We found about seventy people, mainly belonging to the Bindubi and Ngadatjarra tribes, about half of whom had never seen Europeans before. Many photographs that I took on this expedition are now featured in the Aboriginal display at the WA Museum.

We accompanied a number of these people on food-foraging expeditions, and, through an interpreter, learned something about the animals and plants that they sought. On my asking what animal had made a particular track in the sand, the response in the Ngadatjarra language was 'budi-kat'—their version of the English name 'pussy-cat'. This is a typical example of an English word enter-ing an Aboriginal language, for an animal that had been unknown in the area prior to British colonization. Moreover, the word was being used by persons who had never previously seen white people.

Another feature of Nanda culture that Gerritsen links to the Dutch castaways is that their huts were considerably better made and larger than those normally encountered in Western Australia.

Indeed, the reports of early explorers confirm that Aboriginal huts in the area between the Murchison and Irwin rivers were of superior construction, neatly plastered with clay, and grouped together in little 'villages'. It is conceivable that the Dutch castaways played a role in teaching Aborigines how to build such huts, but this need not have been the case: the Aborigines were no doubt quite capable of devising these structures for themselves. The main reason for the high concentration of people living in 'villages' of semi-permanent huts was that Aborigines had an abundant source of food in this area, in the form of the native yam, *Dioscorea hastifolia*.[225] They could therefore sustain a more settled lifestyle, having less need than many other Aborigines in Australia to forage for food over extended areas.

Gerritsen claims that this native yam, or its 'ancestral species', was introduced by Dutch castaways to the area extending from Shark Bay to the Murray River, south of Perth, and that the castaways showed Aborigines how to cultivate it. However, *Dioscorea hastifolia* is a species that is endemic to this part of Western Australia.[226] It does not occur elsewhere in the world and could not, therefore, have been brought from another country by a Dutch castaway. Gerritsen's alternative explanation, that *Dioscorea hastifolia* evolved in south-western Australia from an 'ancestral species' brought ashore by the Dutch, is untenable, as it is clearly not possible for a new species to have evolved in only two or three hundred years.

Although Gerritsen claims that *Dioscorea hastifolia* could not have been introduced to the south-western part of Australia unless it was brought there by the Dutch, he does not apply such an explanation to the occurrence of a similar species, *Dioscorea transversa*, which occurs along the east coast of Australia.[227] In fact, these two species probably had a common ancestor in northern Australia, with separate stocks extending progressively down the coast on either side of the continent and evolving into distinct species over a long time-span, perhaps several million years.

Genetic evidence

In July 1988, I received a letter from Mrs Ann Mallard of Santa Cruz, California, outlining a fascinating hypothesis. She suggested that her deceased husband, Ken Mallard, might have inherited the genetic disease porphyria variegata from a survivor of the *Zuytdorp* wreck. Ann Mallard told me that in 1962, she had married Ken Mallard, a part-Aborigine from Shark Bay, when they were both working in New Guinea. While he was on a course of the anti-malarial drug chloroquine, Mallard suddenly became ill. His condition worsened when barbiturates were prescribed: he experienced vomiting, severe abdominal pains, and delirium, and fell into a near-comatose state. He was lucky to survive this crisis, which was diagnosed as having been caused by the metabolic disease porphyria.[228]

It was originally thought that Mallard had the type of the disease known as acute intermittent porphyria, but subsequently his condition was rediagnosed as porphyria cutanea tarda. He later died of a heart attack, and some time afterwards it was realized that his symptoms, including lesions on the backs of his hands and associated skin sensitivity, were characteristic of porphyria variegata, otherwise known as South African porphyria.

A person with porphyria variegata can go through life almost unaffected, but life-threatening attacks can occur when certain drugs are taken, especially barbiturates, the attacks being associated with high levels of porphyrin in the blood, urine and faeces. The disease is quite common among the white Afrikaners of South Africa, especially in the Eastern Cape, and it has been spread elsewhere as these people have migrated to other parts of the world.

A classic medical-genealogical study by Dean (1971) has shown that all cases in South Africa can be traced back to one Dutch couple, Gerrit Jansz van Deventer and Ariaantje Jacobs van den Berg, who were married at the Cape in 1688.[229] Gerrit Jansz was one of the early freeburghers (settlers) at the Cape, arriving there in 1685, while Ariaantje was one of eight orphan girls sent out from Rotterdam by the *Heeren XVII*, to provide wives for those freeburghers. All girls found husbands within a few months of arriving at the Cape. Gerrit Jansz and his wife had eight children, of whom four can be shown to have had porphyria variegata.

Out of 4.5 million Afrikaners in South Africa, some 800,000 have only twenty family names and are descended from twenty freeburghers who settled at the Cape in the mid-seventeenth century. These people constitute a unique group for the study of inherited disorders, and about 30,000 are believed to carry the gene for porphyria variegata.[230] Dean's study showed that one in two of the descendants of Gerrit Jansz and Ariaantje Jacobs inherited this condition, passing it down through seventeen generations to the present day. Intensive research in several countries has been directed towards identification of the relevant gene, and it has now been shown to occur in chromosome 1. The research results will be published shortly.[231]

Ann and Ken Mallard visited Shark Bay in 1964, meeting Tom Pepper there. Ann enjoyed hearing his stories about the old days, including his account of the discovery of the *Zuytdorp*, and Pepper gave her a copy of my Historical Society booklet on the wreck, which she read with interest. It was some years later, after Ken Mallard had died, that she realized the possible connection between this wreck and his unusual 'South African' disease. She wondered whether it could have been introduced to Aborigines of the Shark Bay area by one of the shipwreck survivors.

After Ann Mallard wrote to me on the matter, I contacted Dr Geoffrey Dean, the world authority on porphyria, who lives in Dublin. On the basis of the medical data that I provided, he confirmed that Ken Mallard almost certainly had porphyria variegata, and expressed strong interest in the possibility that it had been introduced to Australia in 1712 by a survivor of the *Zuytdorp*. As a result of this, Dean made two visits to Cape Town, seeking to determine whether a son of Gerrit Jansz could have joined the *Zuytdorp* when it left the Cape.

Unfortunately, no listing has survived of the new crew, perhaps eighty or ninety persons, who joined the ship there. However, the Cape census of 1695 shows that Gerrit Jansz had two sons at that time, of whom only one is known to have been born to his wife Ariaantje.[232] That legitimate son remained at the Cape throughout his life. Dean wondered whether the second had been an illegitimate child, most likely coloured, born prior to Gerrit's marriage to Ariaantje in 1688. It was common practice for early Dutch settlers to cohabit with Hottentot or Malay slave women before there were white women to marry, and many people among the coloured population at the Cape today can trace their ancestry back to such unions. If Gerrit Jansz did sire an illegitimate son, that son would have been about twenty-five years old in 1712. According to Dean, 'a son by such a union, owning no farm or land, would be much more likely to join a ship, if given the chance, than a freeburgher such as the legitimate children of Gerrit Jansz after his marriage to Ariaantje.' Could such an illegitimate son have joined the *Zuytdorp*, survived the wreck, and introduced porphyria variegata to the Aborigines of Shark Bay? It is an intriguing possibility.

Another possibility, put forward subsequently by Dean,[233] is that the disease did not originate with Gerrit Jansz but with his wife, Ariaantje, and her family. Ariaantje's half-sister, Willemyntje Ariens de Witt, was another of the orphans sent out in 1688 to marry freeburghers at the Cape. Dean has suggested that she may also have carried the gene for porphyria variegata, and that the gene was taken to Australia by her son Hendrik Bibault, who might have been on board the *Zuytdorp* in 1712.

Willemyntje married Detlef Biebow (or Bibault), the first medical practitioner at the Cape, and they settled at Stellenbosch, near Cape Town. In April 1707, their seventeen-year-old son, Hendrik Bibault, became drunk with three of his friends at the mill in Stellenbosch. When the local magistrate arrived, asking them to behave, Bibault struck him with a bag of meal. All four were sentenced to be flogged, and Bibault, as the ringleader, was ordered to leave the Cape. When asked if he had anything to say, he made the historic response:

> *Ik will niet loopen; ik ben een Afrikaner.* [I will not leave. I am an African.][234]

Bibault is the first white man known to have publicly called himself an Afrikaner, and he is honoured for this by a monument in Stellenbosch. The judgment that he leave the Cape was enforced, and Dean has suggested that he joined the *Zuytdorp* when it called there in November–December 1707, en route to Batavia. Dean further suggests that Bibault was still a member of the *Zuytdorp's* crew on its final voyage in 1711–12. Archival research to examine this idea is required.

What is needed now, to test the main hypothesis that porphyria variegata was introduced to Aborigines by a *Zuytdorp* survivor, is more positive evidence that Mallard did indeed have the variegate form of porphyria. This could be achieved by genetic testing of blood samples from his near relatives. On evidence available to date, it seems possible that the disorder can be traced back, through Mallard's mother and grandmother, to his great-grandmother, a full-blood Aborigine named Wuthia, who died in about 1912. If so, one in two of Wuthia's descendants could be expected to have inherited the disease.

I spoke with Sister Stella Rowley, who was the resident nursing sister at Shark Bay for many years, to determine whether she had noted any symptoms of porphyria variegata among Aboriginal and part-Aboriginal families of the area. I quoted the common symptom of skin sensitivity, especially in the form of lesions on the backs of the hands, and told her that Ken Mallard had first developed such symptoms at the time of puberty. Sister Rowley had not noticed any evidence of this nature. Nor did she think it might have been overlooked, as she had been especially vigilant regarding skin lesions, in view of the prevalence, some years ago, of leprosy among Aboriginal and part-Aboriginal communities in other areas of northern Australia.

Thus, I know of no positive evidence of the occurrence of porphyria variegata among Mallard's relatives. However, cutaneous symptoms do not always occur, and people can go through life without knowing that they are carrying the disease. Moreover, medical data at the Queen Elizabeth II Medical Centre show that three other part-Aboriginal people are currently known to have porphyria variegata.[235] There is a need for research to determine, first, whether they carry the gene that marks the disease in South Africa, and second, whether they are descended from Aborigines of the Shark Bay area.

Another rare genetic disorder that has a relatively high incidence among the Aboriginal community in south-western Western Australia is Ellis–van Creveld syndrome, which results in children being born with extra toes and fingers, short limbs, and heart defects. It is estimated that one in thirty-nine Aborigines in this area carries the recessive gene, which is the second-highest incidence known in the world. The syndrome is most frequent among the Amish people of Pennsylvania, who trace their ancestry to the Mennonite sect, which was originally founded in the Netherlands, and whose members migrated to the United States in 1683 to escape persecution. It has been suggested that the disorder could have been introduced to Aborigines by a Dutch survivor of the *Zuytdorp* wreck.[236] However, to date, no connection has been established between the incidence of the syndrome and the Aborigines of Shark Bay or surrounding areas. More research on the genealogy of affected individuals is clearly warranted.

Important avenues for future research on possible links between Aborigines and survivors of the *Zuytdorp* will be through other types of DNA research. As more is learned about DNA characteristics of the various human races, a clear distinction between Aborigines and Europeans, on the basis of their DNA, may be expected. It will probably be possible to determine whether the Aborigines of a particular area have admixtures of genes from other races.

However, there are no surviving full-blood Aborigines in the Shark Bay area. Skeletal material is known in this area where burial sites, such as those at Karkura, have been exposed through wind erosion, but this is unlikely to provide definitive DNA, as the bones are thoroughly weathered and lacking in organic material. In any case, it is impossible to be sure how old they are—some could be older than the *Zuytdorp* wreck. On the other hand, if permission could be obtained to exhume bodies of full-blood Aborigines who died during the past fifty years, it may be possible to obtain relevant DNA results from their remains. Of course, this is an extremely sensitive matter, and nothing could be done without the full approval of the part-Aboriginal relatives of the deceased. However, I do think that such approval might be given, in view of the interest expressed by some of these people when speaking with me about their early ancestry.

Another approach could be to test the ground around Aboriginal soaks and burial sites for the presence of human hair, which could then be used for DNA analysis. Campsites of the *Zuytdorp* survivors could also be tested in this way. Scientists in North America have found that hair is preserved as small fragments in soil for thousands of years, through a wide variety of climates and situations. They have examined many Indian sites in the United States and found traces of hair at all of them, whether or not they are situated in caves or the open air.[237] As a result, they have concluded that human remains, once thought to be rare in ancient sites, are probably very widespread, in the form of human hair. As far as I am aware, this method has yet to be tested in the Australian environment.

The question of what happened to the survivors of the *Zuytdorp* wreck should indeed prove to be a fruitful field for future research.

MY LAST VISIT

ON 14 February 1996, I drove from Perth to the wrecksite for my last visit to the site prior to publication of this book. I arrived there in the late afternoon of a very hot day, having taken more than two and a half hours to cover the rough bush tracks of the last 75 kilometres. Nearing the end of the journey, I drove slowly along my track of August 1954, following the old fenceline south of Ramyard Shed, while noting that the fence itself has now almost disappeared: only two or three posts and scraps of rusty wire remain. Continuing along the track through the belt of thick tea-tree scrub, I marvelled at the fact that I had been prepared to push my vehicle through such formidable scrub, alone and far from any assistance, on my initial visit in 1954. I reflected that if I had not had the courage to do so, I could not have reached the wreck on that day, and the *Zuytdorp* story would never have become part of my life.

Access to the wrecksite is much easier now than it was during the 1950s, but it is still a difficult place to reach; fewer than 200 people go there each year. However, it seems inevitable that a road will eventually be built to facilitate tourist access to this spectacular historic locality. If so, there will be a need to minimize the effects of people and vehicles on the wilderness values of this unique part of the Shark Bay World Heritage Area. The country around the wrecksite should be carefully conserved to ensure that its natural features remain essentially the same as when the *Zuytdorp* survivors came ashore there in 1712.

There were no signs of recent wheel tracks as I drove towards the site, so I knew that the area would be deserted. I camped in the open beside the track, about a kilometre from the coast, enjoying the solitude of this wild place, while vividly recalling the excitement and apprehension of my first visit, more than forty years before. The night was clear and moonless, with brilliant stars. In the background, I heard the relentless roar of the sea crashing against the cliffs—a characteristic sound remembered well from the 1954 and 1958 expeditions.

The sea breeze intensified and the evening became cooler as I sat by my campfire, reflecting on the fearful predicament of the ship's survivors and on my long and rewarding association with the *Zuytdorp*. I thought of the pleasure I have gained from my 'hobby' historical research on this wreck, even though geology has always been the principal interest of my research career. The thrill of discovery in relation to the *Zuytdorp* has remained with me for all this time, as diverse aspects of the story evolved, right up to the writing of the present book. Successive letters and documents received from the Netherlands, Cape Town and Jakarta each contributed to my knowledge of the ship, as did the progressive results of underwater archaeology and other investigations. Especially memorable was the excitement of receiving letters from Mrs Meilink-Roelofsz during the early phase of my research.

Dominic Lamera and his wife arrived at the wrecksite early next morning, in accord with a prior arrangement. I had invited him to meet me there, primarily so that he could show me the places where he had found a human thighbone and evidence of a third survivors' campsite. We also discussed other aspects of the *Zuytdorp* story, and Lamera pointed to the place on the sea-floor where he had recovered the collection of coins and other relics declared under the recent amnesty.

I left the site in the late morning, thinking that although we have come a long way in unravelling the *Zuytdorp* story, some important questions still remain. Can the identity of the persons responsible for major looting of the carpet of silver be proved, and have most of the looted coins been melted down or hidden away?

Is it possible to prove that survivors of the shipwreck did join the Aborigines, and that their genes have persisted to the present day among the part-Aboriginal people of the Shark Bay area?

Positive answers to questions surrounding the fate of the carpet of silver may only become known if someone with direct knowledge of the affair is prepared to 'come clean'—which is not impossible. I am, however, more optimistic that archaeological and genetic research will eventually solve the intriguing mystery of what happened to the *Zuytdorp* survivors. Perhaps these Dutchmen became 'unwilling settlers' in New Holland, more than seventy-five years before the first British colonists arrived in New South Wales.

APPENDIX: MAROONING OF THE *BATAVIA* MUTINEERS

In my Historical Society paper on the *Zuytdorp*, published in 1959, I stated that the two convicted mutineers from the *Batavia*, Wouter Loos and Jan Pelgrom, were 'almost certainly' put ashore at Gantheaume Bay, and that the freshwater source was in Wittecarra Gully, which enters the southern part of the bay near Red Bluff. [238] Soon after this paper was published, I was spoken to by Henrietta Drake-Brockman, who was convinced that the mutineers had been marooned at the Hutt River. She later alluded to this conversation in her book *Voyage to disaster*, outlining her conclusion that the Hutt River was the site in question. Rupert Gerritsen has reiterated that interpretation.[239]

I think it is important to review the evidence for these two locations, as Loos and Pelgrom were the first Europeans to be marooned in Australia, and their eventual fate is relevant to that of the *Zuytdorp* survivors.

In reaffirming my earlier conclusion that the two mutineers were put ashore at the southern end of Gantheaume Bay, I have sought to reconcile Pelsaert's various observations, including course and wind directions, sea-floor bathymetry, latitude determinations, and estimated distances. The most significant of these observations are included on Map 10, which outlines the probable courses followed during Pelsaert's two visits to the place where Loos and Pelgrom were put ashore.

The two 'death-deserving delinquents' were marooned by Commodore Pelsaert on 16 November 1629, at what was described as a 'little inlet'. This was a place where fresh water had been found and there were many signs of the indigenous inhabitants.[240] The inlet had first been noted by Pelsaert on 9 June, after leaving the Houtman Abrolhos in the longboat, but on that occasion the sea was too rough to attempt a landing. The two marooned men were provided with a sampan (or yawl) and appropriate gear, and were given written advice by Pelsaert on what they should do. He gave them the option of either remaining at the present locality, or sailing north for about 50 Dutch miles to the northern end of Shark Bay, where Pelsaert had previously seen other black people. Loos and Pelgrom were advised to make themselves known to the native inhabitants, using 'tokens of friendship', and Nuremberg trinkets and toys, beads, bells and small mirrors were provided for this purpose. They were also advised:

> having become known to them [the blacks], if they will then take you into their villages to their chief men, have courage to go with them willingly. Man's luck is found in strange places; if God guards you, you will not suffer any damage from them, but on the contrary, because they have never seen any white men, they will offer all friendship.

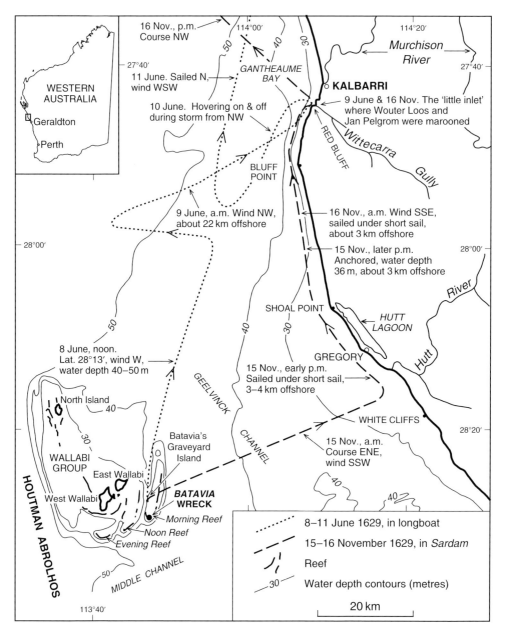

Map 10.
Courses followed by Pelsaert in June and November 1629 when sailing from the Houtman Abrolhos to the 'little inlet' at the mouth of Wittecarra Gully

Their instructions stated that after establishing good relations with the indigenous people, they should seek to determine whether there were any valuable commodities to be obtained in this country, 'be it gold, silver, or anything of value'. They should then urge the blacks to maintain a keen lookout for ships, especially in April, May, June and July, when most ships approached the South Land, and to purposely attract such ships' attention by smoke or other means. It was envisaged that the two murderers might rehabilitate themselves with the company by learning of commodities that could be exploited, and passing on this information after being picked up by a passing ship. However, Loos and Pelgrom were never heard of again.

The inlet was first sighted by Pelsaert on 9 June, the day after he and forty-seven others had left the Houtman Abrolhos in the two ship's boats. His log for those two days is somewhat confused, especially in relation to directions, but this is not surprising, as he was under a great deal of stress at the time. On 9 June—it is not stated whether this was in the morning or afternoon—the two boats reached 'a small inlet as well as low dune land', where they decided to land, but, on approaching the shore, realized that it was too dangerous because of the high surf. They were forced to beat out to sea, in considerable peril because of the big swell that had built up from the west.

The coastline before they reached the inlet and 'low dune land' was described as a 'rocky land, without trees, about as high as Dover in England'. That is indeed an appropriate description of the coastal cliffs between Red Bluff and Bluff Point. Drake-Brockman maintained that in referring to these cliffs, Pelsaert must have meant that they were the same colour as the White Cliffs of Dover, and consequently that he was describing the short stretch of coast known as White Cliffs, 11 kilometres south of the Hutt River. However, this conclusion cannot be justified: Pelsaert, in describing them as being 'about as high as Dover', was simply making a height comparison. Moreover, Drake-Brockman made no attempt to delineate the course that would be required for Pelsaert to have achieved a position south of the Hutt River on that voyage. Such a course would be impossible to reconcile with Pelsaert's log.

Drake-Brockman claimed that the latitude initially given by Pelsaert for the 'little inlet' was 28°13′, which would place it almost precisely at the mouth of the Hutt River. However, this is incorrect: at no stage did Pelsaert suggest in his journal that the inlet was at that latitude. The reading of 28°13′ referred to the boat's position at midday on 8 June, not long before he first sighted the mainland. I believe that the boat must have travelled well north of that position before the inlet was reached on the following day.[241]

The identification of the 'little inlet' as the cove north of Red Bluff is confirmed, more definitively, by observations made on Pelsaert's second visit there in the *Sardam*, five months later. On 15 November, Pelsaert set sail in that ship for the mainland, leaving the Houtman Abrolhos for the last time. His primary purpose was to look for the *Sardam's* skipper, Jacob Jacobsz, and four other men, who had been lost in a small boat during a storm one month before. At the same time, Pelsaert was seeking an appropriate place to land the two criminals, Loos and Pelgrom. It was hoped that the skipper's small boat had been blown across to the mainland; if so, it would have come ashore well north of the Houtman Abrolhos, as the wind had been from the south and south-west during the storm when they were lost.

On leaving the Houtman Abrolhos, the *Sardam* set an east-north-east course for the mainland, arriving there at noon, probably just south of the mouth of the Hutt River. During the afternoon, the ship sailed north along the coast, under short sail, about half a Dutch mile (3–4 kilometres) from the beach, until smoke was seen rising from the hinterland. The ship was then brought to anchor, in case the smoke could be a signal from the missing skipper. The sea-floor was sounded at 21 Dutch fathoms (36 metres), and the ship was close enough inshore (probably 3 kilometres or less) to see anyone who came onto the beach. However, no one appeared, so they decided that the smoke was probably from a fire lit by the native inhabitants. The sea-floor bathymetry of this area shows that the ship must then have been anchored at least 10 kilometres north of Shoal Point (see Map 10).

Next day, 16 November, with the wind blowing a 'topgallant gale' from the south-south-east, the ship weighed anchor and proceeded northward along the coast, close inshore and under short sail, until at noon it reached the inlet where they had wanted to land on 9 June. There they saw smoke rising up at several places, and Pelsaert immediately sent the yawl ashore.

Dr Cornelis de Heer's literal translation of the relevant part of Pelsaert's journal is as follows:

> Here we saw many diverse smokes going up, and being altogether cheered that our people might be there, therefore have I at once sent the yawl to the shore in order to obtain a precise report about the place and the smokes, who there, after a steep point where we had presumed there would be water, found a running-down water, which was brackish on the side of the sea, but fresh higher up.

This translation by de Heer is in accord with a more interpretative version given by J.E. Heeres (1899),[242] which indicated that the men in the yawl, 'after rounding a steep point, where we had expected the presence of water, discovered a running streamlet.' The interpretations by de Heer and Heeres differ from that given by E.D. Drok (in Drake-Brockman),[243] which indicated that the men who had gone ashore in the yawl 'found around a steep corner, there where we thought would be water, running water.' A key difference is that de Heer and Heeres interpreted the Dutch words *steylen hoeck* as 'steep point', meaning a coastal headland, whereas Drok interpreted them as 'steep corner'. Using Drok's interpretation, Drake-Brockman believed that the 'steep corner' referred to a steep-sided bend in the Hutt River, and that the men in the yawl walked, rather than sailed, around it. Certainly, 'corner' is an alternative translation of *hoeck*, but in the context of Pelsaert's journal it seems clear that de Heer and Heeres are correct in interpreting *steylen hoeck* as 'steep point', meaning a coastal headland, and that the men in the yawl sailed or rowed around this feature before going ashore.

Sixty-eight years later, in 1697, Vlamingh referred to the southern end of Gantheaume Bay as a 'brave inlet', defined on its south side by a point that he named Roode Houk (Red Point), and known today as Red Bluff.[244] I believe that Vlamingh's Roode Houk is the same as the *steylen hoeck* of Pelsaert's journal. Vlamingh used the term *houk* (or *houck*) for three such points along the coast, and it seems that this was the word normally applied to rocky headlands by contemporary Dutch navigators. Pelsaert's *hoeck* is simply an alternative spelling of the word.

I think that Pelsaert's 'running-down water', brackish near the sea but fresh higher up, must have referred to a small flow of water in Wittecarra Gully. A small stream flows periodically down this gully after rain, mainly during winter and spring. Only very rarely, perhaps once every fifty to one hundred years, after cyclonic rains, is the flow sufficient to breach the sandbar at the mouth of the gully. Normally, the stream ends in a small salt marsh extending for about 750 metres behind the sandbar. Water flowing into this marsh is salty to brackish for more than 2.5 kilometres upstream, although a number of small freshwater springs issue from the sides of the gully during winter. The only permanent freshwater spring, Wittecarra Spring, is 3.5 kilometres from the coast, beside the north-eastern branch of the gully. It contains excellent water throughout the year, forming a picturesque pool, about 2 metres across and up to 40 centimetres deep, among the roots of tall river gums, which grow in the gully around the spring. The hole in which the water occurs was originally excavated by Aborigines, and it still remains today virtually in its pristine state.

I located this historic spring in 1994, in company with Tom Pepper Junior, the son of the discoverer of the *Zuytdorp* wreck. We were following the bed of Wittecarra Gully, and were enthralled to find a beautiful pool of water at the spring. It still had plenty of water when I visited there again in March 1995, at the end of a very dry summer. The spring lies within Kalbarri National Park, and hopefully can be preserved for the future in its present natural state. I spoke about the spring to Mrs Lucy Ryder, the only part-Aborigine from the lower Murchison River area who is still fluent in the Nanda language.[245] She vividly remembers the 'beautiful water' of this spring, saying that she had last visited it as a young woman about sixty years ago. I asked her its Aboriginal name and she softly responded, '*Wittiecarra*'.

I think that Wittecarra Spring was almost certainly the source of the fresh water found by Pelsaert's party in 1629. Nearby, they noted numerous human footprints, small footpaths leading to the 'mountains', and many columns of smoke, but none of the native people were to be seen—they had apparently concealed themselves completely. The two convicted murderers were put ashore at this place, and its latitude was determined as 27°51′ south. This latitude determination for the 'little inlet' compares with the actual latitude of 27°44′30″ for the cove immediately north of Red Bluff, an error of 6.5′, or about 12 kilometres—well within the common margin of error for latitude determinations at that time.

Willem de Vlamingh also sent parties ashore at this inlet, from his ships *Geelvinck* and *Nyptangh*, on several occasions between 24 and 26 January 1697. Clearly, it was a place where the safe landing of small boats was feasible when wind and wave conditions were favourable.

The British explorer George Grey also attempted to land in the southern part of Gantheaume Bay, on 31 March 1839. However, there was a heavy swell running at the time, and, as a result, Grey failed to see a rocky ledge in front of the beach where he was attempting to land. Both of his boats were smashed after being dumped in heavy surf on rock and sand. He and his men then had no option but to walk to Perth, an epic journey that is vividly described in his journal.[246]

The boats of Pelsaert and Vlamingh must each have landed on one of the two rock-free sandy beaches in the cove at the southernmost extremity of Gantheaume Bay. The smaller of these beaches is immediately north of Red Bluff, while the larger one forms the bar across the entrance to Wittecarra Gully. Grey, on the other hand, apparently chose the second cove north of Red Bluff, known to Kalbarri residents as 'Jakes Corner', to attempt his landing. However, unfortunately for him, the beach in that area is fringed throughout its length by a rocky shelf, which would make a safe landing almost impossible unless the sea was extremely calm.

It is interesting to note that the beach in the little cove immediately north of Red Bluff was used as a boat landing during the late nineteenth to early twentieth century. In a recorded interview, Tom Pepper told me that when he was first working on Murchison House Station in the early 1920s, old station hands told him that sandalwood gathered in the area used to be loaded onto boats from the beach beside Red Bluff.[247] The cove at this locality is still used periodically to moor fishing vessels when the entrance to the preferred anchorage, in the Murchison River at Kalbarri, becomes blocked by sand.

Putting all the evidence together, I conclude that there can be no reasonable doubt that Wouter Loos and Jan Pelgrom were landed in the little cove beside Red Bluff, in the southern part of Gantheaume Bay. If they were not killed by Aborigines or otherwise died soon after being marooned, these two men would have become Australia's first European inhabitants. Their interaction with the indigenous people is likely to have had a significant influence on the attitude of Aborigines towards the next white people to come ashore in this area—the *Zuytdorp* survivors, more than eighty years later.

NOTES

1   The following references have been used in compiling data on the origins and history of the Dutch Republic: Akveld, L.M., Hart, S., and van Hoboken, W.J., 1977, *Maritieme geschiedenis der Nederlanden, 2, Zeventiende eeuw, van 1585 tot ca 1680*: De Boer Maritiem, Bussum; Boxer, C.R., *The Dutch seaborne empire 1600–1800*: Hutchinson, London; Bruijn, J.R., Gaastra, F.S., and Schöffer, I., 1987, *Dutch-asiatic shipping in the 17th and 18th centuries*: Martinus Nijhoff, The Hague; Haley, K.H.D., 1972, *The Dutch in the seventeenth century*: Thames & Hudson, London; Israel, J.I., 1989, *Dutch primacy in world trade, 1585–1740*: Clarendon Press, Oxford; Jaques, A., 1991, *Millennium: Winners and losers in the coming world order*: Times Books, New York; Schama, S., 1987, *The embarrassment of riches: An interpretation of Dutch culture in the Golden Age*: William Collins Sons, London.

2   Jacobs, E.M., 1991, *In pursuit of pepper and tea: The story of the Dutch East India Company*: Netherlands Maritime Museum, Walburg Pers, Zutphen.

3   The following references have been used in compiling data on the VOC, its ships and the route to the Indies: Heeres, J.E., 1899, *The part borne by the Dutch in the discovery of Australia 1606–1765*: Luzac, London; Bruijn, J.R., Gaastra, F.S., and Schöffer, I., 1987, *Dutch-asiatic shipping in the 17th and 18th centuries*: Martinus Nijhoff, The Hague; Crone, G.C.E., 1939, *Onze schepen in De Gouden Eeuw*: Van Kampen & Zoon, Amsterdam; Davids, C.A., 1986, *Zeewezen en wetenschap*: De Bataafsche Leeuw, Amsterdam; Gaastra, F.S., 1991, *De geschiedenis van de VOC*: Walburg Pers, Zutphen; Glamann, K., 1958, *Dutch-asiatic trade, 1620–1740*: Martinus Nijhoff, The Hague; Jacobs, E.M., 1991, *In pursuit of pepper and tea: The story of the Dutch East India Company*: Netherlands Maritime Museum, Walburg Pers, Zutphen; Roos, D., 1987, *Zeeuwen en de VOC*: Stichting VOC Publicaties, Middelburg; Stapel, F.W., 1943, *De Oostindische Compagnie en Australië*: Van Kampen & Zoon, Amsterdam; van Gelder, R., and Wagenaar, L., 1988, *Sporen van de Compagnie de VOC in Nederland*: De Bataafsche Leeuw, Amsterdam; Witsen, N., 1690, *Architectura navalis et regimen nauticum, ofte aaloude en hedendaagsche scheeps-bouw en bestier*: Amsterdam.

4   Schilder, G., 1975, *Australia unveiled: The share of the Dutch navigators in the discovery of Australia*: Theatrum orbis terrarum, Amsterdam.

5   Heeres, J.E., 1899, *The part borne by the Dutch in the discovery of Australia 1606–1765*: Luzac, London; Hasluck, Paul ('Polygon'), 'Dutch castaways—The western coast 300 years ago', *Western Mail*, 2 January 1936.

6   Green, J., 1986, 'The survey and identification of the English East India Company ship *Trial* (1622)': *International Journal of Nautical Archaeology and Underwater Exploration*, vol. 15, pp. 195–204; Henderson, J.A., 1993, *Phantoms of the Tryall*: St George Books, Perth.

7   The sailing instructions issued to the Dutch navigators mentioned the need to avoid the dangerous Abrolhos shoals off Brazil. *Abrolho* (plural *Abrolhos*) is a Portuguese word that, in its nautical usage, means 'submerged rocks, underwater cliffs, or shallow reefs'. It is derived from the Latin *aperi oculos*, meaning 'open the eyes' or 'look out', which in Portuguese is *abre os ohlos*. The Dutch no doubt had the Brazilian Abrolhos in mind when in 1619 they gave the name Frederik Houtmans Abrolhos to similar shoals off the coast of Western Australia.

8   *Instructie om in de May-tijt uyt Nederlandt na Java te seylen*: sailing instructions printed in 1652 for VOC ships sailing from the Netherlands to Java.

9   Bruijn, J.R., Gaastra, F.S., and Schöffer, I., 1987, *Dutch-asiatic shipping in the 17th and 18th centuries*: Martinus Nijhoff, The Hague.

10   Anon., 1647, *Ongeluckige voyagie van't schip Batavia nae de Oost-Indien*: Jan Jansz, Amsterdam; facsimile edn 1994, Hordern House, Sydney.

11   Uren, M., 1940, *Sailormen's ghosts*: Robertson & Mullens, Melbourne; Drake-Brockman, H., 1963, *Voyage to disaster*: Angus & Robertson, Sydney; Edwards, H., 1966, *Islands of angry ghosts*: Hodder & Stoughton, London; Sigmond, J.P., and Zuiderbaan, L.H., 1979, *Dutch discoveries of Australia*: Rigby, Adelaide; Roeper, V.D., 1993, *De schipbreuk van de* Batavia, *1629*: Walburg Pers, Zutphen; Godard, P., 1993, *The first and last voyage of the* Batavia: Abrolhos Publishing, Perth.

12   Stokes, J.L., 1846, *Discoveries in Australia*: T. & W. Boone, London.

13   Drake-Brockman, H., 1955, 'The wreck of the *Batavia*': *Walkabout*, vol. 21, January 1955, pp. 33–39.

14   Pendal, P.G., 1994, *Select Committee on ancient shipwrecks*: Western Australian Legislative Assembly report.

15   Green, J., 1975, 'The VOC ship *Batavia* wrecked in 1629 on the Houtman Abrolhos, Western Australia': *International Journal of Nautical Archaeology and Underwater Exploration*, vol. 4, pp. 43–63.

16   Henderson, J.A., 1982, *Marooned*: St George Books, Perth; Green, J.N., 1973, 'The wreck of the Dutch East Indiaman the *Vergulde Draeck*, 1656': *International Journal of Nautical and Underwater Exploration*, vol. 2, pp. 267–289.

17   de Heer, C., 1963, 'My shield and my faith': *Westerly*, no. 1, pp. 33–46.

18   'Is wreck the Gilt Dragon?': *Daily News*, 19 April 1963.

19   Green, J.N., 1985, *Treasures from the* Vergulde Draeck: WA Museum, Perth.

20   Pendal, P.G., 1994, *Select Committee on ancient shipwrecks*: Western Australian Legislative Assembly report.

21   I believe Jim Henderson, Alan Henderson and John Cowen should each have been recognized, with Graeme Henderson, as primary discoverers of the *Vergulde Draeck*, as they were all in the water when the discovery was made, and all participated in confirming that a wreck had been found. Such a decision would have been consistent with those made by the committee regarding the primary discoverers of the *Batavia* and *Zeewyk*. The case for recognizing Alan Robinson as a primary discoverer is less compelling, because he was not in the water when the discovery was made, and his claim to have found the wreck several years earlier cannot be substantiated. However, historical accuracy should have required that he be recognized at least as a secondary discoverer, without in any way condoning his later destructive actions in relation to the wreck (see p. 152). I also believe that he should have been recognized as a secondary discoverer of the *Tryall* wreck.

22   Halls, C., 1965, 'The loss of the *Ridderschap van Holland*': *The Annual Dog Watch*, no. 22, pp. 3–8.

23   Letter dated 30 March 1713 to The Most Noble Hon. Joannes van Steelant, Councillor Extraordinary of India and Commissioner of the Cape Government, from the uppermerchant Willem Helot, regarding provisioning of the ship *Zuytdorp*: Algemeen Rijksarchief file VOC 4071.

24   Robert, W.C., 1972, *The explorations 1696–1697 of Australia by Willem de Vlamingh*: Philo Press, Amsterdam; Schilder, G., 1985, *Voyage to the Great South Land, Willem de Vlamingh, 1696–97*: Royal Australian Historical Society, Sydney.

25   Halls, C., 1964, 'Two plates, being an account of the Dirk Hartog and Vlamingh plates, their loss, and subsequent recovery': *Westerly*, no. 1, pp. 32–40.

26   Playford, P.E., 1959, 'The wreck of the *Zuytdorp* on the Western Australian coast in 1712': *Western Australian Historical Society Journal and Proceedings*, vol. 5, part 5, pp. 5–41.

27   Journal of the VOC ship *Zeewyk* 1726–27: Algemeen Rijksarchief file KA 9369, partly translated into English by C. de Heer; Edwards, H., 1970, *The wreck on the Half-Moon Reef*: Rigby, Perth.

28   Stokes, J.L., 1846, *Discoveries in Australia*: T. & W. Boone, London.

29   Edwards, H., 1970, *The wreck on the Half-Moon Reef*: Rigby, Perth; Uren, M., 1940, *Sailormen's ghosts*: Robertson & Mullens, Melbourne.

30   Inexplicably, two of these cannon were buried in the grounds of the WA Museum, and were only located and dug up after I raised questions regarding their whereabouts in 1958.

31   Mörzer Bruyns, W.F.J., 1992, 'Navigation on Dutch East India Company ships around the 1740s': *The Mariner's Mirror*, vol. 78, pp. 143–154.

32   Mörzer Bruyns, W.F.J., 1985, 'Prime meridians used by Dutch navigators': *Vistas in Astronomy*, vol. 28, pp. 33–39.

33   Ingelman-Sundberg, C., 1978, *Relics from the Dutch East Indiaman Zeewijk, foundered in 1727*: WA Museum Special Publication no. 10; Ingelman-Sundberg, C., 1976, 'The V.O.C. ship *Zeewyk* 1727: Report on the 1976 survey of the site': *Australian Archaeology*, vol. 5, pp. 18–33.

34   The following principal source material has been used in compiling data on the *Zuytdorp* and its voyages: letter dated 2 November 1957 to P.E. Playford from M.A.P. Meilink-Roelofsz of the Algemeen Rijksarchief, The Hague, giving information on the *Zuytdorp*, derived from Algemeen Rijksarchief files VOC 1760, 9358 and 9800 and OB 1713; letter dated 7 October 1957 to P.E. Playford from M.A.P. Meilink-Roelofsz of the Algemeen Rijksarchief, The Hague, giving information on the *Zuytdorp*, derived from Algemeen Rijksarchief files VOC 1760, 9358 and 9800 and OB 1713; letter dated 25 November 1957 to P.E. Playford from E.W. Petrejus of the Maritiem Museum Prins Hendrik, Rotterdam, giving information relating to the *Zuytdorp*; Bruijn, J.R., Gaastra, F.S., and Schöffer, I., 1987, *Dutch-asiatic shipping in the 17th and 18th centuries*: Martinus Nijhoff, The Hague; Witsen, N., 1690, *Architectura navalis et regimen nauticum, ofte aaloude en hedendaagsche scheeps-bouw en bestier*: Amsterdam; Crone, G.C.E., 1939, *Onze schepen in De Gouden Eeuw*: Van Kampen & Zoon, Amsterdam; Playford, P.E., 1959, 'The wreck of the *Zuytdorp* on the Western Australian coast in 1712': *Western Australian Historical Society Journal and Proceedings*, vol. 5, part 5, pp. 5–41. See also Battye Library files 1164A and B: two files of correspondence and other material on the wreck of the *Zuytdorp* used in preparing my 1959 Western Australian Historical Society article.

35   de Heer, C., 1978, 'Model of the *Zuytdorp*': *Your Museum*, vol. 6, no. 3; de Heer, C., 1990, The ship *Zuytdorp* of the Chamber of Zeeland of the Dutch East India Company: unpublished report for the WA Maritime Museum.

36   Letter dated 13 February 1958 to P.E. Playford from M.A.P. Meilink-Roelofsz of the Algemeen Rijksarchief, The Hague, from Algemeen Rijksarchief file VOC 264; letter dated 25 November 1957 to P.E. Playford from E.W. Petrejus of the Maritiem Museum Prins Hendrik, Rotterdam, giving information relating to the *Zuytdorp*.

37   Day register of the Castle of Batavia, 6 October 1702.

38   Day register of the Castle of Batavia, 5 August 1703.

39   Coolhaas, W.P., 1976, *Generale missiven van Gourverneurs-General en Raden ann Heren XVII der Verenigde Oostindische Compagnie, deel VI: 1698–1713*: Martinus Nijhoff, The Hague.

40   Coolhaas, W.P., 1976, *Generale missiven van Gourverneurs-General en Raden ann Heren XVII der Verenigde Oostindische Compagnie, deel VI: 1698–1713*: Martinus Nijhoff, The Hague; Das Gupta, A., 1979, 'Indian merchants and the decline of Surat c. 1700–1750': *Beiträge zur Südasianforschung*, Südasien-Institut Universität Heidelberg, vol. 40.

41   Coolhaas, W.P., 1976, *Generale missiven van Gourverneurs-General en Raden ann Heren XVII der Verenigde Oostindische Compagnie, deel VI: 1698–1713*: Martinus Nijhoff, The Hague.

42   Soldiers' roll of the ship *Zuytdorp*: Algemeen Rijksarchief file VOC 12034; request book of the ship *Zuytdorp*: Algemeen Rijksarchief file VOC 12244.

43   Ledger of the ship *Belvliet*: Algemeen Rijksarchief file VOC 12742.

44   Letter dated 13 February 1958 to P.E. Playford from M.A.P. Meilink-Roelofsz, giving information from Algemeen Rijksarchief file VOC 264.

45   Day register of the Castle of Batavia, 19, 23 July, 18 August 1711, 18 July 1712.

46   Letter dated 18 March 1958 to P.E. Playford from M.A.P. Meilink-Roelofsz.

47   Letter dated 23 December 1957 to P.E. Playford from P. Scherft of the Rijksarchief in Zeeland, referring to authority given to the Mint-Master of the Middelburg Mint to coin schellings and double stuivers (*schellingen* and *dubbele stuivers*) to the value of 100,000 guilders. Note that a stuiver was one-sixth of a schelling and one-twentieth of a guilder. One mark of silver (264.084 grams) yielded 50 schellings or 150 double stuivers.

48   Letter dated 22 October 1958 to P.E. Playford from W.F.H. Oldewelt, Town Archivist, Gemeentelijke Archiefdienst van Amsterdam.

49   Journal kept in the ship *Belvliet* sailing from the fatherland via the Cape of Good Hope, 1711–1712: Algemeen Rijksarchief file VOC 10459. Much of this material has kindly been translated by Dr Cornelis de Heer.

50   Resolution passed in the Broad Council of the ships *Belvliet* and *Zuytdorp*, Saturday 22 August 1711: Algemeen Rijksarchief file VOC 10459.

51   Resolution passed in the Broad Council of the ships *Belvliet* and *Zuytdorp*, Tuesday 3 November 1711: Algemeen Rijksarchief file VOC 10459.

52   Will of Alexander Wisse, ship's carpenter, in the ship *Belvliet*, signed and witnessed on 23 November 1711: Algemeen Rijksarchief file VOC 10459.

53   Will of Dirck Blaauw, skipper of the *Belvliet*, signed and witnessed on 16 February 1712: Algemeen Rijksarchief file VOC 10459.

54   Inventory and sales account of the sale of goods left by Matthys Roeloffsz, seaman, who died on 12 October 1711: Algemeen Rijksarchief file VOC 10459.

55   Inventory and sales account of the sale of goods left by Steven Dircksz, gunner-seaman, who died on 17 October 1711: Algemeen Rijksarchief file VOC 10459.

56   Inventory and account of the sale of goods left by Johannes Vermeer of Rotterdam, midshipman, passed away the 22nd of January 1712: Algemeen Rijksarchief file VOC 10459.

57   Resolution passed by the ship's council of the *Belvliet* on 25 February 1712: Algemeen Rijksarchief file VOC 10459.

58   Bruijn, J.R., Gaastra, F.S., and Schöffer, I., 1987, *Dutch-asiatic shipping in the 17th and 18th centuries*: Martinus Nijhoff, The Hague.

59   Day register at the Castle of the Cape of Good Hope, 23 March 1712: Algemeen Rijksarchief file VOC 4069; letter dated 2 April 1712 to the Governor General and Council in Batavia from the Governor and Council at the Cape: Cape Archives vol. C1456; letter dated 27 March 1712 to the *Heeren XVII* in Amsterdam from the Governor General and Council at the Cape of Good Hope: Algemeen Rijksarchief file VOC 4067.

60   Leuftink, A.E., 1991, *Harde heelmeesters*: Walburg Pers, Zutphen.

61   Letter to Phillip Playford from Arnold E. Leuftink (undated, but received in March 1990).

62   Boxer, C.R., 1963, *The Dutch seaborne empire 1600–1800*: Hutchinson, London.

63   Boxer, C.R., 1963, *The Dutch seaborne empire 1600–1800*: Hutchinson, London.

64   Schilder, G., 1985, *Voyage to the Great South Land, Willem de Vlamingh, 1696–97*: Royal Australian Historical Society, Sydney.

65   Boxer, C.R., 1963, *The Dutch seaborne empire 1600–1800*: Hutchinson, London.

66   Blankert, A., 1744, *Scheeps-geneesoefening of nauwkeurige aantekeningen wegens de voornaamste ziektens en qualen die op de Oost-Indische vaart en in Indië voorkomen*: Amsterdam.

67   Letter dated 2 April 1712 to the Governor General and Council in Batavia from the Governor and Council at the Cape: Cape Archives vol. C1456.

68   Day register at the Castle of the Cape of Good Hope, 22 April 1712: Algemeen Rijksarchief file VOC 4070.

69   Letter dated 30 March 1713 to The Most Noble Hon. Joannes van Steelant, Councillor Extraordinary of India and Commissioner of the Cape Government, from the uppermerchant Willem Helot: Algemeen Rijksarchief file VOC 4071.

70   Bruijn, J.R., Gaastra, F.S., and Schöffer, I., 1987, *Dutch-asiatic shipping in the 17th and 18th centuries*: Martinus Nijhoff, The Hague.

71   Ledger of the ship *Belvliet*: Algemeen Rijksarchief file VOC 12742.

72   Day register of the Castle of Batavia, 18 July 1712.

73   Proceedings of the Council of Justice at the Cape of Good Hope, 28 April 1712: Algemeen Rijksarchief file VOC 4071.

74   Letter dated 25 November 1712 to the *Heeren XVII* in Amsterdam from the Governor General and Council in Batavia: Algemeen Rijksarchief file VOC 1706.

75   Letter dated 30 January 1713 to the directors of the Chamber of Middelburg from the Governor General in Batavia: Algemeen Rijksarchief file VOC 1816.

76   Letter dated 30 March 1713 to The Most Noble Hon. Joannes van Steelant, Councillor Extraordinary of India and Commissioner of the Cape Government, from the uppermerchant Willem Helot: Algemeen Rijksarchief file VOC 4071.

77 'The ship *Zuytdorp* debit for the following refreshments and other requirements supplied from the stores since she has appeared at this roadstead on 24th March of this year successively until this day when her voyage to Batavia is about to be undertaken'—list of goods supplied from the contracted butchers, trading warehouse, store, wine cellar, equipment store and arms store, signed at the Castle of Good Hope by M. Wysvliet on 11 April 1712: Algemeen Rijksarchief file VOC 10459.

78 Proceedings of the Council of Justice at the Cape of Good Hope—sworn affidavits on 11 March 1713 by Jeronimo Snitquer, 11 March 1713 by Matthys Bergstett, 12 March 1713 by Jan de Heere, and 14 March 1713 by Willem de Vries: Algemeen Rijksarchief file VOC 4071.

79 Leupe, P.A., 1857, *De Houtman's Abrolhos*: Amsterdam; Major, R.H., 1959, *Early voyages to Terra Australis, now called Australia*: The Hakluyt Society, first series XXV, London; republished 1963, Australian Heritage Press, Adelaide; Battye, J.S., 1924, *Western Australia, a history from its discovery to the inauguration of the Commonwealth*: Clarendon, Oxford, facsimile edn 1978, University of Western Australia Press, Nedlands; Villiers, A., 1952, *Monsoon seas*: McGraw-Hill, New York, p. 257.

80 Letter dated 6 December 1954 to Malcolm Uren of West Australian Newspapers Ltd from G.A. Cox, Director of the Nederlandsch Historisch Scheepvaart Museum, Amsterdam.

81 Minutes of the Zeeland Chamber of the VOC for 9 February 1711: Algemeen Rijksarchief file VOC 7255. A petition from the Mint-Master of Middelburg, Adolf de Groene, requested authority to coin 100,000 guilders in schellings and double stuivers. The order for the minting to proceed was issued on 16 February 1711, when it was stated that the money would be carried to Ceylon by the ship *Belvliet* (letter dated 7 October 1957 to Playford from M.A.P. Meilink-Roelofsz, and translations of resolutions of the Chamber of Zeeland by T. Japikse-Jacobs, 8 February 1959). Letter dated 23 December 1957 to P.E. Playford from P. Scherft of the Rijksarchief in Zeeland, referring to authority given by the Chamber of Zeeland to the Mint-Master of the Middelburg Mint to coin schellings and double stuivers to the value of 100,000 guilders. The order was met before 20 May 1711.

82 Letter dated 14 July 1958 to P.E. Playford from Under Secretary for Lands, advising that the proposed new geographic names Zuytdorp Cliffs and Womerangee Hill had been accepted by the Nomenclature Advisory Committee.

83 Drake-Brockman, H., 1963, *Voyage to disaster*: Angus & Robertson, Sydney.

84 Schilder, G., 1985, *Voyage to the Great South Land, Willem de Vlamingh, 1696–97*: Royal Australian Historical Society, Sydney.

85 Playford, P.E., 1990, 'Geology of the Shark Bay area, Western Australia': in *Research in Shark Bay*, eds P.F. Berry, S.D. Bradshaw and B.R. Wilson, WA Museum, Perth, pp. 13–31.

86 In formally proposing the name Womerangee Hill to the Geographic Nomenclature Committee in 1958, I was following local usage on Tamala Station. However, I have since learned that the Aboriginal (Malgana) name for the hill was Nyamera, while Womerangee was the name applied to a small spring on the east side of the hill.

87 Playford, P.E., 1988, *Guidebook to the geology of Rottnest Island*: Geological Society of Australia and Geological Survey of Western Australia, Excursion Guidebook no. 2.

88 *Perth Gazette and Western Australian Journal*, 5, 12, 19, 26 July, 19 August 1834; Moore, G.F., 1884, *Diary of ten years eventful life of an early settler in Western Australia*: Walbrook, London, facsimile edn 1978, University of Western Australia Press, Nedlands; letter dated 6 July 1834 to Colonial Secretary from Stephen Parker: CSR vol. 33/30.

89 Letter dated 14 July 1834 to H.M. Ommanney from Colonial Secretary.

90 Ommanney, H.M., 1834, 'Report on expedition to the northward in the vessel *Monkey* under the command of Captain Pace to search for a supposed wreck': *Swan River Papers*, vol. 13 (typescript), pp. 27–45 (original vol. 14); 'Return of the expedition to the northward in search of the supposed wreck': *Perth Gazette and Western Australian Journal*, 4 October 1834.

91 Henderson, G., 1980, *Unfinished voyages, Western Australian shipwrecks 1622–1850*: University of Western Australia Press, Nedlands.

92 'Second expedition to the northward': *Perth Gazette and Western Australian Journal*, 6 December 1834.

93 Verbatim transcript of interview with Tom Pepper, recorded by Phillip Playford, Peron Peninsula Station Homestead, 30 March 1975.

94   The name 'Bullocksmellum' arose from an incident in the early 1900s, when a mob of thirsty bullocks being driven from Tamala to Murchison House detected the scent of water in rockholes near this place. A rainshed and well were later built there, and Aboriginal stockmen gave the place the pidgin-English name 'bullock-smellum'. The only thing remaining there today is the old well, which had brackish water; the small rainshed, now gone, was used for drinking water.

95   Cruthers, J., Notes on the 1954 *Zuytdorp* expedition of West Australian Newspapers, tendered as evidence before the 1994 Select Committee on Ancient Shipwrecks inquiry.

96   Letter dated 13 February 1958 to P.E. Playford from E.W. Petrejus of the Maritiem Museum Prins Hendrik, Rotterdam.

97   'Jay Winter' (James Cruthers), articles on the 1954 expedition to the wrecksite—'Shipwreck, treasure, on nor'-west coast', 'Bushman's hoard takes us back 242 years', 'Pieces of eight cemented into the reefs', 'How much change does he get for a piece-of-eight?' (Paul Rigby cartoon), 'Eerie caverns open up a new world of discovery', 'Piecing the evidence for a grim flashback to 1712. Why then were there no bones?', 'Dutch blood in our natives—that may be the answer', and 'Always the cry was "Pieces of eight"': *Daily News*, 9, 10, 11, 13, 14, 15, 16, 17 December 1954.

98   Bryan Clark, 'Ship's cache still exists': *Gascoyne Telegraph*, 20 January 1988. In this article, Fred Mallard (brother of Lurlie Pepper and Ada Drage) identifies Tom Pepper as the discoverer of the *Zuytdorp* wreck. Statement by Emma Bingley (sister of Lurlie Pepper and Ada Drage) dated December 1982, identifying Tom Pepper as the discoverer of the wreck: sent to the Director of the WA Museum on 3 July 1983 by Mrs Patricia Brookes of Canterbury, Victoria, tutor in the Victorian Council of Adult Education.

99   Verbatim transcript of interview with Tom Pepper, recorded by John Thomson, Denham, 29 November 1966: Battye Library of West Australian History Oral History Programme, ref. OH26; verbatim transcript of interview with Tom Pepper, recorded by Phillip Playford, Peron Peninsula Station Homestead, 30 March 1975; verbatim transcript of interview with Tom Pepper, recorded by Chris Jeffery, 17 April 1981: Battye Library of West Australian History Oral History Programme, ref. OH419.

100   Minutes of the Shark Bay Road Board for 26 May, 5 August, 1 October 1929.

101   In my opinion, Willie's Shed should be preserved as a unique feature of the historic stockroute from Tamala to Murchison House. When a road is eventually built from Kalbarri to Tamala, this remarkable rainshed could well become a significant tourist attraction. Several smaller sheds that were also erected by the Shark Bay Road Board at regular intervals along the stockroute are still standing, in varying states of disrepair. Ramyard Shed (built by Ernest Drage) is the closest one to the wrecksite.

102   Tom Pepper told me that it would take about two weeks to drive a mob of sheep from Natta through to Gee Gie, progressing steadily at about a mile an hour. After drinking their fill at Natta, the sheep could get nothing to drink before reaching Willie's Shed, nearly a week later. However, they were used to drinking very brackish water at Tamala and would not accept the pure rainwater at Willie's. When water was run into the drinking trough, a sheep would dip its nose in, taste the water, then turn away, despite being very thirsty. The only way to get the sheep to drink would be to dissolve an appropriate amount of salt in the trough, and a 50-pound (23-kilogram) bag of salt was carried with the droving team for this purpose.

103   Edwards, H., 'Zuytdorp's finder dies': *West Australian*, 28 September 1985.

104   I later found that Cook had provided information and photographs for the following article on the '1939' expedition—'Stockman's green bottles find opened up Zuytdorp wreck': *Geraldton Guardian*, 22 March 1983.

105   Courtney, Victor, 'We hunt for treasure on the nor-west coast': *Sunday Times Magazine*, 8, 15 June 1941.

106   'Treasure trove, coins and ingots found': *West Australian*, 12 May 1939; 'Treasure trove, more finds near Murchison River': *West Australian*, 9 September 1939; Uren, M., 1940, *Sailormen's ghosts*: Robertson & Mullens, Melbourne.

107   Courtney, V., 1961, *The life story of J.J. Simons*: Halstead Press, Sydney.

108   Faye, E., 1992, *Life's just a big joke, isn't it?*: Williton Printers, Williton (UK).

109   Cruthers, J., Notes on the 1954 *Zuytdorp* expedition of West Australian Newspapers, tendered as evidence before the 1994 Select Committee on Ancient Shipwrecks inquiry.

110 Letter dated 22 September 1958 to P.E. Playford from J. Schouten, Director of the Stedelijke Musea te Gouda, advising that the clay pipes found near the wrecksite are similar to those of seventeenth-century Dutch origin, except that the name 'Apffenbergh' on one of them is not Dutch and 'sounds German'.

111 'Jay Winter' (James Cruthers), 'History in the finding—Bushman's hoard takes us back 242 years': *Daily News*, 10 December 1954.

112 Letter dated 30 March 1958 to P.E. Playford from Wilfred Burton, advising that the instrument given to him by Tom Pepper (cannonball callipers) was probably then in the possession of Miss Olga Dickson of Cottesloe. I contacted her, and found that she still had the instrument. She eventually agreed to donate it to the WA Museum, and it can now be seen on display at the WA Maritime Museum, Fremantle. Letter dated 29 April 1958 to P.E. Playford from E.W. Petrejus of the Maritiem Museum Prins Hendrik, Rotterdam, advising that 'callipers like those shown in your photo were, and still are, used for measuring round shot and projectiles. In former days these callipers were quite indispensable, especially when cannon of different bores were used.'

113 Three articles by Hugh Edwards on the 1958 expedition to the wrecksite—'Coins, keys, wreckage unravel 250 years of history', 'Zuytdorp was a ship of death', and 'Secrets of Dutch wreck still lie hidden by ocean': *Daily News*, 2, 3, 4 June 1958.

114 Edwards, H., 1962, *Gods and little fishes*: Peter Davies, London.

115 Edwards, H., 1958, Daily journal of West Australian Newspapers' 1958 expedition to investigate the wreck of the Dutch ship *Zuytdorp*, lost on the coast of the Southland, latitude 27 deg. 13 min., June 1712: unpublished manuscript.

116 Letter dated 19 May 1958 to Receiver of Wreck from D.J. Burton, listing items recovered on the recent expedition to the *Zuytdorp* wrecksite: Department of Transport, WA Branch, Australian Archives PT 1473/4, item 58/67, pp. 2–3; letter dated 25 August 1958 to Receiver of Wreck from D.J. Burton of West Australian Newspapers, advising that the company planned to establish a museum of its own to house the relics collected on the recent expedition: Department of Transport, WA Branch, Australian Archives PT 1473/4, item 58/67, p. 6.

117 Playford, P.E., 1959, 'The wreck of the *Zuytdorp* on the Western Australian coast in 1712': *Western Australian Historical Society Journal and Proceedings*, vol. 5, part 5, pp. 5–41.

118 Cramer, M., 1975, 'The first *Zuytdorp* dive': in *Sharks and shipwrecks*, ed. H. Edwards, Lansdowne, Melbourne, pp. 114–119.

119 See also 'Old Dutch wreck site explored for first time': *Geraldton Guardian*, 19 May 1964; and 'Three skindivers investigate Dutch wreck': *West Australian*, 19 May 1964.

120 'Skindivers to survey treasure ship wreck': *West Australian*, 9 May 1968.

121 'Zuytdorp claim by local men': *Geraldton Guardian*, 9 May 1968; 'Geraldton man says Zuytdorp claim made': *West Australian*, 10 May 1968.

122 Letter dated 30 May 1964 to Receiver of Wreck, Geraldton, from Max Cramer: Australian Archives PT1473/4, item 58/67, pp. 11–12 (this letter was forwarded to the Receiver of Wreck, Fremantle, by the Sub-collector of Customs, Geraldton, on 2 June 1964); letter dated 13 May 1968 to Receiver of Wreck, Western Australia, from Max Cramer: Australian Archives PT1473/4, item 58/67, pp. 13–15.

123 'Skindiver finds silver coins near Zuytdorp': *West Australian*, 22 May 1968.

124 Letter dated 31 May 1968 to the Director, WA Museum, from T.H. Brady.

125 Minutes of Special Meeting of the WA Museum Board on 3 July 1968, attended by Messrs Max Cramer and Tom Brady.

126 'Treasure ship at Lancelin': *Daily News*, 9 September 1957.

127 Henderson, James, 'The curse of the Gilt Dragon': *Sunday Independent Magazine*, 15 June 1969.

128 Case R.45/1969, before Mr Justice Virtue, in the Supreme Court of Western Australia: Ellis A. Robinson (plaintiff) v. Hancock Prospecting Pty Ltd and Wright Prospecting Pty Ltd, trading as 'The Independent', Maxwell Newton, Mervyn J. Brown, and James Henderson (defendants), heard 1, 2, 3 April 1970, verdict delivered 8 May 1970; 'Robinson wins libel claim': *West Australian*, 9 May 1970.

129 Henderson, J.A., 1982, *Marooned*: St George Books, Perth, p. 168; Henderson, G., 1986, *Maritime archaeology in Australia*: University of Western Australia Press, Nedlands.

130 Pearson, C., 1976, 'Legislation for the protection of shipwrecks in Western Australia': *International Journal of Nautical Archaeology and Underwater Exploration*, vol. 5, pp. 171–180.

131 The present Executive Director of the WA Museum, Andrew Reeves, regards the Commonwealth legislation to protect historic wrecks as a landmark among government actions over the past thirty years to protect Australia's cultural heritage. State–Commonwealth cooperation in implementing this legislation has been very successful, and Reeves would like to see the concept applied as a model for broader Commonwealth assistance in heritage areas.

132 Debate on the Navigation Amendment Bill: *Hansard*, Federal House of Representatives, 9 December 1976, pp. 3637–3639.

133 Contract between the WA Museum Board and John Cowen (undated, but signed in late November or early December 1965); letter dated 21 November 1972 to the Director, WA Museum, from J. Cowen, in which he raises the issues of a salvage contract and payment of a reward for discovery of the wreck; opinion by Kott, Gunning and Co., barristers and solicitors, dated 29 September 1981, regarding that contract; submission to the Select Committee on Ancient Shipwrecks by John Cowen, dated 28 February 1994; letter dated 12 September 1994 to P.G. Pendal from J.S. Cowen (objecting to findings of the Select Committee).

134 File note by the Acting Director of the WA Museum, R.W. George, dated 6 December 1965, discussing a visit by Alan Robinson.

135 Letters dated 25 April 1994 and 16 January 1995 to P.E. Playford from Naoom Haimson.

136 Robinson, Alan, 1968, 'The Zuytdorp': *Underwater Explorers Club News*, vol. 7, no. 11, June 1968.

137 'Skindiver finds silver coins near Zuytdorp': *West Australian,* 22 May 1968.

138 The map is shown on p. 47 of Robinson's book *In Australia treasure is not for the finder*: Vanguard, Perth.

139 Letter dated 7 June 1968 to the WA Museum Board from E.M. Heenan and Co., outlining a proposal on behalf of Alan Robinson to salvage material from the *Zuytdorp* wreck.

140 Memorandum dated 11 June 1968 to the Director of the WA Museum from Colin Jack-Hinton, Senior Curator, Division of Human Studies.

141 Letter dated 11 June 1968 to Colin Jack-Hinton from T.H. Brady.

142 Memorandum dated 14 June 1968 to the Director of the WA Museum from Colin Jack-Hinton, Senior Curator, Division of Human Studies.

143 Memorandum dated 28 June 1968 to the Director of the WA Museum from Colin Jack-Hinton, Senior Curator, Division of Human Studies.

144 Minutes of Special Meeting of the WA Museum Board, 4 July 1968.

145 'Big project to lift treasure from Zuytdorp': *West Australian*, 10 July 1968.

146 'Wreck group says it will not break law': *West Australian*, 12 July 1968; 'Group not allowed to work wreck': *West Australian*, 13 July 1968.

147 Memorandum dated 17 July 1968 to the Director of the WA Museum from Colin Jack-Hinton, Senior Curator, Division of Human Studies.

148 Henderson, J.A., 1993, *Phantoms of the Tryall*: St George Books, Perth.

149 'Police search for mystery trawler': *Weekend News*, 19 June 1971.

150 'Mystery trawler deserted in N.W.': *Weekend News*, 10 July 1971.

151 Henderson, J.A., 1993, *Phantoms of the Tryall*: St George Books, Perth.

152 File note by Jeremy Green, September 1979, on 'Inspection of cannon (Reg. no. 2409) and site at Shark Bay'.

153 North, N.A., 1976, 'Formation of coral concretion on marine iron': *International Journal of Nautical Archaeology and Underwater Exploration*, vol. 5, pp. 253–258; MacLeod, I.D., 1985, 'The effects of concretion on the corrosion of non-ferrous metals': *Corrosion Australasia*, vol. 10, pp. 10–13.

154 'Another old cannon': *Sunday Times*, 7 October 1979.

155 Robinson, Alan, 1980, *In Australia treasure is not for the finder*: Vanguard, Perth.

156 McIntosh, Alan, 'Tragic end for a top diver': *Daily News*, 3 November 1983; 'No verdict on hanged diver': *West Australian*, 3 November 1983; Schmitt, Hugh, 'Eccentric dies—Good bloke, born loser': *West Australian*, 5 November 1983.

157 'Wrecks have wrecked my life', Alan Robinson's story as told to Mike Worner: *Sunday Independent*, 10 December 1978.

158 van Niekerk, Mike, 'Tarnished treasure, tempestuous tale of "Robbie", WA's rogue wreck hunter', and 'Tragedy of the Batavia': *West Australian Big Weekend*, 22, 29 May 1993.

159 A composite account derived from letters dated 25 April 1994 and 16 January 1995 to P.E. Playford from Naoom Haimson.

160 Press statement, 18 July 1968, by the Chairman of the WA Museum Board, Sir Thomas Meagher, following a visit to the *Zuytdorp* wrecksite by David Ride.

161 'Diver took relics—prosecution': *West Australian*, 8 May 1986; 'Diver breathes sigh of relief': *Daily News*, 8 May 1986.

162 Letter dated 24 January 1970 to the Director of the WA Museum from John Allchin.

163 Letters dated 30 December 1970 to Tom Brady and J. Allchin from the Acting Director, WA Museum.

164 Report on *Zuytdorp* expedition by H.L. Bingham, 9 February 1971: unpublished WA Museum report; 'Wreck yields rich haul': *Daily News*, 2 February 1971.

165 Lovell, A., 1985, *The Mickelberg stitch*: Creative Research, Perth; Lovell, A., 1990, *Split image*: Creative Research, Perth.

166 'Mickelberg's house raided': *West Australian*, 9 May 1983; 'CIB holds on to gold hoard': *West Australian*, 10 May 1983.

167 'Mrs Mickelberg—I never knew': *Daily News*, 10 May 1983.

168 McIntosh, Alan, 'Cliffs of gold—What became of the Perth Mint's missing gold?': *Daily News*, 31 October 1984.

169 Memorandum dated 31 May 1976 to Director, WA Museum, from Curator, Maritime Archaeology, re the *Zuytdorp* wrecksite.

170 'A miser with millions': *People*, 6 May 1953, pp. 5–9.

171 Memorandum dated 16 May 1978 from Jeremy Green, Curator of Maritime Archaeology, to Head, Human Studies, giving details of the dive at the *Zuytdorp* wrecksite on 12 May, when many coins and artefacts were recovered.

172 *Zuytdorp* report, by I.M. Crawford, Head, Division of Human Studies, WA Museum, May 1978.

173 Memorandum dated 7 October 1980 to the Director, WA Museum, from Jeremy Green, Head, Department of Maritime Archaeology.

174 Zuytdorp camp destruction, Geraldton Curator's Report: report signed by G.I. Wallace, the curator, on 16 October 1980, and by I.J. Field, the watchkeeper, on 21 October 1980. Other details were provided verbally by I.J. Field.

175 WA Museum file report listing an inventory of *Zuytdorp* site equipment, belonging to the museum, I. Field and STW Channel 9, that was destroyed by fire or stolen on or about 7 October 1980.

176 Western Australian Police Department, 1980, documents relating to the burning of the museum caravan: document reference 0251194P3, CIB Perth file 80/69600, CIB Geraldton file 80/221-1 (entry 304).

177 Memorandum dated 5 March 1981 to Director, WA Museum, from Head, Department of Maritime Archaeology; letters dated 18, 23 November 1981 to D. Lamera regarding his appointment as warden.

178 Personal communications: 1995, Mike McCarthy and Fairlie Sawday, WA Maritime Museum; 15 February 1996, Dominic Lamera.

179 Information on coins recovered from the *Zuytdorp* is contained in the following: Wilson, S., 1985, 'Coins from the *Zuytdorp*': *Journal of the Numismatic Association of Australia*, vol. 1, pp. 24–30; Wilson, S.J., 1964, 'The significance of coins in the identification of old Dutch wrecks on the West Australian coast': *The Numismatic Circular*, September 1964, pp. 191–195; letter dated 15 March 1958 to P.E. Playford from H.E. van Gelder of the Koninklijk Kabinet van Munten, Penningen en Gesneden Stenen, giving information on coinage recovered from the *Zuytdorp* wrecksite; letter dated 16 April 1958 to P.E. Playford from H.E. van Gelder of the Koninklijk Kabinet van Munten, Penningen en Gesneden Stenen, giving information on silver-copper alloys normally used for various coins.

180 Memorandum dated 20 February 1984 to Director of the WA Museum from Jeremy Green, Head, Department of Maritime Archaeology.

181 *Zuytdorp* feasibility study: by I.M. Crawford, dated 26 April 1984.

182 *Zuytdorp*: report dated 16 July 1984 for ANCODS by I.M. Crawford and J.N. Green.

183 *Zuytdorp* wreck salvage operations: Geological Survey of Western Australia file 279/1984.

184 McCarthy, M., 1993, '*Zuytdorp*: The search continues': *Landscope*, vol. 8, no. 3, pp. 42–48.

185 *Zuytdorp*—a report on the situation to date and proposals to finalise fieldwork and fulfil the WA Museum's obligations re the site: by Mike McCarthy, dated 3 September 1986.

186 Harris, Alex, and Glass, Alison, '275 years on, Zuytdorp yields secrets': *West Australian*, 6 June 1987.

187 Glass, Alison, 'Dutch wreck gives up more of its secrets': *West Australian*, 17 February 1988.

188 'Find worthy of a toast': *Sunday Times*, 20 March 1988; Stanbury, M., and Sawday, F., 1991, *ANCODS 1991 report and catalogue of artefacts*: special publication, Department of Maritime Archaeology, WA Maritime Museum, no. 7.

189 Weaver, F., 1990, Report of the excavations of previously disturbed land sites associated with the VOC ship *Zuytdorp*, wrecked 1712, Zuytdorp Cliffs, Western Australia: report to the Department of Maritime Archaeology, WA Maritime Museum, no. 90.

190 Morse, K., 1988, 'An archaeological survey of midden sites near the *Zuytdorp* wreck, Western Australia': *Bulletin Australian Institute for Maritime Archaeology*, vol. 12, pp. 37–40.

191 The mystery of the *Zuytdorp* survivors has received wide media publicity in Australia and overseas, e.g.: 'Zeelandica': *Provinciale Zeeuwese Courant*, 21 March 1960; 'Zeeuwse kroniek': *Zeeuws Tijdschrift*, 1960, no. 2; 'Lost whites of Australia discovered': *London Daily Telegraph*, 11 September 1990; 'Whites may have settled 70 years before First Fleet': *Weekend Australian*, 8–9 September 1990; 'Dutch castaways our first settlers?': *West Australian*, 8 September 1990; 'Sporen van VOC bij Aboriginals': *Leids Dagblad*, Leyden, 25 June 1991; 'New bid to solve shipwreck puzzle': *West Australian*, 16 March 1994; 'Afrikaner link to Aborigines': *Sunday Times* (South Africa), 20 March 1994; 'Search for proof of first Europeans': *Sydney Morning Herald*, 19 August 1994; 'Skeletons hold the scientific key to one of Australia's great mysteries': *Age*, 19 August 1994; 'Disease may be answer': *Geraldton Guardian*, 20 February 1995.

192 Letter dated 23 April 1958 to P.E. Playford from E.W. Petrejus of the Maritiem Museum Prins Hendrik, Rotterdam, providing advice on the use and design of breech blocks. The breech-loading swivel cannon were used especially to repel enemies attempting to board a ship, and were loaded with small shot, nails and other pieces of metal to spray on the boarding parties. Such breech-loading cannon were known to the British as 'murderers'.

193 Day register of the Castle of Batavia, 4, 8, 17, 18, 22, 28 July 1712: announcing the arrival of the ships *Kockenge*, *Oostersteyn*, *Zuyderbeeck*, *Belvliet*, *Popkensburg*, *Oude Zyp* and *Corsloot* from the fatherland and listing their cargoes.

194 *Perth Gazette and Western Australian Journal*, 12 July 1834.

195 Edwards, H., 1963, 'Mystery of the stone walls': *People*, 22 May 1963, pp. 37–40.

196 Henderson, J.A., 1993, *Phantoms of the Tryall*: St George Books, Perth.

197 Drake-Brockman, H., 1963, *Voyage to disaster*: Angus & Robertson, Sydney; Edwards, H., 1966, *Islands of angry ghosts*: Hodder & Stoughton, London.

198 Heeres, J.E., 1899, *The part borne by the Dutch in the discovery of Australia 1606–1765*: Luzac, London; Henderson, J.A., 1982, *Marooned*: St George Books, Perth.

199 de Heer, C., 1963, 'My shield and my faith': *Westerly*, no. 1, 1963, pp. 33–46.

200 Edwards, H., 1970, *The wreck on the Half-Moon Reef*: Rigby, Perth.

201 'Lost for words, mission to reconstruct the decaying language of Nhanda': *West Australian Big Weekend*, 12 November 1994.

202 *Perth Gazette and Western Australian Journal*, 5, 12, 19, 26 July, 19 August 1834.

203 Reynolds, H., 1981, *The other side of the frontier*: James Cook University of North Queensland, Townsville; reprinted 1982–95, Penguin edns; Grey, G., 1841, *Journals of two expeditions of discovery in north-west and western Australia during the years 1837, 38, and 39*: T. & W. Boone, London, facsimile edn 1983, Hesperian Press, Victoria Park.

204 Rathe, G., *The wreck of the barque* Stefano *off the North West Cape of Australia in 1875*: Hesperian Press, Victoria Park.

205 Drake-Brockman, H., 1963, *Voyage to disaster*: Angus & Robertson, Sydney; Gerritsen, R., 1994, *And their ghosts may be heard*: Fremantle Arts Centre Press, Fremantle.

206 Sharp, E.I., 1985, *E.T. Hooley, pioneer bushman*: Lamb Printers, West Perth.

207 van de Graaff, W.J.E., 1980, 'Transportation patterns of Aboriginal artefacts in the Shark Bay area, Western Australia': *Royal Society of Western Australia Journal*, vol. 63, pp. 1–3.

208 'Dutch castaways our first settlers?': *West Australian*, 8 September 1990; 'Whites may have settled 70 years before First Fleet': *Weekend Australian*, 8–9 September 1990; letter dated 30 November 1990 to P.E. Playford from G.A. Brongers, Openluchtmuseum 'Het Hoogeland', regarding the tobacco-box lid from Wale Well.

209 Bowdler, S., 1990, In search of the *Zuytdorp* survivors: report on an archaeological reconnaissance of a site in the Shark Bay area, to the Australian Heritage Commission.

210 I am indebted to Hugh Edwards for bringing this report to my attention.

211 Letters dated 17 November and 6 December 1958 to P.E. Playford from H.E. van Gelder of the Koninklijk Kabinet van Munten, Penningen en Gesneden Stenen.

212 Gregory, A.C., and Gregory, F.T., 1884, *Journals of Australian explorations*: Government Printer, Brisbane.

213 Gregory, A.C., 1886, 'Inaugural address', *Proceedings of the Queensland Branch, Geographical Society of Australasia*, vol. 1, pp. 18–25.

214 Bates, D., 1944, *The passing of the Aborigines*: Speciality Press, Melbourne.

215 Bates, Daisy M., 'Our Aborigines, Pelsart's Dutchmen': *Sydney Morning Herald*, 28 March 1925. I am indebted to Peter Bridge for bringing this report to my attention.

216 Grey, G., 1841, *Journals of two expeditions of discovery in north-west and western Australia during the years 1837, 38, and 39*: T. & W. Boone, London, facsimile edn 1983, Hesperian Press, Victoria Park.

217 Gregory, A.C., and Gregory, F.T., 1884, *Journals of Australian explorations*: Government Printer, Brisbane.

218 'General intelligence': *Perth Gazette and Western Australian Journal*, 9 August 1861. I am indebted to Hugh Edwards for bringing this to my attention.

219 'In this desert cavern is the sketch of an ancient ship—how come? It's either native art—or an artful hoax': *Weekend Mail* (*Daily News* supplement), 1 October 1955; 'The baffling mystery of Walga Rocks', 'Mystery of Walga ship deepens', 'Expert to study rocks mystery', 'Expert sees Walga "rock ship" as 300 year old link': *Daily News*, 6, 11, 18, 25 November 1968; Elliott, Ross, 'The galleon that sails our desert': *Walkabout*, March 1972; Jack-Hinton, C., 1968, re Walga Rock: unpublished memorandum from Senior Curator in Charge, Division of Human Studies, to Director, WA Museum, reporting on a visit to Walga Rock on 22 November 1968.

220 Herbert, H.K., 9 September 1991, Report on two micro-samples of pigment; Herbert, H.K., 12 November 1991, Report on five scrapings of paint and one rock; Clarke, R.M., 27 February 1995, Report on seven samples from Walga Rock: Chemistry Centre (WA) reports.

221 Gerritsen, R., 1994, *And their ghosts may be heard*: Fremantle Arts Centre Press, Fremantle.

222 'Lost for words, mission to reconstruct the decaying language of Nhanda': *West Australian Big Weekend*, 12 November 1994.

223 Written communication, 1995, J. Blevins and D. Marmion.

224 Playford, P.E., 1964, Report on Native Welfare expedition to the Gibson and Great Sandy deserts: Geological Survey of Western Australia, Record 1964/10; 'Three Woomera tribes see first whites': *Melbourne Herald*, 2 May 1964.

225 Hallam, S.J., 1989, 'Plant usage and management in southwest Australian Aboriginal societies': in *Foraging and farming, the evolution of plant exploitation*, eds D.R. Harris and G.C. Hillman, Unwin Hyman, London; Hallam, S.J., 1979, *Fire and hearth*: Australian Institute of Aboriginal Studies, Canberra.

226 Pate, J.S., and Dixon, K.W., 1982, *Tuberous, cormous, and bulbous plants*: University of Western Australia Press, Nedlands.

227 Elliott, W.R., and Jones, D.L., 1984, *Encyclopaedia of Australian plants*: Lothian, Melbourne; Cribb, A.B., and Cribb, J.W., 1975, *Wild food in Australia*: Collins, Sydney.

228 Letters dated 22 July, 8 October 1988 to P.E. Playford from Ann E. Mallard.

229 Dean, G., 1982, 'Porphyria variegata': *Acta Dermatovener* (Stockholm), suppl. 100, pp. 81–85; Dean, G., 1971, *The porphyrias, a story of inheritance and environment*: Pitman, London.

230 Botha, M.C., and Beighton, P., 1983, 'Inherited disorders in the Afrikaner population of southern Africa': *South African Medical Journal*, vol. 64, pp. 609–612.

231 Letter dated 4 April 1996 to P.E. Playford from Geoffrey Dean; personal communication, 18 April 1996, Enrico Rossi.

232 Letter dated 11 October 1988 to P.E. Playford from Geoffrey Dean.

233 Letters dated 2 February 1990, 29 March 1991 and 4 April 1996 to P.E. Playford from Geoffrey Dean.

234 Cape Archives, 6 March 1707, no. CJ 311.

235 Personal communication, 1995, Enrico Rossi.

236 Goldblatt, J., 1992, 'Ellis–van Creveld syndrome in a Western Australian Aboriginal community': *Medical Journal of Australia*, vol. 157, pp. 271–272.

237 Bonnischen, R., and Schneider, A.L., 1995, 'Roots': *The Sciences*, vol. 35, no. 3, pp. 26–31.

238 Playford, P.E., 1959, 'The wreck of the *Zuytdorp* on the Western Australian coast in 1712': *Western Australian Historical Society Journal and Proceedings*, vol. 5, part 5, pp. 5–41.

239 Drake-Brockman, H., 1963, *Voyage to disaster*: Angus & Robertson, Sydney; Gerritsen, R., 1994, *And their ghosts may be heard*: Fremantle Arts Centre Press, Fremantle.

240 Heeres, J.E., 1899, *The part borne by the Dutch in the discovery of Australia 1606–1765*: Luzac, London; Drake-Brockman, H., 1963, *Voyage to disaster*: Angus & Robertson, Sydney; Gerritsen, R., 1994, *And their ghosts may be heard*: Fremantle Arts Centre Press, Fremantle.

241 Other parts of Drake-Brockman's analysis of Pelsaert's journal are wrong because of her incorrect understanding of Dutch distance measurements. She equated a Dutch mile with 3 English statute miles, whereas the correct figure is 4.6 statute miles, 4 nautical miles, or 7.408 kilometres. There were 15 Dutch *mylen*, equal to 60 modern nautical miles, to a degree of latitude. The generally accepted length of a Dutch mile during most of the seventeenth century and the first half of the eighteenth century was 22,800 Rhineland feet, equivalent to 7.157 kilometres, or 3.4 per cent less than its true length. This measure became known colloquially as the 'Snellius mile', after Willebrord Snellius (or Snell), the Dutch mathematician who made the calculation. In the mid-eighteenth century, the Snellius mile was corrected to 23,700 Rhineland feet 'or a little less', which is equivalent to 7.439 kilometres, or 0.4 per cent too long. However, the measurement made of a Dutch mile by the famous Amsterdam cartographer Willem Janszoon Blaeu was equivalent to 7.414 kilometres, or merely 0.08 per cent too long (Stapel, F.W., 1943, *De Oostindische Compagnie en Australië*: Van Kampen & Zoon, Amsterdam).

242 Heeres, J.E., 1899, *The part borne by the Dutch in the discovery of Australia 1606–1765*: Luzac, London.

243 Drake-Brockman, H., 1963, *Voyage to disaster*: Angus & Robertson, Sydney.

244 Schilder, G., 1985, *Voyage to the Great South Land, Willem de Vlamingh, 1696–97*: Royal Australian Historical Society, Sydney.

245 'Lost for words, mission to reconstruct the decaying language of Nhanda': *West Australian Big Weekend*, 12 November 1994.

246 Grey, G., 1841, *Journals of two expeditions of discovery in north-west and western Australia during the years 1837, 38, and 39*: T. & W. Boone, London, facsimile edn 1983, Hesperian Press, Victoria Park.

247 Verbatim transcript of interview with Tom Pepper, recorded by Phillip Playford, Peron Peninsula Station Homestead, 30 March 1975.

Index